Par for the Ladies

THE EXTRAORDINARY STORY OF THE WOMEN
WHO GOLFED AT NORTH BERWICK

For RACHEL, JAMIE, SARAH and DAVID

Par for the Ladies

THE EXTRAORDINARY STORY OF THE WOMEN WHO GOLFED AT NORTH BERWICK

AILSA FORTUNE

STANTON PRESS

First published in 2016 by:
Stanton Press
Wester Grange
Grange Road
North Berwick
EH39 4QT
United Kingdom
www.stantonpress.com

ISBN 978-0-992792-1-5
A catalogue record for this book is available from the British Library.

Designed by David Booth, Booth Creative
www.boothcreative.com

Cover illustration © John Rigg

Printed in Great Britain by Stephens & George Print Group

CONTENTS

FOREWORD

Catriona Matthew, M.B.E.

I am delighted to write a few words as a foreword to this first account of the history of the North Berwick Ladies' Golf Club and the fascinating story of the women who played over the original Ladies' links (now the Children's Course) and later over the West Links.

I grew up in North Berwick and love coming back to the town, after weeks away on tour. I was lucky that my parents got me into golf when I was quite young. In the summer holidays, I would spend many hours with my brothers going round and round the 9-hole children's course and I remember playing in the children's competitions. My husband and I take our two girls to play there now – it's the perfect course to introduce youngsters to the game.

I joined NBLGC when I was twelve years old and played in all the Ladies' Club competitions and medals. The lady members made me feel very welcome. The West Links will always be one of my favourite courses, even though I have been lucky enough to play on courses all over the world. There is just something special about North Berwick – it really is a traditional links course, with all the quirkiness of an old design. It plays differently every time, is a constant challenge and always great fun.

I believe that encouraging youngsters to play any sport is a good thing and nowadays girls have as many sporting opportunities as boys. Golf is a great choice because you can continue to play and enjoy it for a long time."*Par for the Ladies* highlights the enduring importance of golf at North Berwick and in particular the ladies' game. It is a story that needs to be told. I wish the book every success.

Catriona Matthew

AUTHOR'S NOTE

The idea of documenting the history of North Berwick Ladies' Golf Club came from Anne McCarthy, Lady Captain, 2012-2014. There was no written record of the Ladies' Club, although it had been in existence since 1888 and Anne felt it was long overdue. When I began my research in 2013, it became clear that few documents relating to the early activities of the Club had survived. There were four file boxes held by the North Berwick Golf Club, containing a couple of minute books from the 1970s and 80s; a splendid competition book, detailing the results of almost every ladies' match played between 1919 and 1972; and a single ring-binder folder entitled North Berwick Ladies' Club Archives, 1893-1991. The title belied the content. Most of the documents related to the 1930s and 1950s and contained little of interest. There was, however, a 'List of New Members' dated 1894, and folded within it was another list of 'Ladies admitted as members since the commencement of the club, August 1888'. That list of names provided a small and frustrating clue as to the identities of the original members. The entries were styled in the convention of the time – Miss Meikleham, Miss Napier, Miss MacAndrew – with no indication of their first names. By chance, I uncovered a membership list from 1906, which gave addresses. It was a significant breakthrough. A few of the ladies' names appeared on both lists. I felt I was entering Aladdin's Cave and I didn't want to disturb the genie. The two membership lists were the starting point for building up a biography of each of the ladies and then placing them in a broader social context. My path was set and I followed the thread through the 1890s, the early 1900s, until I reached the 1920s, at which point I could start considering evidence from living memory.

Another valuable source was contemporary newspapers, periodicals and magazines. There was no reference in the archive folder to the official opening ceremony which took place on 5th July 1888. An article in *The Scotsman* of 6th July 1888 offered incontrovertible evidence that the first match of the Ladies' Club took place across the new nine-hole links course the previous day.

> **"In connection with the Ladies' Golf Club, a ladies golfing green at North Berwick was opened yesterday afternoon......A large assemblage of ladies and gentlemen met on the green, when after the company had been photographed, the new course was opened by Mr Walter Dalrymple...."**

The present Sir Hew Hamilton-Dalrymple, 10th Bt., who lives in North Berwick, is a grandson of Walter Dalrymple, the gentleman who drove off the first ball on the ladies' links, and Sir Hew's mother was a Lady Captain of the Club in the 1920s. In him, there was a happy meeting-point between contemporary sources and living memory. Sir Hew recalled anecdotes from the heady days of the 1930s when the North Berwick links hosted high society and golf was the "goff". Deborah Backhouse, whose great grandmother, Eulalie Houldsworth, was a member of the Ladies' Club in the 1890s, put me in touch with individuals whose connections to North Berwick and golf also go back several generations. I have felt privileged to have been given access to family records, archives and some splendid photographs by people whose mothers, grandmothers, great-grandmothers, sisters and aunts were familiar (and sometimes famous) figures on the links in their day and who helped to define the unique character of the Ladies' Club.

ACKNOWLEDGEMENTS

I should like to acknowledge the support, help and encouragement I have received in bringing Par for the Ladies to its 21st century conclusion. My thanks to Deborah Backhouse, Marjorie Baylay, David Booth, Elaine and Robin Carlyle, Lee Carr, Walter Riddell-Carre, Sarah Chaundler, Lord Crathorne, Kay Crocket, Sir Hew Hamilton-Dalrymple, the late Ann Dymond, Bridget Ellwood, David Fortune, Ian Goodall, Sir James Grant-Suttie, Denise Gray, Stewart Greenwood, Pauline Jaffrey, the late John Imlay and Mary Ellen Imlay, Gillian Kirkwood, Anne McCarthy, Elaine McSherry, Catriona Matthew, Anne Balfour-Melville, Sir Francis Ogilvy, Joan Oliver, John Rigg, Jennifer Sharp, Hugh Teacher, Alistair Thomson, Ros Thoresen, Ella Vlandy, Bobby Walker, Ian Watson, Lord Wemyss, Isabelle de Waldner, Hilary Wilkie, Dawn Young, Simon de Zoete, Stewart Auld, Local History Archive Staff at the John Gray Centre (Haddington), Ian Doig and Tantallon Golf Club, the Staff at North Berwick Golf Club.

I am most grateful to everyone mentioned above, whatever the extent or nature of their contribution; all have helped to make possible the publication of this book.

The author would also like to thank the following, in addition to those named above, for permission to use their photographs and reproduce their material:

Mary Evans Picture Library pp82, 121, 128, 149, 178, 181, 182, 199 © Illustrated London News/Mary Evans; © Historic Environment Scotland, pp55, 152; © National Portrait Gallery p140; East Lothian Council Archives & Local History Service pp20,41, 54, 88, 94, 124, 172, 176, 185, 196, 211; ELC Museum Service images pp100,103; Hugh MacKenzie images p111; Women Golfers' Museum pp 70, 73, 76, 122, 131, 135, 136, 220; © St Baldred's Episcopal Church, p34; Amersham Museum p52; Christies *Origins of Golf – The Jaime Ortiz-Patino Collection Catalogue*, p90 extract letter by Mrs Alice Gwynn, entry Kenneth McConkey, quoted p187., I.C.A.S. Archive p33. Photographs from private collections are the copyright of their owners.

The author acknowledges the use of any copyrighted material in this book and has made every effort to identify, trace and contact all copyright holders in order to seek the requisite permissions.

The author has made every effort to ensure accuracy in any statements made about individuals who feature in this book.

BIBLIOGRAPHY

Cossey, Rosalynde, *Golfing Ladies, Five Centuries of Golf in Great Britain & Ireland*, Orbis Publishing, 1984

Dunlop-Hill Noel Ed. *History of the Scottish Ladies' Golfing Association, 1903-1928*, London, Morton, 1929

Kerr, Rev. John, *The Golf Book of East Lothian*, T & A Constable, 1896

Adamson, Alistair Beaton, *In the Wind's Eye*, 1980

Leitch, Cecil, *Golfing for Girls*, London, 1911

Mackern, Louie, Ed., *Our Lady of the Green; A Book of Ladies Golf*, with chs by Amy Pascoe and M. Boys Lawrence & Bullen, 1899

McAndrew, J., *Golfing Step by Step*, 1914

Mair, Norman, *Muirfield, Home of the Honourable Company (1744-1994)*, Mainstream, 1994

Stringer, Mabel, *Golfing Reminiscences*, Mills & Boon, 1924

Sayers, Doreen, *100 years of Golf in North Berwick, 1857 to 1962*, Stephenson Press, 1994

Savage, Peter, *Lorimer and the Edinburgh Craft Designers*

Wentworth, James, Ed., *A Centenary Celebration*, Scottish Ladies' Golf Association, 2004

Records of the North Berwick Golf Club, held at the National Library of Scotland

Pook, Liz, *Legends of the Ladies' Links, Dorothy Campbell, Part II*, p10, Through the Green, June 2008

Golf Illustrated, with which is incorporated 'Golf' Vols1-XXVIII, 1893, 1898-1906 & 1915

The Ladies' Golf Official Year Book (various years), The Golf Agency, Edinburgh and London

The Letters of Arthur Balfour & Lady Elcho, Ed. Ridley & Percy

The Autobiography of Margot Asquith, Thornton Butterworth, 1920

North Berwick Golf Club Records [ACC 11578] National Library of Scotland

Murrayfield Golf Club www.murrayfieldgolfclub.co.uk

Haddingtonshire Courier Archive, Local History Archive, John Gray Centre, Haddington

www.scotlandspeople.gov.org

www.ancestry.com

Quotations from newspapers and periodicals were accessed through the following URLs, July 2016, in the National Library of Scotland Licensed Digital Collection.
https://auth.nls.uk/ldc/goto.cfm?rid=60; https://auth.nls.uk/ldc/goto.cfm?rid=17;
https://auth.nls.uk/ldc/goto.cfm?rid=38; https://auth.nls.uk/ldc/goto.cfm?rid=115;
https://auth.nls.uk/ldc/goto.cfm?rid=10

CHAPTER ONE

'The Flutter of Petticoats'

"We must apologise to the Ladies for having said so much about golf at North Berwick without lifting our hat to them or taking any notice of their cosy little links and their gay gatherings thereon."
(John Kerr, *Golf Book of East Lothian,* 1896)

Writing in his *Golf Book of East Lothian*, in 1896, John Kerr did not foresee the impact of women on the game of golf. His precise and detailed history of the development of golf in East Lothian introduces female golfers as a delightful sideshow, rather than an integral part of the sport. He justifies this portrayal by pointing out that as the Ladies' Club was formed only a few years before his book was written, there is little of its history recorded and therefore one supposes little of interest. How mistaken he was! The resolution and unwavering enthusiasm of the small band of women who joined the club when it was first formed in 1888, to play golf on a properly laid out course, contributed to the evolution of North Berwick into one of the great golfing venues, with a reputation that stretched beyond these shores. Although some sort of parity with the men over the links was achieved by 1936, it was over a century from the founding of the North Berwick Ladies' Golf Club, before the women were fully integrated into the North Berwick Golf Club.

There were women golfers at North Berwick long before the Ladies' Club was formed. Kerr singles out the Anderson girls, daughters of the Rev. F. L. M. Anderson, Rector of St Baldred's the town's Episcopal Church, and Violet Chambers of the Chambers publishing family, as being notable for "playing the gentleman's round". He dares to suggest that they played with a style that some men "might well have tried to emulate". Although these young women stood out as good golfers, men found the "flutter of female petticoats" disagreeable

Lady Tennant (1868-1943), a member of North Berwick Ladies' Golf Club for many years, was born Marguerite Miles. In 1898, she married the widowed Sir Charles Tennant, whom she had met on the golf links at Biarritz.

on the long course and felt that the generally inferior standard of play among the ladies interfered with their own enjoyment of the game.

Kerr's views apart, it is not absolutely clear from where the pressure came to set up the Ladies' Club with its own short course, whether from the men, anxious that as golf increased in popularity their time on the course would be limited, or from the ladies themselves who wanted to be able to play on their own account and not at the whim of their men-folk. The notion that it was a male-dominated decision is given credence by the fact that once it was set up, the Ladies' Club was run and managed almost entirely by a group of gentlemen from the existing 'men only' New Club, formed in 1880, as an offshoot of the original North Berwick Golf Club:

> **"Several gentlemen interested in extending the amenities of the burgh, and desirous of providing recreation for lady visitors during the season, have taken steps to lay out a new golfing course for the ladies, which it is anticipated will be much appreciated."**
>
> (*Haddingtonshire Courier* 25 May 1888)

Among these men was William Gibson Bloxsom, a member of the North Berwick New Club, who is credited with first promoting the idea. It was driven forward by Walter Dalrymple whose family owned the links as far as the borough boundary, where a stone wall ran across the course. Walter liaised with Mary Constance Nisbet Hamilton, owner of the adjoining Archerfield estate, which stretched from North Berwick and ran west as far as the village of Gullane four miles away, to come to an agreement about terms and conditions of setting out a ladies' course on her land.

Mary Constance Nisbet Hamilton (1844-1920) owner of the land upon which the Ladies' Course was laid out. In September 1888, she married Henry Thomas Ogilvy and she and her husband adopted the surname Nisbet Hamilton-Ogilvy.

Miss Nisbet Hamilton had come into a vast inheritance on the death of her mother Lady Mary Nisbet Hamilton, in December 1883, and was said to be one of the wealthiest women in Britain. The extent to which she agreed to the proposal for the course because it furthered the efforts of lady golfers in their quest for some sort of parity with the men, is questionable. In terms of her position in the community, it was a good move and there were several obsequious references in the local press to the "considerate kindness of the proprietrix". Nevertheless she drove a tough bargain for the privilege of playing golf over her land. There would be no period of notice to quit, if at any future time she changed her mind. The ground had to be enclosed with approved fencing and gates, at the Club's expense. The course was strictly private and only members "who may each be accompanied by an attendant to carry clubs" were allowed to enter, but never on a Sunday and never with dogs,

✶ The term 'mixed doubles' was often used in the early days of golf instead of the current term 'mixed foursomes'. (See Kerr p135)

horses or carriages! As the course was to be laid out over part of Ferrygate, a farm on the Archerfield estate, the rights of the tenants had to be addressed. The compromise was that from June to September "only sheep shall be allowed to pasture on that ground" – and so at least no pigs, hens or cows could disturb the ladies' play! The annual rent was set at a reasonable £15.

The other 'interested' gentlemen, apart from Walter Dalrymple and William Bloxsom, were Benjamin Hall Blyth, George Dalziel and David Allan Stevenson and together they made up the first committee that ran the Ladies' Club. It was not an unusual set up for a group from the committee of a men's golf club to run the ladies' club, and the North Berwick ladies demured. "The ladies of the North Berwick Club very wisely leave its management in the hands of the gentlemen," explained John Kerr.

The notion of the men in control, however, made some women restless and there were attempts elsewhere to encourage women to run their own clubs. One lady golfer commented on the anomaly of the men being in charge: "It's like setting an elephant to do embroidery!" For the time being, the North Berwick ladies were happy that the gentlemen ran their golfing affairs. The entrance fee was 2s 6d and the annual subscription 5s. Within months of the club opening there were over seventy members. In addition, several men were admitted either as 'Gentlemen Life Members' or 'Gentlemen Honorary Associates'. This entitled them to play on the ladies' links and participate in the mixed doubles* matches, held every year, although their entry fee and annual subscription were each set at a higher rate of 10s. In addition, the gents' privileges were limited during the busy summer months, as they were not allowed on the course after 4.00pm, without being accompanied by a lady member!

View to the ladies' links and the Marine Hotel – while the focus is on the men's game, two ladies can be seen playing over their course in the background, c.1890.

The first hole of the new nine-hole course was in front of the town's most stylish hotel, the Marine, from whose large lounge windows, residents had a fine view of the sea and the distant Fife coast and could now also look forward to hours of entertainment watching the lady golfers show their skills. The boundary wall provided a hazard at the second hole on the way out and the ninth on the return. The main part of the course was set out on the grass park, known as Saugh's field, above the first part of the North Berwick links. Efforts had been made to produce excellent turf and good greens and there was no doubt it was going to be a popular addition to the existing facilities. Thinly veiled reservations were expressed, however, during the laying out of the course in May, in *The North Berwick Advertiser and East Lothian Visiter*, which commented: "a new set of short holes will shortly make the park the rendezvous of the fair sex and the cynosure of all male eyes – not, we hope, to the detriment of golf in the open". In other words, it would never do for the men to be put off their game by eyeing up the women! The description of the course in the *Haddingtonshire Courier* 25 May 1888, as "very pretty", again smacked of the usual patronising tone which greeted many female sporting endeavours. The article continued in the same vein, with a confident assertion that "the lady players will thus be enabled to enjoy the invigorating pastime to which so many of them are partial, secure of interruption or danger from the long driving of the males".

The ladies could feel relatively secure from any other real or imagined threats from the men, within the precincts of the small club house which was erected immediately to the west of the offices and stabling of the Marine Hotel and a short step from the first tee. Within the clubhouse, the men had to fall in with the constraints of a straight-laced Victorian society and for the sake of propriety could go no further on the premises than the club room.

THE LADIES' COURSE

1. Marine .... 70 yrds.
2. Kaimend ...... 60 yrds.
3. Ferrygate ..... 120 yrds.
4. Plantation .... 140 yrds.
5. Woodend ...... 90 yrds.
6. Centre Park . . . 115 yrds.
7. North Park .... 70 yrds.
8. Green Hollow . 100 yrds.
9. The Home .... 170 yrds.

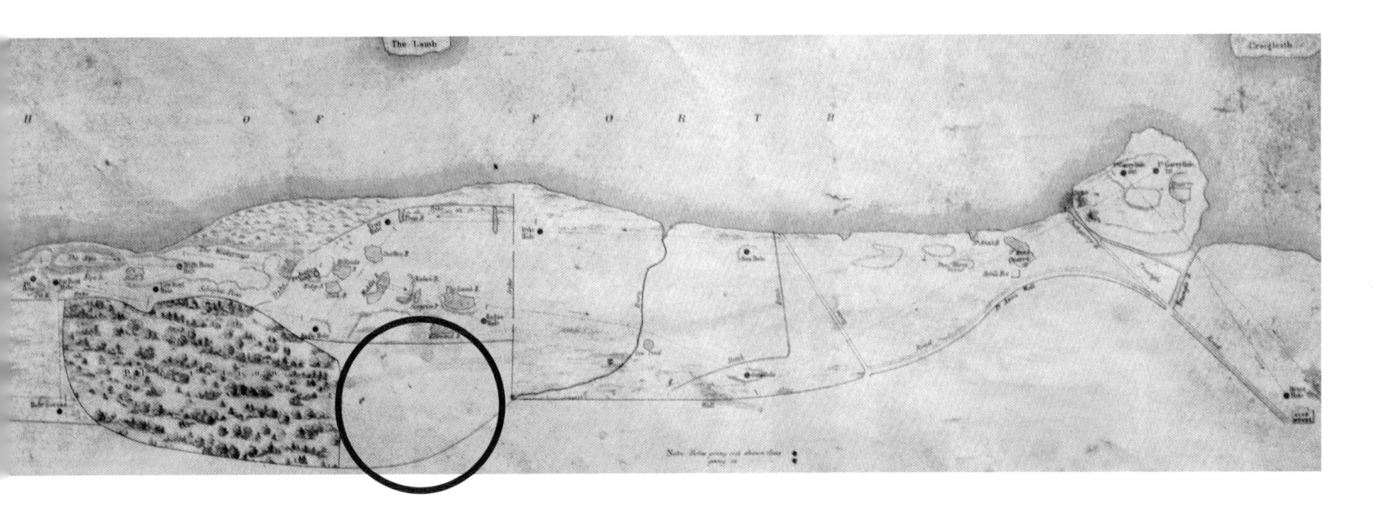

A plan of the North Berwick Links c.1880s, before the Ladies' Course was laid out to the right of the plantation.

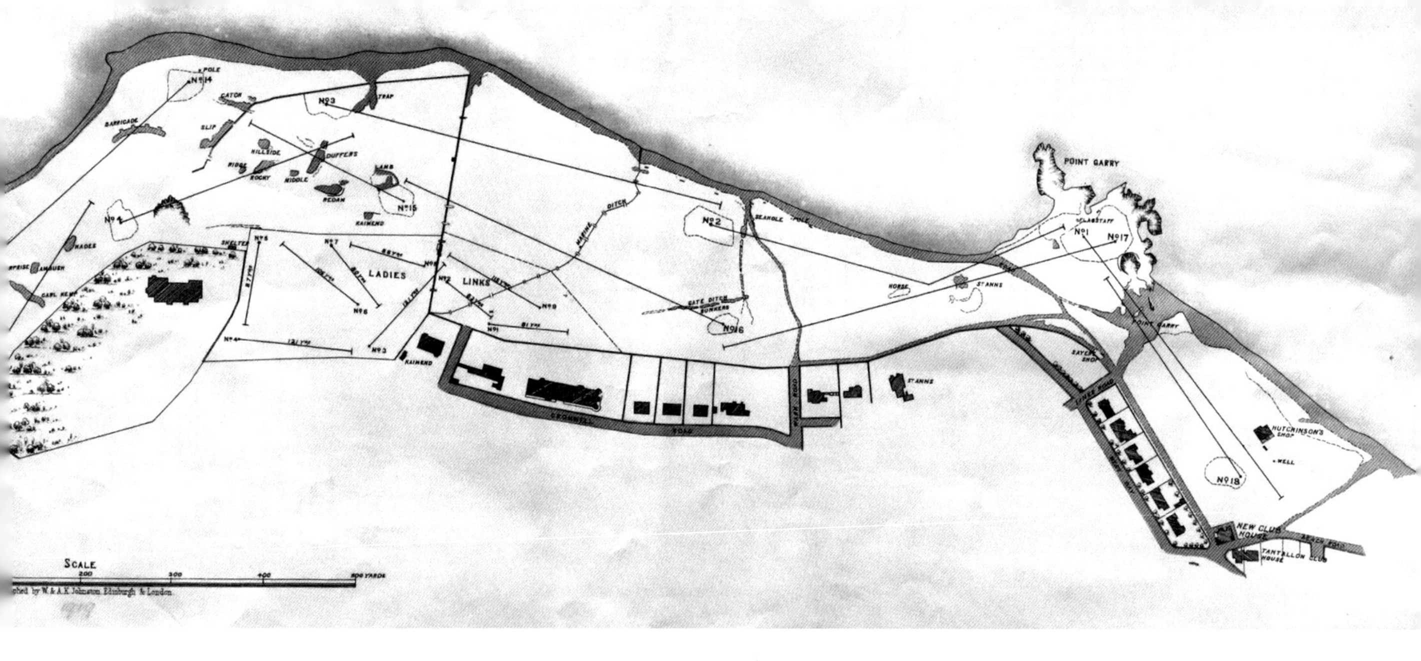

A plan of North Berwick Links after the Ladies' Course was laid out.

CLUB HOUSE RULES

13. The Club House shall be opened from 1st May to 30th September at 9 A.M., and from 1st October to 30th April at 10 A.M., and shall be closed not earlier than 4 o'clock nor later than 8 o'clock according to the time of year. The hours for closing shall be posted on the notice board of the Club.

14. The Club House shall not be open on Sundays.

15. The Club House is only open to Members and Honorary Associates, who may however introduce guests and may entertain them to tea, but the guests may only remain in the Club House while the Member who introduced them is present. Gentlemen, whether Members, Honorary Associates or Guests may enter the Club Room only.

(Extract Rules 13 to 15 of the North Berwick Ladies' Golf Club)

The Opening Ceremony

The official opening of the North Berwick Ladies' Golf Club took place on Thursday 5th July 1888. Afternoon tea was served to golfers, guests and officials of the Club, in the grounds of the Marine Hotel, which were laid out with lawns and flower beds to the east. The 'assemblage' then moved through a doorway in the hotel's north boundary wall, on to the green, where they were photographed. The ceremony was marked by Walter Dalrymple driving off the first ball. Perhaps it was tactful to invite the man who had promoted the idea of the ladies' club to conduct the opening ceremony, but it seems strange that a lady was not asked to perform this role. Immediately afterwards, however, seventeen ladies and Walter Dalrymple were dispatched in pairs, by starter Tom seventeen ladies and Walter Dalrymple were dispatched in pairs, by starter Tom Dunn, to play the opening game of two rounds, on the new course. The showery weather did not dampen the enthusiasm of either players or spectators. There was a tie for first place between three young lady members of whom much was to be heard in future on the green - Margaret Gillies Smith, Florence Anderson and Blanche Anderson. Margaret Gillies Smith triumphed in the play-off, with a single round in 35. She was sixteen years old.

PARTICIPANTS IN THE OPENING MATCH, JULY 1888.

- Miss Gillies Smith and Miss A Dalziel
- Mrs Husband and Miss M Wakelin
- Miss Sprott and Miss H Jarvie
- Miss E Wyllie and Miss Spens
- Miss M Sprott and Miss Jarvie
- Miss E Bruce and Mr Dalrymple
- Miss F Anderson and Miss S Jarvie
- Miss B Anderson and Miss E Campbell
- Misses C and A Gillies Smith and Miss A Gillies Smith

Resting between shots! Sir Walter Hamilton-Dalrymple with his two young sons on the links at North Berwick c.1894.

The Men who ran the Ladies' Club

Walter Dalrymple was the eldest surviving son of Sir John Dalrymple 7th Bart. of North Berwick and succeeded to the baronetcy on the death of his father in December 1888. The Dalrymples had been closely associated with the 'goff' in the borough as long as anyone could remember. They owned much of the land in and around North Berwick, including the West Links, where golf had been played from around the turn of the nineteenth century. Golfing on the West Links was formalised in 1832, when the North Berwick Golf Club was established by a group of local landed gentry and aristocracy. Walter's great uncle, Sir Hew Dalrymple Hamilton 4th Bart., though not a founder member, was elected to the club during its first year. Walter's uncle,

TOM DUNN

Green keeper and professional at North Berwick, Dunn was thought to be responsible for laying out the Ladies' Course in 1888. During the winter of 1888-89, he went to work in Biarritz. So impressed was he with the ladies' green there, he commented that it was second only to the Ladies' Course at North Berwick – a possible reinforcement of his own skills! Tom died in May 1902.

Sir Hew Dalrymple 6th Bart., fondly referred to as 'Laird of the Links', held the club captaincy for a record twenty years, from 1867 to 1886. News of his death, in April 1887, was met with outpourings of deep regret by fellow members of the North Berwick Club, and it was noted in the minutes that he always had had the interests of the club at heart. In truth, he had been a bit of an autocrat and it had probably been quite difficult to remove him from the captaincy of this elite gentleman's club, the access to which could only be attained if one had acceptable credentials, namely land and pedigree.

Sir Hew's brother John, who succeeded to the title, lived mainly in London and had little interest in North Berwick, and so the mantle of the 'Laird of the Links' was placed on the shoulders of Sir Hew's nephew, Walter Dalrymple. Walter would undoubtedly have felt under pressure from both the tradition of his forebears and the expectation of the tightly-knit golfing fraternity, to make a mark on the North Berwick golf scene – interesting, then, that he chose to champion the ladies' cause! His personal circumstances may have swayed him. In the years since his marriage, in 1882, to Alice Clifford, she had given birth to three daughters. Did he foresee a time when he would have daughters as companions on the links if there were no sons? Walter would be aware of the burgeoning interest in the ladies' game nationwide and the potential economic benefit to North Berwick of developing a good short course, predominately for the ladies, who regularly accompanied their men folk to Scotland's golfing mecca. In fact, a few weeks after Walter opened the Ladies' Club, his first son Hew Clifford was born, followed a year later by another son, John.

Benjamin Hall Blyth, the Chairman of the 1st Ladies' Committee was a principle advocate and organiser of the Ladies' Club.

Benjamin Hall Blyth, Chairman of the Ladies' Committee, had long-established connections with North Berwick. He was brought up in Edinburgh, but as a child was a frequent visitor to North Berwick where the family had a house, Park End Villa, in the Westgate. His father, also Benjamin Hall Blyth was a prominent railway engineer and after his premature death in 1866, young Benjamin became involved in the family business as a civil engineer and was partly responsible for the construction of Waverley Station. In 1872, he married Millicent Taylor. Their first child, a boy, Benjamin Edward was born in April 1875, but died a few weeks later. Their daughter Elsie Winifred, who was born in 1877, shared her father's passion for golf from an early age. The family home was at 17 Palmerston Place in Edinburgh, but, in 1888, Hall Blyth built a large house, Kaimend, in North Berwick, immediately beyond the Marine Hotel and looking across the West Links, where he could repeat the pattern of his childhood and enjoy regular games of golf. Like many of his prosperous middle class contemporaries, he was a member of several golf clubs and sat on several committees. At six foot five in height, with a booming voice and a hearty appetite, he was in all respects a larger than life figure with a forceful character and strong opinions. Did his affection and ambition for his only surviving child, a daughter, override any prejudice he may have harboured about women on the golf course? Certainly at the opening ceremony he was reported to have rebuffed any suggestion that setting up a ladies' course was purely male selfishness to get the ladies off the long course. He emphasised that the idea was conceived to allow the ladies to play more golf. Elsie was immediately signed up for membership of the new Ladies' Club, and although she was then a child of eleven, she was soon holding her own in club competitions. There is a fine irony in Hall Blyth's early involvement with the Ladies' Club, as his granddaughter, Millicent Couper, became one of a handful of Scotland's greatest women golfers to have cut her teeth on the Ladies' Course at North Berwick.

William Bloxsom, first Secretary of the NBLGC.

David Alan Stevenson (1855-1917), like Hall Blyth, was also part of an illustrious engineering dynasty and they knew each other beyond the golf course. The families lived in close proximity in Edinburgh's West End. David's grandfather Robert had built the Bell Rock lighthouse and the family firm of D. & T. Stevenson, of which David and his younger brother Charles became partners in 1878, were responsible for the design and construction of almost every lighthouse off the coast of Scotland, including the Bass Rock lighthouse, in 1902. Their first cousin was Robert Louis Stevenson, one of Scotland's best-known literary sons, and from David's early childhood, the extended Stevenson clan made the journey from Edinburgh to North Berwick every summer, where they rented houses close to the beach and where the children were introduced to the game of golf. While RLS "despised this activity (golf)", for David, golf became an important means of relaxation and enjoyment. David was a bachelor when he became involved in the Ladies' Club, but he and his brother had been brought up in a household with four older sisters and a female cousin, who were avid golfers. After he married in 1892, he and his wife Annie went on to have two daughters, Dorothy and Kathleen, both of whom were impressive golfers and members of the Ladies' Club.

From a different perspective, William Gibson Bloxsom made unsparing efforts to make the Ladies' Club a success. The son of a commercial traveller, born in 1849, William Bloxsom did not have the advantages of birth of Walter Dalrymple, nor the useful social connections with North Berwick of Stevenson and Hall Blyth. He was brought up as an only child in suburban Morningside, on what was then the outskirts of Edinburgh. He was clever and his ambitious parents saved enough for him to enrol in the Edinburgh Institute, where he excelled in mathematics. He trained as an actuary and by the age of twenty nine he was involved in the setting up and management of the Scottish Metropolitan Life Assurance Company and soon after was elected a fellow of the Institute of Actuaries. In 1876 he married Jane Anne, the daughter of Charles Wilson Murray, a merchant with the highly successful trading company, Jardine Matheson, in Hong Kong.

In 1877, William and Jane had a daughter Mary Agnes, but the following year, just four weeks after the birth of their son Charles Gibson, Jane died from postnatal complications. She was twenty three years old. William's widowed mother Agnes moved in and took over the task of bringing up her grandchildren. William Bloxsom continued to build up his business and in his leisure time he took up golf. He joined several clubs, including Muirfield, but he was most active in North Berwick, where he was secretary of the Tantallon Club for many years. Tantallon had been founded in 1853, by a group of local merchants who played over the North Berwick links. It had a more democratic approach to membership, in contrast with the elitist membership rules governing the North Berwick Golf Club. In 1888, Bloxsom enthusiastically embraced the idea of a ladies' club and put himself forward as a committee member. Perhaps he was motivated by a desire to promote a wholesome activity which would keep his motherless daughter occupied as she grew into a young woman and allow him to pursue his love of the game. He duly signed up his eleven year old Mary Agnes, as one of the first members of the new Ladies' Club.

The last of the quintet of men who took on the running of the Ladies' Club in 1888, was George Dalziel, a friend and neighbour of Stevenson in Edinburgh. Dalziel, a solicitor, was married with three children and spent several weeks each year at North Berwick, where golfing appeared to be his main leisure activity. He was a great wheeler and dealer and bought up a large number of properties in the town. His main North Berwick residence was a large house on West Bay, overlooking Point Garry. He could literally step out of his house onto the golf course. George Dalziel must have encouraged his children to learn to play golf, as his daughter Annie was one of the early leading lights of the ladies' club and took part in the celebrated opening match.

George Dalziel one of the founders of the NBLGC.

Accommodating the Ladies

Annie Dalziel almost certainly played golf at North Berwick long before the laying out of the new ladies' course. In fact, ladies' golf had been thriving in North Berwick since about 1869, when the most easterly section of the West Links was set aside for their play. The chief instigator of this innovation had been Sir Hew Dalrymple 6th Bart. It was the side show of an ambitious plan to

Rules of the North Berwick Ladies' Golf Club

MEMBERSHIP

1. The club shall consist of –

(2) The existing Gentlemen Life Members

(3) Gentlemen Honorary Associates

COMMITTEE

2. The Management of the Club shall be in the hands of the Committee.

3. The admission of Members shall be in the hands of the Committee.

4. The committee shall have power to add to its number.

5. The Committee shall have power to alter and amend these rules, and to frame such further rules and bye-laws as may at any time be found necessary.

The foreground of this photo, c.1890, is where the ladies played golf before their nine-hole course was laid out. It was little more than a putting green and is where the municipal putting green was set up in the 1920s.

extend the main course westwards to create a bigger and better course for the men. When Sir Hew had been elected Captain of the North Berwick Club, in 1867, and with his mind, no doubt, set on creating his own golfing legacy, he planned to make the North Berwick Links surpass any other golfing ground in Scotland. Accommodating the ladies was a surprisingly egalitarian and far-sighted gesture, and was a response to the increasing number of female golfers. The move followed the opening of the ladies' golf club at St. Andrews, which had taken place in September 1867 and was generally accepted to be the first of its kind:

> **"A ladies' golf club, quite a new feature in the golfing circle, has recently been instituted at St Andrews. The game may easily be carried out in any place where 50 to 100 square yards of ground can be obtained and with as great facility as the popular game of croquet. The implements required for practice are a putter, a cleek and ball, and no doubt golf will become a favourite game, not alone with the ladies of St Andrews, but throughout the kingdom."**
>
> (*Aberdeen Journal* 16 October 1867)

Perhaps Sir Hew was astute enough to figure out that incorporating something similar for the ladies, on the edge of the links, would keep North Berwick at the cutting edge of golfing developments and make his beloved burgh a fashionable destination during 'The Season'.

A few ladies' clubs were established in the wake of St Andrews: Westward Ho! in 1868, Musselburgh and Wimbledon in 1872 and Carnoustie in 1873. In reality most of the early ladies' courses were little more than glorified putting greens, but once a club had been established they adhered to a set of rules. At North Berwick, ladies' tournaments took place regularly, throughout the 1870s and 80s, before the club was established. They were popular events and always drew a crowd of onlookers. There was always great encouragement given to young girls to participate in the competitions and there were rather nice prizes to be won: most often a piece of jewellery, but sometimes, a set of golf clubs, which in those days generally consisted of five clubs. An early recorded ladies' golf competition, on Saturday 26th September 1874, attracted the usual crowds as twenty players set off on the links. The ladies were favoured with the presentation of prizes by the town's Provost Brodie, who took a keen interest in the game. The first prize was a handsome brooch won by a Miss Greenhill.

In the 1880s, Violet Chambers was one of the first good lady golfers to come to public attention in North Berwick. Her frequent presence on the links,

Sir Hew Dalrymple, 6th Bart., who created the first facilities for ladies to golf in North Berwick.

SIR HEW DALRYMPLE, BART.
'The Laird of the Links'

among so many men, attracted comments in the local press. Violet was born in 1861, one of six children of Robert Chambers (secundus) and was brought up in a household where there were as many literary influences as sporting ones. Her grandfather, Robert Chambers, a man with a towering intellect, was a founder member of the renowned Chambers' publishing company, with his older brother William. There is a statue of William in Chambers Street, Edinburgh (named after him in recognition of his public service as Lord Provost in the 1860s), which was created by an up-and-coming sculptor John Rhind. The Chambers and the Rhinds would have been well known to each other and branches of both families are to be found in North Berwick in the late 19th century and on the links there. Violet's father Robert, a partner in the family firm, had an excellent reputation as a golfer and in 1862 had published an amusing little book about the sport, *A Few Rambling Remarks about Golf.* He was Captain of Tantallon from 1880 until his premature death in 1888, at the age of fifty six from cirrhosis of the liver.

Violet Chambers, one of the early women golfers in North Berwick.

Violet and her siblings had a privileged upbringing. Chambers' Publishing was enjoying a golden era. Chambers' Encyclopaedia was selling well, Chambers' English Dictionary was published in 1872 to great acclaim and the company was rapidly becoming the largest English language publishers in the world. The family home was at 10 Claremont Crescent in Edinburgh, but summer holidays were spent in North Berwick, where in 1872, Robert Chambers had a huge red sand-stone house built at the east end of the town, on raised ground above the original East Links. He called his house St. Baldred's Tower. For the Chambers' children – girls and boys – an ability to play golf was regarded as a useful accomplishment within their social circle.

Dorothy Campbell, one of Scotland's greatest women golfers, learned to play golf on the North Berwick links, at a very young age, some years after Violet Chambers. In an article published in *Golf Illustrated* in 1915, she wrote: "I believe that the first woman who played on the links at North Berwick was Miss Violet Chambers and I have often heard my mother say that she was almost mobbed when she first started, as the sight was such a surprise to the conservative people of the town".

Violet certainly did have a following in North Berwick and perhaps she should be acknowledged as the woman who contributed most to encouraging ladies' golf in North Berwick. On Friday 4th September 1887, we find her presenting the prizes, rather than participating in the game, at the annual Ladies' Golf Tournament, although she was only twenty six. The first prize was the Miss Chambers' Medal, played in a scratch competition for young ladies over fourteen. The medal was solid silver and a miniature copy was given to the prize winner to keep. The competition was two rounds of what could reasonably be called the original ladies' links, lying to the east of the West Links. The younger girls played a handicap competition over nine holes.

It is often commented that many of the early lady golfers were spinsters and this raises a suspicion that married ladies' golfing was frowned upon. To an extent this is true and married ladies were slow to come forward. In this particular tournament, however, the majority of the players were girls rather than women, but convention, particularly among the middle and upper classes, was to address any young girl as 'Miss' and that continued if, or until, she married. Among the younger participants on September 4th, were Miss Elizabeth McCulloch and Miss Harriet McCulloch, who were aged 13 and 10 respectively.

Elizabeth, Harriet and their elder sister Edith, aged 17, were the daughters of David McCulloch, agent (or manager) for the North Berwick branch of the British Linen Bank and unlike many competitors, they lived locally. Edith qualified for the scratch competition on September 4th and won the silver medal with an impressive round of 61. Four of Dorothy Campbell's older sisters, Louise, Edith, Madeline and Muriel also competed, but didn't carry off any prizes on that occasion. Dorothy was four at the time and according to her own recollections was still a year away from swinging a club over the links.

In 1889, Violet Chambers moved to London and although she made frequent visits to North Berwick she scarcely participated in the new Ladies' Club. Her literary career seemed to supersede her golf, after the publication of the first of many novels, *And They Too*, later that year. In June 1891, she married a fellow Scot, Clarens Tweedale, who encouraged her to continue writing. She became as celebrated in London as she had been in North Berwick and could count among her friends, the great Liberal Prime Minister W.E. Gladstone (who visited her in North Berwick) and poet Robert Browning. She was reckoned to be one of the most talented and versatile young women of her day. In 1910, she was featured in *Every Woman's Encyclopaedia* as a "woman of all works":

Robert Chambers, Violet's father had a fine reputation as a golfer.

"She can paint a landscape and cook a dinner; she can write a book and make a shirt; she can etch a sporting scene and embroider the finest designs; she is a brilliant pianist and has the reputation of being one of the best political speakers of the day."

(*Every Woman's Encyclopaedia*, vol. 2 pp1380, 1910-1912)

She did not always receive such unreserved praise, as in the comment made on her novel, *What shall it Profit a Man?* in the periodical *Golf! A Weekly Record* of December 17th, 1897: "Mrs Tweedale's novel writing is not so good as her golf at North Berwick used to be – for that was first class!" At least the critic knew a good golfer when he saw one!

The Rev. F.L.M. Anderson outside the parsonage with his 2nd wife and two of his daughters, the elder of whom is carrying a couple of golf clubs.

Apart from Violet Chambers being singled out for her excellent golfing, in the early days, the Anderson girls, daughters of the Rev. Fortesque Lennox Anderson, Rector of St Baldred's Episcopal Church, were also feted for their accomplished play. The Rev Anderson had arrived in North Berwick in 1867 to become the first Rector of the new church. By 1872, the family were settled in the parsonage, in York Road, which was conveniently situated halfway between the golf course and St Baldred's Church. At that time, Fortesque and his wife Charlotte had five young daughters, Helen Maud, Edith, Meriel, Florence and Blanche and a son, Lennox Stuart. The following year, Charlotte, pregnant for the seventh time in as many years, died during the premature delivery of a still born daughter. Nannies and governesses were brought in to the Anderson household to help bring up the motherless children, the eldest of whom was seven. As part of the coping strategy, each child was sent off to board at school in Edinburgh, as they reached the age of eleven. The Rev. Anderson threw himself into affairs of the church, creating a reputation as a learned yet sociable parson with a wealthy, admiring and expanding congregation. He spent as much of his spare time as possible on the golf course, with his children following suit at weekends and during the school holidays. There was further sadness in the family when Edith succumbed to a heart condition and died in June 1876, aged nine. In October 1882, the Rev. FLM Anderson married his children's young governess, Emma Sidley, and had three more children.

The four surviving Anderson sisters played in a ladies' tournament at North Berwick in September 1885. There were two matches, one for over 12s and one for 12 and under. Maud Anderson, then aged nineteen and playing off scratch, lifted the first prize – a set of clubs, while Edith McCulloch, the Bank Manager's eldest daughter won the handicap prize of a gold bracelet. The winner of the younger girls' competition was Violet Sprott, the ten year old daughter of another North Berwick cleric, George Washington Sprott, Minister of the Church of Scotland, St Andrew Blackadder. The Rev. Sprott and the Rev. Anderson had much in common: both had lost their wives in childbirth, shortly after moving to North Berwick; both then had to deal with the subsequent death of a child and take full responsibility for the upbringing of their very young families; and both were committed to play the key roles that were expected of the Parish Minister and the Rector within the community. But it was their status as 'men of the cloth' that gave their families an opportunity to mix with the gentility who flocked to North Berwick for the summer season and who built enormous holiday houses on the outskirts of the town and dominated activities on the west links. The Sprotts, Andersons (and McCullochs) were among few local families whose manners, education and accomplishments made them welcome participants among the new golfing set, whose regular presence was redefining the town as a fashionable resort.

Ladies in a supporting role

The popularity of North Berwick had begun to increase dramatically, after the opening, in 1850, of the North Berwick railway line, a spur off the main London to Edinburgh line, and from that time visitors poured into the town during the summer months. A reflection of this could be seen in the number of new houses that were built on the outskirts of the town, which up until then had consisted of little more than the High Street and a cluster of buildings around the harbour. A few houses appeared in the East Bay, but the major expansion was to the west of the town and started around 1860, when a large free standing stone house was built overlooking the golf course, for a Mr

This early print of ladies golfing at Westward Ho! (Royal North Devon Club) was presented to Elsie Grant Suttie, a member of The North Berwick Ladies' Golf Club, by the Devon Club, after she won the Ladies' British Open there in 1910.

Campbell. The house was Inchgarry and the owner was Mr Thomas Buchanan Campbell, a wealthy Edinburgh metal merchant and grandfather of Dorothy Campbell. Inchgarry was Thomas Campbell's summer and weekend retreat and after he died there in September 1875, his eldest son William, Dorothy's father, took it over and the family continued to spend the summer months in North Berwick.

Almost all the ground immediately to the south of the links was rapidly developed over the next few years, largely by the Edinburgh professional and business classes, eager to have a stake in Scotland's new golfing paradise. They were almost all building second homes. They were joined by a number of the English upper classes, who were taking in either golf or 'the waters' as part of their seasonal tour north of the border, which was generally organised around grouse shooting and salmon fishing. Some of the old East Lothian landed gentry already had property in the burgh, such as the Dalrymples, while others travelled in from their country estates, stayed with friends or rented: all made sure they were present in the town to enjoy the 'goff' during the season.

The establishment of the North Berwick Golf Club, in 1832, had brought golf to the fore in the burgh. Membership of the golfing fraternity was largely an upper-class affair and this elite group called the tune regarding golfing activities in the town. According to John Kerr (p82): "[In those days,] there were a few enthusiasts, with club and ball, but the inhabitants generally were indifferent toward the game". This apparent apathy of the local population could have been because of golf's social exclusivity. A contemporary account contradicts Kerr's view. The Rev. Balfour Graham, parish minister, writing in the *New Statistical Account of Scotland*, in 1841, stated: "The prevailing game of the parish is the golf". The truth is likely to lie somewhere between. There were, in fact, plenty of working-class men and boys in the town, who found their way on to the links by caddying and later became professional golfers. What is certain is that in North Berwick, in the mid nineteenth century, few women played golf.

The ladies, however, were regularly to be seen supporting their men-folk at the great annual meetings of the North Berwick Golf Club. It was customary for the ladies to accompany their husbands, watch them play and sit down with them to lunch. For many years, before the men's club house was built, a magnificent lunch was laid out in a tent on the green, with food and drink provided by the members. On one occasion, the tent was donated by Lady Anne Baird, wife of Sir David Baird, founder member and first captain of the North Berwick Club. Why she should have made the gift and not her husband is unclear, but her contribution is interesting in that it demonstrates a sort of tacit approval of the gentlemen's domination of the game, yet it puts down a marker that the women wished to be included.

The Fair Sex Gets Its Green

In a way, it was the need for a more permanent home than a tent for the North Berwick Club, which precipitated change in the golfing habits among the old county members and ultimately led to the setting up of the Ladies' Club. As the North Berwick Club had at most between fifty and sixty members, there were never sufficient funds to build a club house. By the 1860s and 70s, there was increasing pressure from the new moneyed classes, who had arrived, from Edinburgh and beyond, in order to golf. They had joined the Tantallon Club, but many of them sought a closer association with the grandees who ran the prestigious North Berwick Club and who jealously guarded entry to its privileged ranks. In 1880, a solution was reached: rather than broaden the membership of the old North Berwick Golf Club, another golf club, the New Club, was formed and the money raised from the first 120 members enabled a permanent club house to be built, on the site of the old tollhouse, close to the first tee. Sir Hew Dalrymple facilitated the scheme, by purchasing the tollhouse and feuing the site to the new club. However, there were now at least 120 wives and daughters of the New Club members, who were no longer content merely to be spectators: they wanted to play.

It had become clear to the men that "the fair sex would not rest content until they got a green to suit themselves" and once they had accepted the inevitable - that the advance of women on the golf course was not going to be stemmed - they moved rapidly to launch the Ladies' Club. The entire project took just three months to complete. There was all-round satisfaction on that Thursday afternoon of July 5th 1888, as the first members of the North Berwick Ladies' Golf Club tee'd off on their excellent course, invigorated by the sea air and buoyed up by the prospect of greater golfing challenges ahead. The newly appointed chairman, Benjamin Hall Blyth could not, however, resist reminding the ladies of their debt of gratitude to the men - "Great expense has been incurred", he chaffed and wondered whether there were ever going to be enough lady members to defray the cost. He should have had more faith. The Club was an instant success. By the end of August there were thirty seven members and rising. It was soon apparent that the ladies could enjoy the Royal and Ancient game as much as their male counterparts:

"Look pleasant when your efforts fail
And when the wind is in your sail,
And balls are flying down the gale
Play Steady!"

CHAPTER TWO

The Ladies Sign Up: "Where is it all to end?"

"Golf, the rage of our northern Brighton, has seized on the fair sex who would not rest content till they got a green to suit themselves."
(*The Scotsman*, 11 July 1888)

On Friday 3rd August 1888, the first monthly competition for the newly formed North Berwick Ladies' Golf Club was played over the ladies' course. A large crowd gathered in the warm sunshine to watch. Most were the leading lights of the North Berwick golfing society and parents of the young ladies participating in the match. The reporter from *The Country Gentlemen* magazine picked out those with a bit of celebrity status for his readers. Most notable and glamorous among them was the Marchioness of Tweeddale, whose husband's extensive East Lothian estates lay around the village of Gifford, with the beautiful mansion Yester House at its centre. She was a keen supporter of the idea of the ladies' club, though not a member. She was accompanied by Sir George (a member of the North Berwick Club) and Lady Houston-Boswall, who had come up from their Blackadder estate in Berwickshire. Walter Dalrymple made it his duty to attend. The Ladies' Club Chairman Mr Benjamin Hall Blyth was there with his wife to cheer on their daughter Elsie. Mr and Mrs Gillies Smith were supporting their three daughters, two of whom carried off the honours – the eldest, Margaret, winning the club's silver medal with a wonderful score of 64 over two rounds of the ladies' links and Coventry securing third place after playing a tie against a Miss Wylie.

"During the season ladies can be seen in quiet corners busily engaged in practising swings with different clubs." (J. McAndrew, Golfing Step by Step, 1914).

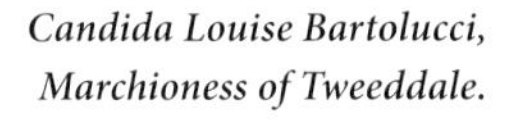
Candida Louise Bartolucci,
Marchioness of Tweeddale.

The scene that August day had been played out on very many occasions during the golfing season at North Berwick over the previous fifty years, when there were Club competitions for the gentlemen, or organised matches between some of the better known band of professional golfers (at the time, all men). In those days, the rare events in which the ladies played, had always caused a stir and brought out a crowd. What was significant in August 1888 and in the future was that, with the formalisation of the ladies' game through the setting up of their Club, they could now be confident of 'disporting themselves on the green' without fear of censure.

Many of the early members of the Ladies' Club were the wives and daughters of wealthy, upper-middle-class Edinburgh families, who lived in large terraced houses, either in the Georgian New Town close to the city centre, or in the newer Victorian West End. Some of these families had been holidaying regularly in North Berwick from the 1850s and 60s, when it was only the men who were to be seen out of the golf course. Generally speaking, the men played and the ladies spectated. By the 1880s, golfing in the little seaside burgh began to carry with it a certain caché, beyond just the county set. The Edinburgh ladies were anxious to be part of that social milieu. One way of being noticed was to appear on the links to watch one of the many golf matches and competitions that took place during the summer months. Another means of announcing one's presence in the town was by leaving one's name and North Berwick address with Miss Hope at her stationer's shop in the High Street. This meant it would appear on the Visitors' List which was published every week in the local newspapers. Calling cards could then be exchanged and invitations delivered and received. Miss Hope performed this function for years and then suddenly, in January 1889, she announced that she had disposed of her stationery and fancy wares business and was about to emigrate to Australia to join her brother. Within weeks she had gone and a Mrs Brownlee took her place, without a break in the publication of the all-important Visitors' List.

THE NORTH BERWICK VISITORS' LIST, 22 AUGUST 1888

Cromwell Road

Agsacre	**Mr and Mrs Gillies Smith and family, Edinburgh**
No.2	**Mr and Mrs Fleming and family, Edinburgh**
No. 3	**Mr and Mrs Younger and family, Edinburgh**
Greenhythe	**Dr, Mrs and Miss Orphoot, Edinburgh**
Kaimend	**Mr and Mrs Hall Blyth, Edinburgh**
Springfield	**Mr George Brown and family, Edinburgh**
Rock Ibris	**Mrs Black and family, Edinburgh**
Springbank	**Mr and Mrs Hector Smith and family, Edinburgh**
Gordonbank	**Mr and Mrs Jopp and family, Edinburgh**

(North Berwick Advertiser and East Lothian Visiter, 22 August 1888)

A mischievous sketch, probably drawn by Lady Wemyss, of Constance Nisbet Hamilton-Ogilvy golfing.

Another group of the early members of the NBLGC were the wives and daughters of successful Glasgow business men and industrialists, who perhaps considered the east coast resort more genteel than any options on the west. Their expectations of being integrated immediately into the county set were raised too high. In 1888, not a single one of the lady members of the new golf club belonged to the East Lothian nobility and gentry, as might have been expected – that is to say, no wives and daughters of the members of the old North Berwick Club joined the NBLGC in its opening year. Most were not yet ready to challenge the conventions of their class; they would have had to seek their husbands' permission and it remained their husbands' duty to protect them from the coarseness of unrefined society! These families, however, such as the Tweeddales at Yester, the Wemyss at Gosford and the Hamilton-Ogilvys at Archerfield, had their own private courses, where their ladies could play unobserved by the general public. The first among the county set to break ranks and join the Ladies' Club, in September 1889, was the Hon. Lady Hay, who belonged to the Hays of Yester. There was an initial hesitancy from any of the married ladies to join, but their daughters flocked to become members. This surge of young blood in the newly-formed club may explain, in part, the incredible success rate of its members in early competitive golf.

Within days of the silver medal competition, Mrs Gillies Smith, married lady though she was, did not delay in stepping forward with her three daughters, to be among the very first women to sign up for membership. The newspapers talked about the ladies' enthusiasm for golf in North Berwick as "the rage of our Northern Brighton". Until then, it had been par for the course for the ladies' involvement in the game to be ignored by the sporting press, although there was endless coverage of men's golf. However, that was beginning to change and accounts of the activities of the significant numbers of new ladies' clubs began to appear in several publications. The disapproving attitudes towards women's open participation in sport, so prevalent among the Victorian middle classes, were beginning to relax. The sight of women golfing was becoming more normal and, as this comment in *Bailey's Monthly Magazine of Sports and Pastimes* of December 1888 suggests, was presenting a challenge to men as to how to deal with it:

> **"And today in Scotland ladies play golf as well, and some of them wield their clubs in such fashion and to such purpose as to occasionally lead men to consider where it is all to end!"**

Perhaps, some already realised that the ladies could not be tucked away on 'their cosy little links' forever.

Margaret (Rita) Gillies Smith and her two younger sisters, Coventry and Adelaide, dominated club matches in the first decade of the Ladies' Club, but Margaret remained the truly outstanding golfer. They were born and brought up in Edinburgh, with their two brothers (their younger brother died from kidney disease in 1885), in a large Victorian four storey terraced house at 35 Drumsheugh Gardens, at the heart of Edinburgh's salubrious West End. The family also had a house in North Berwick, 'Agsacre', in Cromwell Road, which overlooked the ninth tee of the ladies' course. It was designed and built for them, in 1879, by architect Dick Peddie and had ten bedrooms and a tennis court in the grounds. The girls were educated at home by a German governess, but with the encouragement of their mother, Maria, they had ample opportunity to practise their strokes during the summer months. Every Sunday, during the summer, the family worshipped in St Baldred's Church, a five minute walk from Agsacre. Their father Adam Gillies Smith, a son of the manse and educated at Aberdeen University, was a chartered accountant. In 1855, he had become one of the first members of the Society of Accountants, the forerunner of the CA Institute and at the peak of his career was Manager of the North British and Mercantile Insurance Company.

Adelaide Gillies Smith, one of the early good lady golfers at North Berwick.

Adam Gillies Smith had high expectations of a solid career path for his surviving son and hopes of decent marriages for his three daughters. He was to be disappointed. The girls appeared to be more interested in success on the golfing green than in catching the eye of a suitable young man. In 1888, his son Cecil embarked on a law degree and was already proving to be an excellent golfer, often partnering his eldest sister in mixed doubles matches, but tragically, in 1896, he died after suffering a stroke. He was 26 and on the threshold of a brilliant career as an advocate. It was a terrible blow to the family. Adam Gillies Smith's faith sustained him and he immersed himself in local affairs in the town. When he died in January 1900, at the age of 72, his obituary painted a picture of a good family man:

> **"Mr Smith in his own home and among his own people always appeared at his best. Pleasant and kind…he was an excellent host and a most agreeable and entertaining companion."**

Mrs Gillies Smith died in 1903. The strong bond of family seemed to keep the three sisters (none of whom ever married) together. They rattled around in Agsacre, until they sold it in 1919 and bought a more manageable house, The Latch, on the east Bay. Golfing activities had been largely suspended in the 1914-18 war, and, after it was over, the sisters dropped out of competitive golf. During the war, Margaret had signed up for the Voluntary Aid Detachment and had given service to her country as a field nurse in Salonika (Greece) and in France, behind the trenches. She was greatly respected in North Berwick for her bravery. Between the wars, all three sisters devoted a good deal of time to charitable causes, in particular raising money for the British Red Cross Society. They were never short of invitations among polite society in the town. Sir Hew Hamilton-Dalrymple remembers the sisters coming to tea at his parents' home, The Lodge, in Quality Street in the 1930s, when he was a young boy, and on another occasion, them taking a trip out to the Bass Rock with his family – by then, they were simply three bright elderly ladies, their golfing days far behind them.

In later years, they spent much time in their cottage, Taighsgoil, in Aberfeldy and perhaps became a little eccentric. On more than one occasion, Coventry wrote letters to *The Scotsman*, detailing sudden and extraordinary rumblings and vibrations of their cottage windows, enthusiastically picking up on the suggestion that the disturbances were earthquakes! Perhaps, she was seeking excitement in a life that had become too dull and in which opportunities had passed her by. The sisters each died peacefully in old age at Taighsgoil, away from the North Berwick ladies' links, where they had attracted such admiration and demonstrated so much skill as young golfers, in an age where they were truly ahead of the game. (The Gillies Smith sisters' golfing triumphs are detailed in chapter 5)

Mrs Lucy Smith, wife of Hector, Manager of the National Bank of Scotland, joined the Ladies' Club on the 10th August, with her friend and Edinburgh neighbour, Maria Gillies Smith. (The Hector Smiths lived at 33 Drumsheugh Gardens.) Lucy had four sons, who were educated at Loretto, the youngest of whom was killed in action at Loos in 1915. Her involvement with the Ladies' Club, like that of many other early members, was set around summertime visits to North Berwick and she had dropped her membership by 1906.

One married lady who made her formidable presence felt on the links and in the town was Mrs Mary Caroline Outhwaite. Daughter of a wealthy Yorkshire banking family, she and her husband Lt. Col. Francis Outhwaite had moved to Scotland in 1884, on his retirement from the army and built a large house, Craigforth, on the headland, between Earlferry and Elie, overlooking the golf course there. At about the same time, they rented Westfield, on Links Road, North Berwick, during the summer golf season, but became so attached to the house, they bought it in January 1888 for over £3000. Their two sons, John Henley and Thomas, were both excellent golfers and John, in particular, established a reputation on the Scottish amateur golfing circuit. Mary Outhwaite was one of the first members of the North Berwick Ladies' Club and a keen competitor. Her reputation locally was not, however, for her golfing prowess, but as someone who held rather forthright views. One day, when she was being driven in her coach past a new windmill at Fentonbarns, just outside North Berwick, the horse bolted, nearly causing a serious accident. Mrs Outhwaite would not rest until the Fentonbarns farmer, William Ford, had been brought to court for contravening the Roads and Bridges Act in erecting the windmill too close to the public highway. In the end the case was dismissed and Mary Outhwaite remained unmoved by any adverse publicity she received as a result.

St Baldred's Episcopal Church in Dirleton Avenue c.1888. It was nick-named the 'English Church', as so many visiting golfers from south of the border worshipped there. The Rev. FLM Anderson is standing on the far right of the group of clergy and choir.

The Outhwaites, in common with many other English visitors to the town, worshipped every Sunday in St. Baldred's Episcopal Church. The church had been built at the west end of North Berwick, in 1862. There was no golf on Sundays and the visiting gentlefolk flocked to hear the sermons preached by the Rev. Anderson. In 1892, Francis Outhwaite paid for a stained glass window, in the church, in memory of his mother Frances, who had died in 1891. It was one of nine exquisitely crafted windows made by Messrs. Clayton & Bell of Regent Street, London, for St Baldred's and although the Outhwaites also golfed at Elie, where Mrs Outhwaite was Secretary of the Elie and Earlsferry Ladies' Club, this act was indicative of the Outhwaites' over-riding desire to be well-remembered in North Berwick. In August 1896, Mary Outhwaite helped to organise a three-day ladies' golf tournament at the Elie Club, at which Margot Asquith, the new young wife of H.H Asquith MP (and later Prime Minister) presented the prizes. In June the following year, Mary's husband Francis suffered a fatal heart attack at the age of forty nine. Two years later in July 1899, her 25 year old elder son John (Jackie), a Lieutenant in the 2nd battalion the Gordon Highlanders, fell victim to an outbreak of enteric fever, on a posting to Dagshai, in India, and died. An obituary in the *Dundee Courier* noted he had already made a mark in the amateur golf championships and his death had cut short a promising career in golf. The two sudden and unexpected bereavements brought to a close her North Berwick golfing days and although she continued as Honorary Secretary of the Elie and Earlsferry Ladies' Club, she no longer played. She dressed in black for the rest of her life, dying in Elie in 1933, at the age of eighty three.

Margot Tennant golfed at North Berwick before and after her marriage to Herbert Asquith in 1895. He became Prime Minister in 1908.

The Anderson girls would have been well-known to Mrs Outhwaite, both through their appearances on the North Berwick links and their regular attendance at their father's bidding, at St Baldred's on Sundays. In 1888, there were three sisters at home in the Rectory, Helen who was 22, Florence 18 and Blanche 16 and their brother Lennox Stuart. In October 1885, Meriel Anderson was married to the Rev. Cecil Nash, an Episcopal minister, who had a comfortable living in Aberdeenshire. Meriel was just seventeen and her husband ten years older. In the wedding photo, taken outside St Baldred's, the expression on Meriel's face, somehow lacks the radiant smile of a new bride. She looks timid and fearful. The marriage, however, would have brought relief to her father; he would be free of the responsibility and expense of at least one of his daughters. This was important; in 1882, he had married the children's governess Emma Sidley, who was half his age and started a second family. For Meriel, golfing would become secondary to attending to her duties as the Rector's wife and within a few years, there were three little Nashs, who required attention. Of the sisters, Florence and Blanche were the great golfing enthusiasts and both played a strong game. It has been said that their father would not allow them to join the club, but records show they were there from the start. Both had taken part in the Club's inaugural game, in July, both tying for first place. Florence came second in the Club's silver medal competition, the following month, but it was Blanche's game that matured into something exceptional, breaking course records and entertaining the crowds with her graceful style and her full swing. Maud and Florence married, in 1891 and 1893 respectively, while Blanche's main focus remained golf.

Meriel Anderson's marriage to the Rev. Cecil Nash in 1885. Her sisters are bridesmaids.

When fifteen year old Elizabeth Napier joined the Ladies' Club on the 10th August 1888, she was no stranger to the game. She had connections to North Berwick and golf, through both of her parents. Her mother, also Elizabeth, was part of the illustrious Stevenson family and sister of one of the club's founders David Allan Stevenson and when she married an Edinburgh lawyer, Alexander Napier, who was already a member of the New Club, it was almost inevitable they would maintain the family tradition of North Berwick golfing summers. In the handicap competition in August, the young Elizabeth won fifth prize after playing off a tie. She also had the lowest scoring single round of 36 off a handicap of 7. Two days later in the scratch competition, she was not so well on form and completed the two rounds of nine holes in 87. In 1897, Elizabeth married the heir of the Glenbervie estate in Kincardinshire, Arthur Badenoch Nicolson, but continued to play as a member at North Berwick.

Louisa Hope Stevenson joined the Ladies' Club on August 28th 1888 and participated regularly in the club competitions, always a steady player, but never a shining star. She typified the early membership. She was young (24), single and came from a wealthy, educated, well-connected, Edinburgh family, who belonged to the chattering classes of the day and who had adopted the fashion of spending summer holidays in North Berwick. Her father was the Rev. Robert Horne Stevenson, Minister of St George's, Edinburgh and a Moderator of the Church of Scotland. Her mother was Frances Cadell and descended from the great entrepreneurial and industrialising Cadell family, who had established the Carron Ironworks in 1759. Her great grandfather John Cadell developed salt and vitriol works close to Cockenzie, where he lived in the large Jacobean mansion Cockenzie House, which is still a focal point in the village today. Louisa's grandfather Robert Cadell, became a publisher, who made his fortune by gaining the sole publishing rights over Sir Walter Scott's novels. Louisa's father, who was fifteen years older than her mother, died in 1886, at the age of 73. For the next twenty years Louisa stayed at home as companion to her mother and then, in January 1905, quite unexpectedly, at the age of 40, she married Alexander Gordon Fraser Sinclair. Sinclair, ARSA, was a landscape and portrait painter of some renown. He was a member of a group known as the Society of Eight, which included John Lavery and Patrick Adam, both of whom had golfing connections with North Berwick (see Ch 3).

Ethel Bilton at fourteen was the eldest of seven siblings of Lewis and Hannah Bilton and in 1888 enjoyed a spell as a member at North Berwick. She broke no records as a golfer. In common with several young Club members, her family was well off. Her mother was the daughter of a Liverpool shipbuilder, John Grayson of H & C Grayson Ltd and her father an Edinburgh solicitor and a partner in the firm Skene, Edwards & Bilton. The Bilton children enjoyed a comfortable upbringing. Their father was a member of the General Assembly of the Church of Scotland and the Queen's Rifle Volunteer Brigade and both parents were involved in charitable works. In the summer, the family took a house, The Knowe, in Marmion Road, North Berwick. Sporting activities, including golf were encouraged. In December 1893, the family's, hitherto, untroubled existence was rudely disrupted by the death of nine year old Gavin Bilton in a freak accident at home, when he fell and sustained a fatal head injury. An odd episode surrounded his death; rumours circulated that Gavin had died as the result of an accident on the rugby field at The Academy, where he was at school. The rumours were so widespread that the school's Rector, R.J. Mackenzie, wrote a letter to *The Scotsman*, with Mr Bilton's agreement, disclaiming them. A dark cloud hung over the family for a long time. As an adult, Ethel left her North Berwick golfing days behind and, unlike many of her social contemporaries, she pursued a career; she worked as a matron in a boys' boarding school. Most women from her background would have lived on private means, if they couldn't find a suitable husband! She appears to have settled in England.

The Bell sisters, Eleanora and Janet signed up for the club in its early days and although now forgotten, established a fine reputation as excellent golfers in club competitions. Eleanora was twenty when the club opened and was still playing off a handicap of 4 in 1915 at the age of fifty seven. The girls lived in Grosvenor Crescent in Edinburgh's west end, with their widowed mother. Their father Benjamin Bell, a sheriff advocate and cousin of Dr Joseph Bell, on whom Arthur Conan Doyle based Sherlock Holmes, had died in 1886 and the golfing influence came largely from their mother. Their elder sister Margaret had married an Edinburgh Chartered Accountant, Hugh Blair, and joined the club as Mrs Blair. Her daughter Janet continued the family tradition and not only was a scratch player at club level, but also had a LGU (Ladies Golf Union) handicap of 7.

The Macandrew sisters, Margaret and Isabella, also from an Edinburgh family, were direct contemporaries of Eleanora and Janet Bell and early members of the Club. They competed in the second contest for the scratch medal of the Club on 24th August 1888, but were the only players that day who made no returns. Although they were Club members for over twenty years, from that time they seem to have steered clear of competition, but continued to play for enjoyment.

Among the several sets of sisters who graced the new links were twins, Mathilda Wakelin and Rachel Husband. Rachel had married William Husband, a bank employee, in March 1881, at her father's home, Rosehill House, in the picturesque village of Inveresk which lies close to Musselburgh. (It was still a common practice in Scotland, for the minister to come to a bride's home to conduct a marriage ceremony, in the company of family and a few close friends, followed by a simple wedding breakfast.) The girls' father, John Wakelin, had built up a thriving business as an oil and seed merchant in the 1850s. He golfed at Musselburgh, but it was unlikely any of his daughters (there were six in all) would learn to play at that time. Rachel was encouraged to play golf by her husband, who was a member and later secretary at Royal Musselburgh. He was also a member at Tantallon. William Husband rented rooms in North Berwick in the summer and so while Rachel practiced her strokes on the ladies' links with Mathilda, William could strike out on the long course. In the match to celebrate the opening of the ladies' links in 1888, both women appeared near the bottom of the scoreboard. Rachel died from cancer in 1897. Mathilda remained single and stayed at home looking after her widowed father. She died at Rosehill House in 1928, aged 80.

The Montgomerys were the archetypal middle-class, professional Edinburgh family who spent their summers in North Berwick golfing and socialising. William Montgomery, a lawyer, who lived and worked in Rutland Square in the centre of Edinburgh, had four daughters and three sons. In term time, the boys were sent off to Glenalmond an elite public school in Perthshire, one of whose founders was William Gladstone. The girls stayed closer to home and simply crossed Edinburgh's principal thoroughfare, Princes' Street, each morning, to the Young Ladies' Institution in Charlotte Square.

In March 1888, William died quite unexpectedly, at the age of 58, after succumbing to an acute streptococcal infection, erysipelas, which was commonly called St. Anthony's fire, because of the large red swollen, painful patches which appeared on the face or arms and legs. Nowadays it is treated swiftly with antibiotics, but it could be a killer in the late nineteenth century and William died within a fortnight. He had not written a will: the school fees were outstanding and the grocer, the butcher and the dressmaker were all waiting to be paid. It must have been a trying time for Mrs Montgomery. Nevertheless, in August, the family kept to their usual routine and spent the summer in North Berwick. For the youngsters, the links provided a relief from the sadness of the preceding months. The Montgomery sisters were competent golfers and keen competitors and were quick to sign up for the Ladies' Club. The three younger girls, Meta, Alice and Ethel became familiar figures on the ladies' course, taking part in the monthly competitions. This pattern continued for several years, until marriage or other interests took them south of the border.

The Montgomery's association with the Ladies' Club didn't end there. The youngest Montgomery son, William Harold, was appointed agent of the North Berwick branch of the British Linen Bank, in about 1900, a position he retained for the rest of his working life. In 1908, he married the daughter of a Wiltshire solicitor, Dorothea Godiva Mann, who quickly became involved in the North Berwick ladies' golfing scene. She was a good golfer, playing off a handicap of 6 in 1915. In August 1919, her two daughters, Betty aged 10 and Jean aged 9 were the youngest competitors for the Ladies' Gold Medal, which was won by David Stevenson's daughter Kathleen and in which young Jean returned the worst score of the day – 124, for two rounds of the 9-hole course. The Montgomery girls' next recorded appearance was in the children's competition, the following year, in which Betty restored family honour by winning the third handicap prize of ten shillings. As a footnote, Dorothea's husband William died suddenly of a heart attack, while golfing on the West Links in December 1937, at the age of sixty eight.

By coincidence, there was a high percentage of fatherless daughters who were members at North Berwick in the early days of the Ladies' Club and begs the question, from whom did the impetus come to take up golf? For a woman, active participation in any sport could still raise eyebrows. Yet it seems, these relatively young widowed mothers, left with the responsibility of bringing up a family of several children, must have encouraged their daughters, as well as sons, to get out on to the golf course. Viewed against a broader context of late Victorian Britain, the question of women's rights was constantly being aired and traditional social and political restrictions on women were beginning to be lifted. Modern mothers were determined their daughters should enjoy freedoms not available to them and be better prepared for an independent life.

Men golfing and women spectating was a familiar scene at North Berwick until more women took up the game in the 1890s. (Lithograph by Thomas Blacklock c.1892).

The daughters of a prosperous Glasgow family were among the members of the Ladies' Club. Mary Louisa (16) and Janet Spens (15) were the two eldest daughters of William George Spens, company secretary of one of Scotland's burgeoning Life Assurance Societies and their mother was the Hon. Mary Borthwick. There were seven children – four girls and three boys. Every year, the family spent the month of August in North Berwick. The girls took part in the club competitions with enthusiasm, but only moderate success, cheered on by their mother in the crowd of spectators. In about 1896, the Spens moved to Edinburgh and continued to visit North Berwick in the summer months, renting Winterfield Lodge, a large house overlooking the links. They were often joined by William's brother Nathaniel and his family, who lived in London. The family maintained their golfing connection to North Berwick for many years. Two of William's daughters married – Mary Louisa, in 1895, to army officer William Stirling, and, in 1904, Alice married George Jardine, whose family part-owned the Gartcosh iron & steel works. Janet and her younger sister Ariana continued to live at home, spending the summers golfing in North Berwick. Late in life Janet married a widowed Anglican priest, the Rev. Arthur Herbert Powell. She had probably met him when he visited golfing relatives in North Berwick. Ariana never married and died in the house she had shared with her parents at 44 Albany Street Edinburgh, in 1954.

Some of the large houses built overlooking the links, including Agsacre (the Gillies Smith's house) and Winterfield. The Marine Hotel is on the right, c.1890.

In July 1888, the three Jarvie sisters, Agnes (22), Helen (20) and Susan (12) arrived in North Berwick with their widowed mother Elizabeth and their three brothers, from Blantyre in Lanarkshire. They lived there with their grandmother, in the old mansion house of Millheugh. They rented Fidra Cottage in the Westgate, close to the links, for the entire summer season. They joined the club as soon as it started up in July and the girls took part in the opening match. They were in North Berwick until October and played in all the club matches. But none of them played great golf and even with generous 'allowances' (handicaps), they still finished a long way down the field. Within a few years their membership lapsed and so did their brief association with the North Berwick Ladies' Club.

Julia Elderton's connection with the Ladies' Club was also short-lived. Her father, Frederick, was manager of a life assurance company in Glasgow and rented Park House, a large villa (now the local branch of the RBS) in the centre of North Berwick for the summer, from Anne Dall, widow of local merchant, James Dall. Julia, aged 20, was one of the very first club members and a keen competitor. But the following year, July 1889, at the start of the family holiday and a few days before the ladies' handicap competition, Julia's mother became ill and died at Park House. It was the end of the Elderton's holidays in North Berwick and of Julia's membership of the Ladies' Club.

The house immediately next to Park House was Blenheim House, the summer residence of Walter Maximilian De Zoete. The house was in the Westgate, an extension of the High Street and the back entrance opened onto the links. The De Zoetes were among the first English families to dip their toes in the sea at North Berwick and quickly discovered all the advantages offered by the town and the great golfing opportunities. Walter's father Samuel had been a stockbroker and Chairman of the London Stock Exchange and after his father's death in 1884, Walter continued in the family business. He was an excellent sportsman, but golf was his passion and he was renowned as an extremely good amateur golfer. The annual family visits to North Berwick, where Walter was a member of the New Club, were primarily for golfing.

Walter and his wife Dorothy had five daughters and one son and seemed to have had no hesitation about their two elder daughters, Edith, fourteen, and Winifred Mary, twelve, joining the Ladies' Club. On Thursday August 30th 1888, Mr and Mrs De Zoete joined the spectators to watch their daughters take part in the handicap competition over the ladies' course. There was a buzz of excitement as the Marchioness of Tweeddale, who had gifted the first prize of a gold bracelet set with pearls, was to be there to present the prizes. On the day, a note of apology arrived to say that a death in the family had made her presence impossible. However, the appearance of the Archbishop of York and the Lord Advocate was enough to engage the interest of the crowd when there was a lull in the match. Winifred had a happier outing than her older sister and came eleventh out of a field of forty one. She completed eighteen holes in 83 strokes and her handicap of 14 gave her a score of 69, ten strokes behind the winner Miss Thomas, whose handicap of 36 gave her a distinct advantage over the rest of the field.

Edith de Zoete practising her golf swing in the garden, c.1888.

The following week, Walter De Zoete, playing off scratch, won the North Berwick Club gold medal with a round over the main course of 62. The Earl of Wemyss was elected club captain at the meeting before the match and, afterwards, a fine lunch was served in the marquee erected beside the home green to "a large party of ladies and gentlemen". While Miss Edith De Zoete had the privilege of attending the lunch with her parents, Winifred was left at home with the nanny and her younger siblings!

Spectators following a match on the links at North Berwick.

Miss Shearer first appeared on the list of ladies admitted as members on 28th August 1888 and took part in the Club handicap match the following day. The order of play had already been drawn and she was given a bye into the second round, and with an allowance of 20 strokes, she finished half way down the field with a net score of 68. In the September meeting, Thomasina Maude Shearer and her partner Miss Mary Meikleham were first to tee off at 3.15pm. There was a record entry of forty four and so the competition was stiff. Thomasina's handicap had been reduced to 14 and she finished a respectable ninth, with a net score of 74. Margaret Gillies Smith won the Gold Medal with a fine scratch score of 69. There was an unusually large crowd of onlookers, who had probably turned out as much to see the Chief Secretary for Ireland, A. J. Balfour presenting the prizes, as to watch the golf.

Thomasina was brought up in Edinburgh, but after her marriage in June 1893 to Harry Smith Murray, she lived in a fine Victorian mansion Glenmayne, in Galashiels. Harry's father, John Murray, had set up a wool trading business with William Sanderson in 1844 and married William's sister, Isabella. The business had become a huge success with interests in Australia, New Zealand and South America. After his father's death in 1892, Harry continued in the business, but sold his interest at the end of the First World War. Thomasina and Harry had no children. Thomasina retained her membership of the Ladies' Club as Mrs Murray and various members of the Murray family continued to golf at North Berwick for many years.

One of the members whose permanent home became North Berwick was Ethel Wylie. Her father had been a stockbroker in London and Edinburgh and died in 1869 when Ethel was 10 years old. There were eight children and it seemed to be the lot of the two daughters Margaret and Ethel to stay at home as companions to their widowed mother, who had a house on the east bay. Ethel was enthusiastic about golf and played regularly and steadily in club competitions over the next few years, eventually bringing her handicap down to 4 in 1892. Once a year when there was a mixed foursome match, Ethel would partner her brother Napier, who became a member of the Ladies' Committee. Ethel never married. She remained in her mother's house and died there in 1935 at the age of 75.

Margaret Gillies one of the great women golfers to come out of North Berwick, in the early days of the Ladies' Club.

For Mary Jane Meikleham, the Ladies' Golf Club provided a welcome outlet for her quiet social life. She had been born and brought up in North Berwick, where her father David Meikleham had been a prominent town councillor and Provost in the 1850s. He had earlier had a rather unusual career as an engineer to the Ottoman government and later distinguished himself by setting a record for growing ripe black Hamburg grapes in March, 1860 at the back of his house. The grapes, which he sold for 14 shillings a lb., graced the table of Napoleon III, in Paris, a few days later. Financial success allowed her father to buy the gracious old Muirfield House on the edge of Gullane, as a family home, in the 1860s. Mary Jane was still living at home when her parents and one of her brothers died in the 1880s, and so she and her surviving brother, both unmarried, remained close companions until he died suddenly in 1894. Mary Jane was a familiar figure on the ladies' links almost until her death in 1905. She should be remembered, however, for her generous bequest of Muirfield House and grounds to establish a convalescent home for the Royal Edinburgh Sick Children's Hospital. To fulfil her legacy the old mansion house was pulled down and Sir Robert Lorimer designed a purpose-built home for the children in 1909.

Fifteen year old Elizabeth Mylne was an enthusiastic participant in early club matches. Her mother was also a member, but she seemed more inclined to watch her eldest daughter compete rather than participate. Miss Mylne, for all her initial enthusiasm was rarely up with the leading ladies when the results came in. The family spent the summers at North Berwick with her mother's sister, Jane, and various cousins at Rock Ibris in York Road. Later her younger sisters joined the club. One cousin was killed in the Great War another married Harry Auldjo Jamieson, and lived for many years at Nether Abbey, in Dirleton Avenue, now an iconic small family-run hotel in the town. Elizabeth may have continued golfing for years: the Club records hold few clues. She never married and died in 1955 at the age of 82, in a house in Magdala Crescent in Edinburgh, a stone's throw from where she was born and brought up at 21 Eglinton Crescent.

Several of the early members passed through the annals of the club without making much of a mark, but from the start there was a hard core of enthusiastic and very accomplished young golfers, who turned out for almost every match. In the Club's first year there were four major competitions across the ladies' links. In the opening match in July, Margaret Gillies Smith, Florence and Blanche Anderson tied, with Margaret Gillies Smith winning the deciding round. Margaret Gillies Smith maintained her splendid form for the remainder of that season and won every scratch event. Blanche and Florence Anderson, Ethel McCulloch, Ethel Wyllie and Margaret's younger sisters and several others were all snapping at her heels. These young women were not only taking on each other, they were challenging the perception that ladies were to be indulged by the male golfing hierarchy when they tapped a golf ball gently across the green – not raising their arms too high, lest it should be considered unladylike. The North Berwick ladies, however, were playing to win and it would not be long before many of them would become discontented with their short course and demand equal rights on the long course too. That took a long time to achieve, but the 'NBLGC First *Members*' – i.e. those on the list of ladies admitted between August 1888 and September 1892 – no matter what their standard of play, all helped to carry the fine reputation of their Club far beyond its boundary wall and maintain its prestige to this day.

Sir Walter Hamilton-Dalrymple concentrating on golf with his sons and a generation later, Sir Walter's grand-daughters striding out to the links for a game of golf.

CHAPTER THREE

The Fair Exponents of the Game

"In gracefulness of play, women usually excel men."
(J. McAndrew, *Golfing Step by Step*, 1914)

"Golf is also flourishing among the fair sex here", wrote 'Man about Town' in *The Country Gentleman* of 26th January 1889, on the growing popularity of golfing in North Berwick. The men, who had regarded North Berwick as their own playing field for so long, had to accept that the Ladies' Club had been a marked success in a very short period and already had a very large membership:

> **"The enthusiasm and friendly rivalry displayed by the fair exponents of the natural game is considerable and the frequent and interesting scratch and handicap contests are invariably well-attended. Altogether, the [North Berwick] Ladies' Club has been the means of giving a powerful stimulus in this district to the popularity of golf as a pastime for ladies."**

Lady Wemyss, the second wife of Francis Charteris, the 10th Earl of Wemyss, was a brilliant golfer and often played at North Berwick. She is featured in more detail in Ch 5.

As the second season of the NBLGC opened in June 1889, there was some trepidation among the committee and members that the initial enthusiasm of the previous year would continue. On the day of the first competition, the sun shone and brought out a crowd of onlookers. The committee and their wives were there in full force, as if to set an example. Among them were Sir Walter and Lady Hamilton-Dalrymple, Mr Bloxsom and Mr & Mrs George Dalziel. Twenty members competed, including five sets of sisters. These young ladies were at the core of the club's activities in the early days: Eveline, Edith and Madeline Campbell, three of the six older sisters of Dorothy; Edith, Harriet and Ethel McCulloch, daughters of the manager of the North Berwick branch of the British Linen Bank; Mabel and Violet Sprott, daughters of the Church of Scotland Minister; Florence and Blanche Anderson, two of the several daughters of the Rector of St Baldred's, Fortesque Anderson and Margaret, Ada and Coventry Gillies Smith. Annie Dalziel, Mary Bloxsom and Elsie Blyth, whose fathers were on the Ladies' Club Committee, Mary Stevenson, sister of Committee member David Stevenson, all turned out for the first meeting of the season. Elizabeth Napier and Ethel Bilton, daughters of the Edinburgh set, whose families habitually spent their summers in North Berwick, also took part. What they had in common was youthfulness, enthusiasm and good golfing skills. Already the bar was being raised because of the keen rivalries which were developing among them:

> **"Golf continues to gain ground as a pastime for ladies and the standard of play at many ladies' golf clubs is rapidly improving."**
>
> (*Golf: A Weekly Record*, 1890)

By 1890, the activities of the North Berwick Ladies' Club and its outstanding players had become a talking point, south of the border. London visitors sent letters to friends at home, describing the excitement surrounding the annual meeting of the Ladies' Club and how the Gillies Smith sisters had swept the board in the competitions for the gold medal and for the beautiful gold bracelet, gifted by the Marchioness of Tweeddale. North Berwick was repeatedly referred to as 'the Brighton of Scotland' or other such nick-names, which underlined its growing importance as a fashionable resort, while Scotland in general was held up as leading the growing trend for women to aspire to a healthier life-style by taking up golf:

> **"It is becoming more and more fashionable for English ladies to play at golf, and as every healthy outdoor game is a thing to be desired, this importation from North Britain is to be commended. Among both sexes in Caledonia, it holds a fascination that the South can hardly realise."**
>
> (*The Pall Mall Gazette*, Wednesday 3 September 1890)

Elsie Blyth, daughter of one of the Club's founder members, Benjamin Hall Blyth.

The healthy living theme was re-echoed in *The Women's Penny Paper* of 6th September 1890, with particular reference to North Berwick:

> **"The annual meeting of the Ladies' Golf Club, North Berwick, has just taken place and the brightness and healthiness of those who took part in it, seem to prove that women are gaining ground in all manner of physical exercise."**

The entry for the July 1889 handicap competition was twenty four, with several new members taking part. One of the most interesting of these was the Hon. Mrs Edith Lyttelton, wife of the Hon. Robert Lyttelton. Before her marriage in 1884, she was an acclaimed concert singer, performing on occasions in the Royal Albert Hall before Queen Victoria. Singing was in her blood; both her parents were professional opera singers and musicians. Her father was Sir Charles Santley and mother Gertrude Kemble. In spite of Edith's pedigree and her beautiful singing voice, she was not encouraged to continue a career after marriage. However, she quickly discovered the joys of golfing at North Berwick. With a net score of 83 she trailed home well behind the leaders.

The competition was held over the ladies course and the five best scores were Elsie Blyth 78, less 20 – 58; Blanche Anderson 68, less 8 – 60; Ada Gillies Smith 70 less 8 – 62; Mary Bloxsom 93 less 30 – 63; Annie Dalziel 77 less 12 – 65. The individual handicaps were handed out immediately before each match and some of the allowances seemed very generous. Blanche Anderson's raw score of 68 was the best round of the day. Ada and Coventry Gillies Smith went round in 70, their sister Margaret in 71 and Blanche's sister Florence had the next best raw score of 73. These five young women were outstanding golfers and competitions always had an extra edge when they were taking part. The prizes were presented by the Rev. Fortescue Anderson and it must have given him pleasure to make an award to 17 year old Blanche, one of his young daughters.

By August that year, news of the excellence of the ladies' course and the standard of play had spread. There was such a large entry for the autumn gathering, fifty two in all, that the starting time had to be brought forward an hour, from the usual 3.30pm. It was the height of the season and visitors arrived in droves to watch the match. The 'blue ribbon' of the meeting was the scratch gold medal, which was to be kept by the winner. There were several fantastic handicap prizes – a gold brooch, a gold bangle, a silver pin tray, a set of gold sleeve links and 5th prize was half a dozen pairs of gloves – essential for any ladies' wardrobe!

Spectators at a golf match at Kilspindie c.1900. This scene is typical of the interest shown in golf matches at the time.

As always, there was an insatiable curiosity to know who else was in the crowd. It was becoming almost mandatory for gossip columns, local and national, to comment on the social aspect of the golf as much as on the skills the ladies demonstrated. As more high-profile visitors arrived from London, more journalists followed to find stories of the great and good at leisure, to fill the society columns of their newspapers and journals.

Apart from the ever-present committee members and their wives – Sir Walter and Lady Hamilton-Dalrymple, Mr and Mrs Benjamin Hall Blyth, the Dalziels and the Stevensons – new faces were to be seen among the spectators on the teeing ground. Mrs Mary Henrietta Mitchell and her husband R. A. H. Mitchell, the great Eton and Oxford cricketer, were among the influx of English visitors. Frank Tennant, son of Sir Charles Tennant, whose family had made a fortune with a highly successful chemical company near Glasgow, was watching the ladies' competition that day, with his wife Annie. His father had been golfing in North Berwick since the late 1870s. John Earnest Laidlay, the current Amateur Golf Champion, arrived on the scene with his new young wife, Jane, who was Annie Tennant's sister. The De Zoetes, the great London stock broking family, were present. John Menzies, son of the founder of the Edinburgh stationers, had a house on the West Bay and was to be found in the crowd that day with his sister Isabella, a keen golfer.

Frank Tennant with his sister Margot Asquith.

The high standard of golfing, on the afternoon of 23rd August 1889, kept the attention of both spectators and press fixed on the green. Margaret and Coventry Gillies Smith tied for the gold medal and played off, only to tie again. The third time Margaret came out on top and won the gold medal. Coventry was rewarded by receiving a replica! Alice Montgomery, Mabel Sprott, Elizabeth Napier and Louisa Stevenson each carried off one of the handicap prizes.

In September, the competition entry was even higher than in August and the spectators more numerous. *The Glasgow Herald* commented on the "quite remarkable" success of the Ladies' Club and ventured to suggest that was very much due to the "energetic efforts of the committee of management and its courteous secretary Mr W Gibson Bloxsom"! The visitors thronged the ground hoping to see the Irish Secretary A.J. Balfour present the prizes, but he had to leave unexpectedly to deal with some urgent political business. A substitute was quickly organised – Adeline Harvey, the wife of Richard Musgrave Harvey, did the honours. The Harveys who lived in a splendid mansion in Portland Place in London, had recently discovered North Berwick and returned every summer until Mrs Harvey's death in 1902. Their substantial wealth came from trading connections in the West Indies. Their young daughter, also Adeline, was golfing that afternoon, but the prizes went to the more experienced players, Edith McCulloch and Florence Anderson.

John Laidlay, Amateur Golf Champion, husband of member Jane Laidlay.

At the autumn meeting the following year, 29th August 1890, there was an issue with handicapping – and the weather! So many competitors, who were not regular golfers, came forward (it was suspected, for the excellent prizes) that the club officials abandoned the usual handicapping system and announced that only those with a handicap of fourteen or under would be eligible for the first prize and a maximum handicap of eighteen would apply for the other prizes. The scramble to win the handicap awards was felt to be detracting from the main event of the meeting – the competition for the merit gold medal! The pouring rain thinned out the crowd of onlookers, although club members and their guests could take shelter in a marquee erected on the edge of the links. Ben Sayers had taken over from Tom Dunn as the starter, the previous year, and sent the fifty six competitors off in pairs. In the event, Margaret Gillies Smith came through well ahead of the rest of the field with 61 for two rounds of the ladies' course to win the gold medal again, and also the first handicap prize of the beautiful gold bracelet, set with pearls, which had pulled in so many 'punters'. The bracelet was gifted by the Marchioness of Tweeddale, who, as she placed it round the winner's wrist, announced how much pleasure it gave her to see Miss Gillies Smith win!

The late September meeting had a record entry of sixty six ladies - and an even bigger crowd. For the first time the meeting lasted the whole day. In the afternoon, the excitement mounted as the mixed foursomes competition took off. It attracted the best players in the club. Margaret Gillies Smith teamed up with the Rev Fortesque Anderson, known to all and sundry as the 'golfing Rector'.

They were beaten into second place by Margaret's younger sister Ada and her partner, Frank Dalziel, son of committee member George Dalziel. Mr Dalziel senior and the other committee members watched the day's events with deep satisfaction, no doubt proud of the major part they played in its organisation.

In the October competition of 1890, Miss Agnes Louisa Tyrwhitt-Drake, visiting North Berwick from Great Shardeloes in Buckinghamshire and whose family claimed descent from Sir Francis Drake, was invited to present the prizes, all of which she kindly donated. She also took part in the match, tying for first place in the handicap awards and taking home one of her own prizes! The scratch prize was won by Eveline, one of the Campbell sisters – all of whom showed early promise at golf some years before little Dorothy appeared on the scene.

The Tyrwitt-Drake family photographed on the steps of their home, Great Shardeloes in Buckinghamshire. The family regularly golfed at North Berwick.

The first summer meeting of the NBLGC was always held at the end of June and heralded the start of the golf season in the town. June 1891 was little different from previous years: a large crowd gathered at the teeing ground opposite the Marine Hotel; the weather threatened rain but brightened later; Mr Bloxsom's arrangements for play were commendable; the course and greens were in good order and there were plenty of decent prizes to be won. The McCullochs, the Andersons, the Gillies Smiths, the Sprotts, the Campbells, the Biltons, Mary Bloxsom, Elsie Blyth, Mary Stevenson and Ethel Wylie, all playing off handicaps of 14 and under, came out for a sporting match. As so often happened, however, few of the first-rate, regular players came near the top of the results list. They were almost always defeated by the ladies who played infrequently or badly and had huge handicaps. Only Blanche Anderson and Ethel McCulloch got anywhere near any of the prizes in the opening match. The winner was Isabella Bourhill, whose maximum handicap of 36, turned her actual score of 85 to a startling 49.

Miss Isabella Bourhill may be at the bottom of a curious story which centres on an artefact in the North Berwick clubhouse trophy cabinet – a golf ball with a ladies' hairpin firmly embedded. There is an explanation given on an old but undated scrap of paper:

> **"The ball was driven from a tee going to the 4th hole. The drive was half-topped and hit the top of the bunker in front and travelled a further 50 yards. It was found to have been impaled on one leg of a hair pin, which penetrated about ½ an inch."**

The golf ball and the hairpin are there to see, but what is absent is any firm proof that this occurred on North Berwick links. On 17th October 1899, a story appeared in *The Scotsman*, that a Mr Alexander Bourhill, a well-known

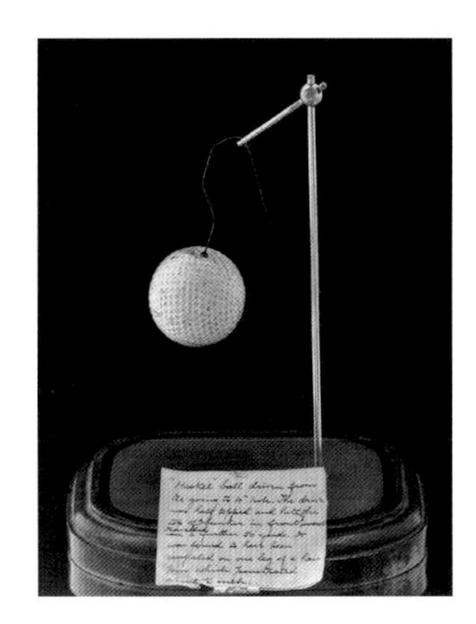

The lady's hairpin embedded into the golf ball.

scratch player at the Royal Musselburgh Club, drove a ball which struck the face of a bunker. After Bourhill had taken three shots to get the ball out of the bunker, he discovered that it had picked up a lady's hairpin, "one prong of which had embedded itself to the depth of an inch right in the gutta and the remainder of the wire was curiously twisted outside." For some time the ball with its "odd adornment" was on view at the Royal Musselburgh Clubhouse and then it disappeared. Only a suspension of disbelief could lead to the conclusion there were two separate incidents and so the question is how did the ball and the hairpin become part of the North Berwick Club lore? Any answer is supposition. However, although Alexander Bourhill lived at Musselburgh, his niece Isabella not only lived in North Berwick, but was a member of the Ladies' Club! The trail ends here, but the hairpin stuck in the golf ball can still be viewed today – at North Berwick!

In August 1891, the name, Mrs Jane Laidlay, appeared on the membership list of the Ladies' Club. She was out on the golf course within a year of having her first baby – quite a bold step to take in those days. She probably was able to get away with it, firstly because she was John Earnest Laidlay's wife and secondly she was very young. John Laidlay's victories in the British Amateur Golf Championships in 1889 and 1891, were fresh in the mind and his arrival on any links caused a frisson of excitement:

> **"Golf has been in vogue during the past week over the links at North Berwick to an extent that must have satisfied the most ardent admirers of the royal pastime. Brilliant gatherings were held on the green on Wednesday and Thursday and at the ladies' course on Friday....... Amongst the visitors to the links in the course of the week, exceptionally distinguished in the golfing world, were the amateur champion Mr J E Laidlay and the ex-champion, Mr Horace Hutchinson."**
> (*Golf: A Weekly Record of Ye Royal & Auncient Game*, Friday 11 September 1891)

At the time, the John Laidlays rented Strathairly House near Largo in Fife, within striking distance of St Andrews, but not too impossible a distance from North Berwick, where J. E. was a member of both North Berwick and New Club. In August the following year, 1892, Jane Laidlay persuaded her sister-in-law, Theophila, to join the Ladie's Club. Theophila was the wife of John's older brother Andrew, a practising barrister, in the south of England. They had recently moved back to Scotland, as Andrew had inherited the family home Seacliffe, on his father's death. The house held a magnificent position on high ground looking out towards the Bass Rock in the Firth of Forth, four miles east of North Berwick. It was where John Ernest Laidlay and his siblings had been brought up and learned to swing their clubs and practice bunker shots on the soft sandy beach. At some point during the 1890s, John Laidlay bought a piece of land to the west of North Berwick to build a new mansion house for himself and his family. It was partly a desire to recreate his beloved childhood home and partly, one suspects, to live up to people's expectations of him and not to be outdone by his brother moving into the splendid Seacliffe. The result was a large, rather heavy-looking mansion, but which nevertheless enjoyed a marvellous position on the edge of the eighth fairway and a view across the Firth of Forth. He called it Invereil.

The Laidlay family story is one of great triumph and tragedy. The triumph is John Laidlay's success as one of the greatest amateur golfers of that era. The tragedy is centred round his brother Andrew and Seacliffe, designed and built by Scots architect David Bryce in the 1840s, and the Laidlay family home since 1856. On the evening of the Sunday 27 July, 1907, Andrew Laidlay was reading in the library, with his usual glass of port. The evening was warm; there was a breeze; the window was open and Andrew had probably dozed off. Perhaps it was a sudden gust of wind that blew the curtain, which knocked against the oil lamp and started the fire. Whatever the exact circumstances, the fire spread quickly and engulfed the whole house. Theophila and her daughter, asleep upstairs, were awakened by a kitchen maid and escaped, in their nightdresses, by knotting bed sheets together and climbing onto the porch roof. Andrew Laidlay perished in the fire. The house was completely destroyed and Theophila and her two children made a new home in one of the properties on the Seacliff estate. Theophila continued her membership of the Ladies' Club until she moved to the Borders in the 1920s.

On September 8th 1893, the weekly magazine, *Golf* announced the results of *The Gentlewoman* Competition, which involved participants returning six consecutive scores of 18 holes. The first two prizes went to two members from North Berwick Ladies' Club, Miss Evelyn Campbell and Miss Orphoot, who completed the six rounds with a score of 417. Miss Campbell received a Mappin & Webb dressing bag and Miss Orphoot, a gold olive-wreath bracelet, from the London Goldsmiths and Silversmiths Company. Mary Orphoot had joined the Ladies' Golf Club, with her mother (also Mary), in September 1889 when she was 21. Their garden door opened on to the first tee of the ladies' links, making it seem almost an extension to their grounds.

Invereil, the North Berwick home of John and Jane Laidlay.

Mary Orphoot's father Peter had bought the large sandstone house on the links in 1880. It was immediately adjacent to the Marine Hotel and was built at about the same time, 1875, and designed by the same architect,

An early image of the Marine Hotel and the newly built houses in Cromwell Road c.1880.

MARINE HOTEL.

William Beattie. As a young man, he was articled to David Bryce, who was renowned for developing the Scots baronial style and designing extravagant mansion houses, for example Laidlay's Seacliffe. When he returned to his father's practice, George Beattie & Sons, William, inspired by Bryce, took the family business up-market. In the centre of Edinburgh, he was responsible for the design of the Carlton and the North British (Balmoral) Hotel and the redesigning of Edinburgh's flagship department store, Jenners. Greenhythe, although modest compared to Beattie's other works, was typical of the other houses being built close to the links during this period. It was spread across three floors. The front porch opened into a large square hall, with a morning room to the south, and dining room and lounge, to the north, with wonderful views over golf course and the sea. A billiard room led off the lounge. Almost fifty percent of the ground floor was given over to the service area. There was a large kitchen, a servants' hall, a general larder, a milk larder, a meat larder, a wash house and scullery, a coal store, a sticks & buckets room and a wine cellar. There were six bedrooms on the first floor, and up in the attic, sleeping accommodation for the domestic servants.

Dr Peter Orphoot was a well-known Edinburgh dentist who had run a successful business at 113 George Street for many years. He was one of the first practising dentists in Scotland and had received instruction from the dental pioneer, Dr John Smith, while a medical student at Edinburgh University. He was a founder member of the Edinburgh Dental Dispensary, which later became the renowned Edinburgh Dental Hospital, in Chambers Street. When Peter Orphoot finally retired from his Edinburgh dentistry practice, he couldn't resist building up a small private practice at Greenhythe and he was still much in demand. If toothache troubled the great and good who golfed at North Berwick during the summer months, they beat a path to Greenhythe, where the offending tooth could be soothed with oil of cloves, drilled and filled, or swiftly extracted. In September 1887, the Rev. William Houldsworth, who was up from London for the golfing season with his family, was having his golfing ruined by a painful tooth. He wrote in his diary on Monday 26th September: "toothache so bad that got Dr Orphoot to pull the one bothering me." Either Orphoot got it wrong or Houldsworth had more than one rotten tooth, as he went back to the dentist on Tuesday and Wednesday, when it seems Orphoot suggested he give his face a chance to recover. By Thursday he was in such pain he didn't attempt to golf. On Friday, Orphoot finally identified the real problem tooth and filled it. Houldsworth noted with a tinge of irritation that it had cost him two guineas for his pains.

The pattern followed by the Houldsworth family when they arrived earlier in September was typical of many visiting golfing families at North Berwick. They travelled to Scotland by train for the summer, always sending a few of their chosen staff on ahead. During the late 1880s and 90s, they would often spend August in Nairn (a very smart golf resort) and September/October in North Berwick. In September 1887, they came direct from London, taking the sleeper from St Pancras at 9.15pm. They arrived at Edinburgh at 7.30am, breakfasted at Waverley Station and caught the 9.20 train to North Berwick, where they were met at the station and taken to the Marine Hotel. It was a beautiful day and the Rev. Houldsworth bought grapes for his children as a treat. The following day he was on the golf course and played a round of golf with General Brewster in the morning, and a second round in the afternoon with Hutchinson, De Zoete and A. J. Balfour. He got his "name down for the club" and managed to find time to have a quick round of golf with his wife Eulalie "on the small links", which at that time were set out at the start of the long course. Two years later in September 1889, with the Ladies' Club in full swing, Eulalie and her elder daughter Lillie, who was eleven, became members. If Eulalie had hesitated about membership the previous season, she found courage to join forces with the small handful of other married lady members, who believed it was perfectly feminine and becoming to take up golf, in spite of their marital status. For the Rev. Houldsworth, he was probably relieved that he would have more time to concentrate on his own game, with his male counterparts.

The *Golfing Annual* declared that in 1891 there were 395 golf clubs in existence of which 34 were ladies' clubs. Of the 206 clubs in Scotland, 13 were ladies. The figures, of course, point to a huge discrepancy between the sexes and would explain the anxiety many women, especially married women, felt

A portrait of Lillie Houldsworth aged about 11 in 1889.

about joining a club. The steely determination of the female golfing vanguard ensured that the game continued to increase in popularity and become a socially acceptable pastime for married ladies. A Ladies' Golf Union was formed in 1893, with its headquarters in London, to promote the interests of ladies' golf and in June 1893 the first (British) Ladies' Golf Championship was held at St Anne's in Lancashire. Lady Margaret Scott, a young English aristocrat was the first lady champion. She was revered among the golfing ladies south of the border, where her play was described as 'dashing, fearless' and 'fascinating' and she went on to win the championship for three consecutive years. How she would have fared against any of the North Berwick lady cracks or any other Scottish lady golfer, will never be known; there was intense disappointment among the organisers that they had failed to attract a single entry from Scotland. There were anguished cries from the English correspondents in the *Golf* magazine, 16th June 1893:

> **"What can be the reason for this neglect on the part of the ladies of Scotland? It is difficult to imagine a reason, seeing that no effort has been spared on the part of the Ladies' Golf Union to make the competition thoroughly representative."**

There is no clear answer, but by contrast, in 1893, the North Berwick Ladies' Gold Medal meeting was attracting a great deal of interest, both from Club members and spectators. Among the ladies there was a fierce desire to unseat the eldest Gillies Smith sister, Margaret, who had thus far monopolised the annual event. She had won it on five successive occasions. On 25th August, 1893, the day of the gold medal event, the initial relief among the competitors that Margaret Gillies Smith was indisposed, was short-lived – her sister Ada came up to the mark and kept the gold medal in the family: "The merit honours were carried by that excellent exponent of the game, Miss Ada Gillies Smith," announced the golfing press. Ada also broke the course record with a score of 62 for two rounds. It is worth noting Blanche Anderson came close with a score of 64.

The coveted Club Gold Medal, won by Margaret Gillies Smith on five consecutive occasions.

Among the unsuccessful competitors for the gold medal was Mabel Sprott, the 27 year old daughter of the parish minister, who had golfed on the links from childhood and had been one of the early club members. Her score was a reasonable 75, but she could be excused for lack of focus. Her marriage to Henry Mortimer Rush, head of Merchiston Castle Preparatory School was to take place the following week, on the first of September. On the day, her golfing friends, male and female, turned out for her wedding at St Andrews

Parish church on the High Street. After the marriage, she and Henry lived on the school premises and there was little opportunity for golf in term time and, in addition, she soon had three young daughters to look after. Like several of her contemporaries, once married, the carefree days on North Berwick links were often curtailed!

In September 1893, Florence Anderson followed her close friend Mabel Sprott to the altar, when she married Major Charles Sawyer of the 1st North Lancashire Regiment, at St Baldred's Church. Although Florence was not such a crack golfer as her younger sister Blanche, she was still considered one of the best lady golfers in North Berwick and played off scratch. Marriage for a woman most often meant going wherever her husband's career took him. For Florence, that meant being the wife of an army officer in India. However, Florence was particularly strong-minded and a few years later, the Sawyers were back in North Berwick, with their young family, and Florence was once again enjoying golf on the links!

The merit gold medal of the North Berwick Ladies' Club finally 'left the possession' of the Gillies Smith family, in August 1894. Elsie Blyth, who had been the youngest competitor in the very first club competition for the silver medal in August 1888 at the age of eleven, was a popular winner. It seemed a just victory for the daughter on one of the founder members. Elsie triumphed with the fine score of 62 for the two rounds each of nine holes, but even so, was closely followed by Margaret Gillies Smith and Miss Madeline Campbell both at 63. Townspeople and visitors alike turned out to watch the match. The Scotsman reporter picked out the 'names' among them. The suave and elegant Lord and Lady Ribblesdale excited most interest among the crowd. Charlotte Ribblesdale was a daughter of Sir Charles Tennant and sister to Margot Asquith and Frank Tennant. When they visited North Berwick, the Ribblesdales would either stay at Frank's house, Hyndford, above the links at the west end of the town, or, as on this occasion, as guests of the Earl and Countess of Wemyss at Gosford House, ten miles along the coast towards Edinburgh. In the evening after the match, Lady Ribblesdale presented the prizes to the successful lady competitors. Her ladyship awarded a handsome embossed silver blotting pad to Miss Blanche Anderson, the lady winner of the mixed doubles tournament on the previous day. In moving a vote of thanks to Lady Ribblesdale, Sir Walter Hamilton-Dalrymple praised her skills as a sportswoman and expressed the hope that she too would soon join the other ladies in golfing on their fine links! Sir Walter's comments seemed to reflect the trend that it was becoming acceptable for aristocratic ladies to take up club membership (as their husbands had done years before them), rather than relying on the private courses of their friends for a round of golf.

Lady Ribblesdale sister of Margot Asquith.

Mixed doubles on the Ladies' Links c.1890s.

The mixed doubles tournament was always the most popular annual event for the lady members, particularly, one suspects, as so many of them were as yet unattached. Of the fifty new members who had joined since January 1892, thirty eight were unmarried and the mixed doubles gave both sexes an opportunity for a little subtle flirtation on the green. If the partnerships are analysed in 1894, however, it looked more like a careful chaperoning exercise than a match-making opportunity, and in any case, several of the young ladies were still in their teens. Ethel McCulloch, Blanche Anderson and Ada Hunter partnered their brothers; Miss Adeline Harvey and Elsie Hall Blyth played with their fathers and although 21 year old Gerald Harvey managed to partner young Miss Nellie Graham, and Elsie Mylne partnered Frank Dalziel, no lasting romantic attachment came of it!

Shared golfing interests did lead Walter Cunliffe into the arms of Miss Edith Boothby in 1896. Edith was one of eight children of a retired army Colonel, Robert Tod Boothby, Eton and Cambridge educated, who lived in St Andrews and sometimes took a house in North Berwick for the golf season. Edith had been a member at St Andrews Ladies' Club, since 1880, when she was twelve years old. She joined the North Berwick Ladies' in September 1892, at the same time as her elder sister Charlotte, who was married to Scottish Provident manager, James Graham Watson. Walter Cunliffe was widowed in 1893 and lonely. He was a great sportsman, tried his hand at golf and loved country pursuits. It is not certain on which golf links Edith and Walter met, whether St Andrews or North Berwick, but they married in July 1896. Walter's father Roger Cunliffe, a very successful billbroker had died the previous year, leaving Walter and his siblings an estate worth over one million pounds. He also left Walter Headley Court farm, a good acreage in a beautiful location near Epsom. The old Elizabethan farmhouse at Headley Court was reconstructed in 1899 into a huge mansion house, designed by Edward Warren and this was where Walter and Edith brought up their two sons and three daughters. Walter and his brothers owned a merchant bank, Cunliffe Brothers, which was not always as successful as their father's enterprises had been. However, Walter was personally highly regarded in the city and was appointed Governor of the Bank of England in 1913 and had the task of calming the jittery money markets at the outbreak of war in 1914. As a result, he was created a hereditary peer. Walter's career path meant his life became London-centric, and although Edith's brother, Robert (father of Lord Boothby, Tory MP and one time minister in Churchill's war-time coalition government)) kept up his golfing at North Berwick and she continued visiting in the summer, Edith had dropped her membership of North Berwick Ladies' Club by 1906.

In September 1894, the ladies challenged the gentlemen, single-handed and on level terms, to a match across the ladies' course. On previous occasions, the women had been completely trounced, "succumbing to the superior prowess of the sterner sex" (*Glasgow Herald* Friday 21 September 1894). For some reason, the ladies agreed to the match being played across 36 holes, therefore giving the men a distinct advantage, if the restrictions imposed by the ladies' dress were also taken into account. The six best women stepped forward, hoping to demonstrate a general improvement in the ladies' game – Margaret and Ada Gillies Smith, Madeline Campbell, Annie Dalziel, Ethel McCulloch and Ada Hunter. There was a particularly high turn-out of spectators for such an event and the match between Stuart Anderson, the Rector's son and the redoubtable Margaret Gillies Smith was the most eagerly anticipated. Stuart Anderson was as fine a young golfer as anyone; the previous year he had won both New Club and Tantallon gold medals playing off scratch and had reached the final of the Irish Open Championship. The first round of the Ladies' Club challenge was close run, with Gillies Smith trailing by two, but she failed to pull ahead and was ultimately beaten by 6 over the 36 holes. All was not lost, Margaret's younger sister, Ada, brought honour to the ladies by defeating Edward Blyth, brother of Benjamin Hall Blyth, by 4.

By 1895, another young player was beginning to make herself known in the ladies' events. At the annual autumn meeting of the Ladies' Club, twelve year old Dorothy Campbell, playing off a handicap of 16 (net 58), won the first handicap prize. Ada Gillies Smith and Blanche Anderson tied for the scratch prize with scores of 62. Dorothy eclipsed her older sister Muriel and several other stalwarts such as Mary Orphoot, Harriet McCulloch, as well as an up-and-coming English golfer Hilda Sant, who had adopted North Berwick as her favourite course and joined the club.

In July 1896, it was Blanche Anderson, who carried off the scratch prize with an excellent score of 63. Mrs Gordon Robertson (Blanche's sister Helen Maud) won the first handicap prize in the same competition with a round of 70, her handicap of 13 bringing her net score to 57. In September 1897, Blanche Anderson won the gold medal again, with a score of 63 and Madeline Campbell was second. Dorothy Campbell's name was appearing more frequently among the list of winners of the handicap prizes and by 1897 she was playing consistently off seven at the club.

Although many of the ladies appeared on the golf course swinging their clubs with grace and hitting the ball with commendable accuracy, there was always room for improvement. There was no shortage of golf instructors in the town. Ben Sayers and David Grant were two of the most sought after. Hilda

DAVIE GRANT (1860–1903)

Davie Grant was an illegitimate child, born in Leith and brought up by an aunt. As a young man he worked with Ben Sayers making golf balls and moved to North Berwick after his marriage in 1881 to Isabella Thomson, whose family came from the town. They brought up a family of ten children, while Grant established his reputation as a professional golfer and teacher. His death in June 1903, at the age of 43, was widely reported in the golfing media. *Golf Illustrated* carried the story in their column 'On the Ladies Links', in recognition of Grant's popularity with the lady golfers, many of whom had taken their first swing of a club, under his exacting direction. His reputation was as a golf instructor, rather than as a great player; his 'weak physique' prevented him achieving real success. He suffered from tuberculosis, the eventual cause of his death.

Ben Sayers was a great success at teaching golf – here he is instructing Lady Wemyss at Kilspindie c.1900.

Sant, a young English member who lived in London, engaged Sayers to teach her at North Berwick and soon established a reputation, south of the border, as one of the best all-round lady golfers. Sayers was a great success as a teacher and so widespread was his reputation, he was called upon to give lessons to several Royal golfing ladies – HRH the Princess of Wales and HRH Princess Victoria – travelling to Windsor to do so. The Duchess of Connaught booked up Sayers to give lessons to her and her daughter Princess Patricia of Russia, after a golfing holiday in North Berwick.

Gradually, new talent took the place of the old. By late 1897, North Berwick was able to bathe in the glory of Edith Orr's magnificent success at the Ladies' Championship at Gullane, earlier in the year and for a while, the crowds and the press looked expectantly for a glimpse of any one of the six Orr sisters on the links. As a result, the success of any other young woman at the North Berwick meetings was down-played, the view constantly expressed that had Miss Edith Orr taken part the result would have been different. This attitude, though short-lived, must have been disheartening for players like Blanche Anderson, who had entertained the crowds at North Berwick with remarkable consistency in her game for years and, on Friday 23rd July 1897, set a new course record with a score of 26 for a single round. In fact, Edith Orr and her sisters were more often to be found on the ladies' course at Nairn during the golfing season, than on their home links at North Berwick.

The July meeting was extraordinary because of the high scores across the board and was another indication of the exceptional standard of play of the North Berwick Ladies. When seasoned golfer Edward Blyth presented the prizes, he expressed the view that it was doubtful the record established that day would ever be broken. He could not have done his homework; Blanche Anderson won the scratch award in 63, yet a month earlier Rita Gillies Smith had completed two rounds of the course in 60!

In July 1897, the Ladies' Tournament was held for the first time over the long course and not over the ladies' links. There was much teeth-sucking among the gentlemen about this novel departure. Some were quick to justify it by suggesting that, as the Ladies' Championship at Gullane had demonstrated, it was acceptable now and again for ladies to play over the long links, as it was 'very conducive to improvement in the play of the fair exponents of the game'. The ladies were left in no doubt that this was a special concession by the gentlemen of the New Club and it would not be a regular occurrence.

Only the top notch players in the club entered the competition. They included twenty year old Mary Bloxsom (daughter of WG Bloxsom), who had participated in club events throughout her teenage years. She was a consistently good golfer and sufficiently accomplished to have competed in the Ladies' Championship at Gullane, earlier in the year, when she was defeated in the second round. The North Berwick Ladies' Club was about to enter its tenth year and Mary had been a member from the start. In the July tournament, she beat club stalwart Edith McCulloch in the first round, but came up against Edith Orr in the second and, not surprisingly, was defeated. After 1898, her appearances in competitive tournaments became less frequent; she had contracted tuberculosis and her condition gradually deteriorated, in spite of her father's best efforts to find a cure. She spent time at the Dunblane Hydropathic, where she could have rest, fresh air and a healthy diet. The mid-Victorian Hydropathic Movement believed that disease could be eradicated by 'taking the waters' and Hydropathics flourished across Britain. They fulfilled a purpose as recuperation centres rather than as the cure centres they were purported to be. It is likely that Mary moved to the small eight-bed sanatorium at Dunblane for the final weeks of her short life. She died there on 10th January 1903, aged just twenty five. Her father William Bloxsom, who had been a steadfast supporter and promoter of the Ladies' Club, left North Berwick and his numerous golfing connections, remarried and moved south.

At the 1898 July meeting of the club, while Mary Bloxsom was beginning to suffer from a lack of energy with the onset of her illness and was trailing at the bottom of the results board, her old friend Annie Dalziel won the scratch award in 59 for the double nine-hole round. It was an excellent score and a few years earlier would have set the record, but by this time there were a number of players who were able to complete two rounds in 60 or under. There was little doubt the overall standard of the ladies' play was improving, whether or not the gentlemen were willing to acknowledge it.

In the final club tournament of 1898, fifteen year old Dorothy Campbell narrowly defeated sixteen year old Marion Houldsworth, one of the daughters of the Rev and Mrs William Houldsworth. The girls were well-matched and were two of the youngest and brightest members of the club and there was little to choose between them in excellence of their play. Dorothy Campbell went on to win a clutch of golfing titles, placing her among the 'greats' in the international golfing Hall of Fame. Marion Houldsworth, however, continued to play in North Berwick, every summer, when she came up from London with her family. In 1907, while Dorothy was competing in the final of the Scottish Ladies Championship, Marion was marrying 'the boy next door' Hugh Wyld. Marion continued golfing, but it was simply one of many activities in a well-rounded family life. More than a century later, in North Berwick, there is an aura surrounding Dorothy Campbell's name and a commemorative plaque on the

A portrait of Marion Houldsworth aged about 7 in 1889.

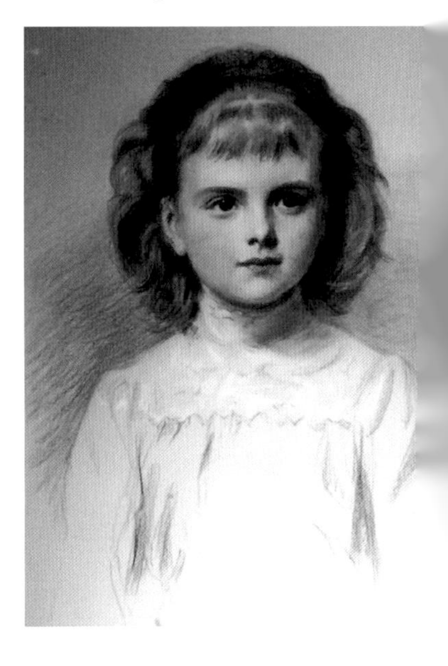

Campbell holiday home, Inchgarry, at the end of West Bay Road. A few hundred metres away is the Houldsworth's summer home, originally Anchor Villa, but re-named Cranston in 1911. The Houldsworth descendants still own Cranston and Marion's grand-daughter Deborah Backhouse plays an excellent game of golf across the links, when the family arrive for their annual summer sojourn.

Marion's daughter Barbara Wyld continuing the family tradition of golfing at North Berwick in the 1930s. She is seen here on the course with Eileen Tweedie, another Ladies' Club member. The Marine Hotel is in the background. The young boy in the photo is caddying for one of the players, the other caddy is just out of the picture to the right.

Yet golf was still exclusive rather than inclusive, especially for women. While there was an artisan club in North Berwick - the Bass Rock Club - there was no equivalent for women. Perhaps the wives and daughters of the artisans would have liked to play, but they were not encouraged to join the Ladies' Club and it is unlikely they could have afforded it. Working class women were too busy keeping body and soul together to think of golf. Golf may well have been flourishing among the 'fair sex' in North Berwick in the 1890s, but only among those fortunate enough to be on the right side of the class divide.

CHAPTER FOUR

The Orr Family Phenomenon

"The success of Miss E. C. Orr in 1897 was more anticipated, as she was on her own links, and the fame of her own and her sisters' play had already reached the south."

(*Golf Illustrated*, 7 April 1899)

Edith Constance Orr triumphed in the fourth British Ladies' Golf Championship, held over the links at Gullane, a small village four miles distant from North Berwick, in May 1897. She was playing out of the North Berwick Ladies' Club and was an overnight sensation. The Open result was even more extraordinary because the runner-up and silver medallist was Edith's older sister, Theodora, and a younger sister Aimie reached round four. Edith Orr was revered as one of the great golfing women of her day, but after her championship victory, she never sought to build on her victory and she and her five sisters never again entered a major championship match. As a result an aura of mystery has developed around them.

There were eight Orr siblings: six girls and two boys - Theodora, Edith, Aimie, Ada, Ethel, John, Hilda and Norman. The family home was 21 Woodside Terrace in Glasgow. Theodora the eldest was born, possibly prematurely, in a hotel at Wemyss Bay, a favourite spot for wealthy Glasgow folk, in September 1869, and the youngest Norman was born at North Berwick in 1884. Their parents John and Frances Orr were both members of the wealthy Glasgow cotton manufacturing fraternity. John Orr had built up a thread manufacturing business K. F. & J. Alexander & Co., which he ran in partnership with his brothers and Frances' father was a Glasgow calico printer. They married in

The six Orr sisters in their garden, all set for a round of golf, c.1893.

1863, when Frances was 20 and John 40. There were miscarriages and a still birth before their daughter Theodora – 'a gift from God' – was born in 1870. Six children followed in fairly quick succession, but by the time Norman was born, John Orr was 59 and his health was beginning to decline. He died in 1887 from prostate cancer.

THE ORR FAMILY

John Orr died 18 February 1887, aged 63.

Frances Bethia, his wife, died in 1913, aged 70.

Theodora born 1869, died 1914, aged 45, in Edinburgh.

Edith Constance born 1871, died 1955, aged 84, in North Berwick.

Aimie Louise born 1872, died 1971, in North Berwick, in her 99th year.

Ada Mary born 1873, died 1951, aged 78, in Middlesex.

Ethel May born 1876, died December 1941, aged 65, in Surrey.

John Arthur Orr born 1879, died in action on 22 October 1914, during the first battle of Ypres. He was 35.

Hilda Grace born 1880, died on 9 February 1955, aged 75, in the Whitehall Hotel, London.

Norman Charles Orr born 1884, died 8 April 1923, on the frontier between India and Afghanistan. He was 39.

Like many families in their income bracket, they left the smoky city in the summer months and headed for the coast and the golf links. The Orrs were part of the group of Glasgow families, who came to North Berwick during the season. In the summer of 1884, the fact that Frances was heavily pregnant didn't cause John Orr to modify holiday plans and on 6th August, Norman was born at Winterfield Lodge, the house they had rented that year, overlooking the links. John Orr was a keen golfer and employed a well-known local professional golfer Davie Grant, a week at a time, to improve his golf. Whenever John Orr was occupied elsewhere, he made sure he got his money's worth from Grant and set him to teach golf to his children. As a result the children learned to play golf when they were quite young. The Orrs were regular visitors to North Berwick, over the following decades, but neither

Frances nor her daughters joined the Ladies' Club in its early days, although it seems they were members from about 1895.

The family also golfed at Nairn in the summer months, usually August, in line with the fashion among other wealthy Scottish golfing families, and the family was well-known on the golf courses at Dornoch, Machrihanish and St. Andrews. On Saturday 25th August 1894, Horace Hutchinson, the acclaimed amateur championship golfer, played a round of golf with Edith, a remarkably fine player. Although Hutchinson moved 3 holes ahead on the way out, at the final hole the scores were even and only when Edith missed a putt was Hutchinson able to claim the match by 1 up. This extraordinary level of success, a women standing her ground against one of the best male golfers of the day, helped to secure Edith's reputation ahead of the 1897 Open and maintained it long after.

John Orr exercised strict control over his children, particularly his daughters. He was relentless in encouraging them to develop their golfing skills. When the family spent the summer at Machrihanish, the girls often played three rounds a day, most often carrying their own clubs, which must have built up their strength and was certainly not the normal practice at that time. Rumours have circulated in recent times that John Orr was an over-bearing father who forbade his talented daughters to compete in golf matches, for fear they would be subjected to the corrosive influences of the betting that accompanied the championships. It doesn't quite add up; when John Orr died Theodora was 17 and Edith 16 and the others were too young to participate in competitive golf.

When he knew he was ill, John Orr made careful provision for his beloved Frances and their children. He appointed Nathaniel Spens, son of an old family friend, to look after his affairs. (Both the Spens and Orr families golfed in North Berwick during the summer months and the Spens girls are featured in chapter 2.) John Orr's last will and testament was designed, consciously or sub-consciously, to hold his family together. If Frances wished to sell the family home, another should be bought which would provide a home where all his children could stay together until they married. He had high expectations that his six daughters would marry, but if any of them didn't, his presumption was that they should continue living together in the same house. The details of how much pocket money each child should receive and when, and the amount to be given to his daughters for their trousseau upon marriage – only if the daughter's choice was approved by his wife, or the trustees – suggests a loving, but controlling parent. There was provision for an annual allowance of up to £3000 to be paid to Frances for the rest of her life – to be withdrawn only if she remarried. There was extra money available for his two sons to continue their education after eighteen, but not his daughters, unless they required training for a 'profession'. The annual allowance for each child at eighteen was £60, a decent sum in those days. When the boys were twenty four, they were to be given control of the shares their father had left: the girls had to accept an annuity paid out at the discretion of the trustees!

After her husband's death, Frances continued to visit North Berwick during summer. In 1895, she rented Tantallon Lodge, in York Road. By that time, all the children were active in a variety of sports: they cycled; they played tennis; the boys played cricket and they all golfed. The girls also learned the piano. In 1896, Frances took a big step and sold the family home, 21 Woodside Terrace in Glasgow, and purchased a substantial Victorian villa, St Margaret's, in Dirleton Road, North Berwick. It comprised 3 public rooms, a billiard room, 8 principal bedrooms, 3 servants' bedrooms, 3 bathrooms, 2 WCs and a refrigerator house. This 'appliance' constantly caused problems and there were complaints that it didn't keep the food cold. Although the family was well-provided for, there were not vast amounts of spare cash. Household accounts reveal that when the dining room carpet was worn, it was repaired by darning the worn patch – and not replaced with a new carpet! There was, however, the luxury of a tennis court laid out in the garden and most importantly the house was situated a five minute stroll from one of the finest links courses in Scotland.

The six Orr sisters must have been a captivating sight on the North Berwick links – Theodora, Edith Aimie, Ada, Ethel and Hilda were all considered good golfers and they tended to go out onto the course together and compete against each other. Although they were all members at North Berwick Ladies' Club, their names are rarely to be found among the lists of competitors for any of the club medals and tournaments. The three older sisters seemed to burst onto the competitive golfing circuit, in 1897, when they entered the Ladies' Championship, at Gullane. It was the first time since its inauguration that it was to be held in Scotland. Their entry almost seemed like a whim.

The Event : The Ladies' Open Championship, May 1897

> **"Such an event would increase [in popularity] and become one of the most attractive gatherings of the year. If a championship was held in such places as St Andrews, North Berwick and Eastbourne, they would attract many a fair golfer."**
>
> (*Golf* magazine November 1890, letter by Toots, Glenalmond, Perth.)

The lady competitors gathered in front of the Gullane Clubhouse at the start of the 1897 Ladies' Open Golf Championship.

Early talk of establishing a ladies' championship had suggested that such an event could be staged at a venue like North Berwick, where, it was argued, it would pull in the crowds and in time "become one of the most attractive gatherings of the year": but this was not to be. On the first occasion that the Ladies' Open Championship came to Scotland (May 1897), it was held at Gullane, a golfing village a few miles along the coast to the west of North Berwick. It was the fifth Open Ladies' Championship. The first one had taken place at Lytham St Anne's, near Liverpool, in 1893, organised by the Ladies' Golf Union (LGU), which had been formed earlier that year.

Entry to the competition was through clubs affiliated to the LGU and North Berwick Ladies' Club had chosen not to affiliate. In its first four years, the championship was heavily criticised for its narrow representation of women golfers. Part of the problem was that women from only a handful of Clubs were eligible to take part, but a bigger issue was the absence of the Scottish lady golfers, who had been reluctant to travel south and who up until then had not shown 'any great interest' in the event. Possibly expense was a factor. However, in May 1897, the Scottish ladies came forward in droves to compete on familiar territory. In the event, no fewer than fourteen entrants were members at North Berwick, although four of those represented other clubs for the championship. Bringing the competition to Scotland certainly broadened its appeal.

The Championship was to take place over four days, 25th to 28th May, on the Gullane course. There was a record entry of 102 ladies. Before it got underway, a couple of warm-up competitions were held, with seventy two of the entrants participating, all anxious to do well. The first was a stroke competition held on the private course at Archerfield on Saturday 22nd. The omens were looking promising for the Scottish players, with Annie Maxwell (NBLGC) coming in a clear leader with a round of 83, seven strokes ahead of her nearest rival. The current Ladies' Champion Amy Pascoe, member for Woking in Surrey, had a most unfortunate round according to the English press, when she went into 'bad country', played two poor holes and scored 96. In the next pre-championship event, held at Gullane on Monday 24th, Miss Pascoe fared little better and the prizes went to three North Berwick members: the first to Theodora Orr, second to Maud Aitchison and third to Annie Maxwell!

Amy Pascoe must have felt huge pressure to repeat her previous championship success, although she herself was quite sure one of the Orr sisters would win. She thought that there was little to choose between the three who were competing, Theodora, Edith and Aimie. In her view they were the most exceptional golfers she had ever seen!

The competition proper began on the morning of 25th May 1897 in fine weather. The greens were described by golfing journalist, 'Lady Di', as in 'ticklish' condition. Amy Pascoe and Issette Pearson were among the most fancied English players. According to Lady Di, Mrs Pascoe spent the days before the competition practising her putting, rather than wearing herself out, like many of the other ladies, (the Orr sisters excepted) by going round the course an average of three times a day.

Spectators gather to watch the ladies tee off at Gullane, 1897.

At the end of the second day and the third round, the Scottish press was suggesting a rout of the English players. Miss Pascoe and Miss Pearson had both been knocked out. The *Aberdeen Weekly Journal* (Thursday 27 May 1897) referred to it as the 'Overthrow of the English Golfers'. At that stage it was hard to predict which one of the Scottish ladies would lift the trophy, as most of the North Berwick contingent – Blanche Anderson, Madeleine Campbell, Elsie Blyth, the Maxwell sisters and the Orr sisters – were still in contention.

By the time the fourth round was reached, hopes of an English champion were fading; eleven of the sixteen remaining players came from north of the Tweed and of those, eight were members at North Berwick, although not all playing out of the NBLC. On Wednesday, the fine weather had turned to drizzle and the mood of several of the English players matched the deteriorating conditions. Lady Di commented rather ruefully in her sports column in *Hearth and Home* that the success of the North Berwick Ladies was one of the remarkable features of the championship. At this stage, it was inevitable that several of the North Berwick players came up against each other. Annie Maxwell beat Elsie Blyth by two up and one to play in a thrilling match. In the fifth round, Edith Orr defeated Blanche Anderson for a place in the semi-final and her sister Theodora defeated Annie Maxwell for another. It was rather fortuitous for golfing history that the Orr sisters did not meet until the final on Friday 28 May!

The two other semi-finalists were Miss Kennedy from Rhyl in Wales and Maud Titterton, who was a member at Portobello, and later at Musselburgh, but played on many occasions at North Berwick. Maud Titterton had defeated Madeleine Campbell in a close match to secure her semi-final place. She then faced Edith Orr in the semi-final, in the swirling mist and pelting rain on the morning of the 28th. She played a fine all-round game, but Edith played better, making only a single error at the twelth, when she put Miss Titterton's ball into the hole! (In 1908, Maud Titterton finally clinched the Ladies' Open Championship, when it was played for the first time at St Andrews. On that occasion, North Berwick player, Dorothy Campbell, was the runner up.)

Maud Titterton playing in the semi-final of the Ladies' Open Championship against Edith Orr, Gullane 1897.

When the moment for the start of the final of the Ladies' 1897 Championship arrived, on Friday 28th May, the rain was pouring down. The crowd, undeterred, stood their ground. The match between Theodora and Edith Orr turned out to be uneventful, except that the spectators were entertained to a display of first-class golf. Edith triumphed over her elder sister four up and three to play. Benjamin Hall Blyth, as ever in the foreground of all important local golfing occasions, presented the cup and medals. He took the opportunity to advise the ladies to play more often over 18-hole courses and not confine themselves to their own 'short greens'. It was an encouraging development and an early sign of softening male attitudes to women being regarded as a nuisance on the 'long course'. It was the advice he had already given to his own daughter, Elsie, when he realised the potential she had. The previous day, he had watched Elsie's narrow defeat, in the fourth round of the championship, after an exciting match against another strong North Berwick golfer and friend, Annie Maxwell. Hall Blyth also made the point that he thought the additional competitions and prizes that surrounded the meeting were a distraction to the main event and were detrimental to the high standard of golf played and were in danger of trivialising the event. His words were noted and changes made in future championships. It was another step forward in raising the importance of the ladies' game.

To receive the Championship trophy was a great moment for Edith. Her exceptional golfing talent was articulated in the following comment: "She drives a good ball with a free easy swing, but it is her iron play which marks her perfection as a golfer. On the green she is deadly, being always well up and leaving nothing to luck." (*Golf: A Weekly Record*, Friday 4 June, 1897)

Mr Talbot Fair, representing the LGU thanked the Gullane Club for staging the event and expressed a keen desire for the Scottish ladies to compete the following year at Great Yarmouth. His words fell largely on deaf ears. Few Scottish lady golfers made the journey south the following year – and certainly neither Edith nor her sisters. It would seem that the single triumph of one of them, satisfied the sisters' collective ambition.

The June meeting of the NBLGC was the occasion chosen to recognise the achievement of Edith Orr in lifting the champion's trophy at Gullane and to acknowledge the honour that her victory had brought for Scotland, the Lothians and of course her own Club, by presenting her with a beautiful little travelling clock.

Throughout the championship event, the English ladies were impressed by the play of the 'Scotties' and felt outclassed. Years later Mabel Stringer (1868-1958), one of the competitors and a great promoter of women's golf, recorded in her book *Golfing Reminiscences*: "The natives were not very kind to us: they kept severely to themselves, they derided our efforts and were uncomplimentary about our red coats, which were worn with club colours, ties and hatbands and medals across their chests." She remembers the lack of hospitality they received as southerners and the fact that they were made to pay to the utmost farthing for everything: "One day at tea in the school, which was used as a club, two or three of us chose a table in the window overlooking the links; when we were given our bill, we found we had been charged nearly double the sum we had paid the preceding day, and were told the extra charge was for sitting in the window."

Mabel's memory of the weather was that it was awful throughout, although, in fact, it had been quite pleasant at the start when she was competing – she was knocked out in the second round. She complained that their clothes were never dry and: "our smart, stiff sailor hats were limp and misshapen and our beautiful 'red jackets and showy garments' as the natives derisively dubbed them, lost all their smartness." She did, however, recall the one really glorious day, which was the 'sawbeth' when a number of the English players went for an excursion to Tantallon Castle. But on the Monday, when the serious business resumed, the English players were "given a salutary lesson in taking a back-seat gracefully and sportingly, for three Scots lassies headed the stroke competition, Miss Orr, Miss Aitchison and Miss Annie Maxwell. The English players were dismissed one by one."

NBLGC MEMBERS WHO TOOK PART IN THE 1897 LADIES' CHAMPIONSHIP

(NB the Aitkens played out of Falkirk Tryst and Bloxsom and Aitchison played out of Edinburgh.)

Edith Orr (winner)
Theodora Orr (silver medallist)
Aimie Orr (4th round)
Annie Maxwell (5th round)
Mary Hay Maxwell (4th round)
Blanche Anderson (5th round)
Mary Orphoot (2nd round)
Elsie Blyth (4th round)
Madeleine Campbel (5th round)
Edith McCulloch (1st round)
Maud Aitken (4th round)
Agnes Aitken (3rd round)
Mary Bloxsom (2nd round)
Maud Aitchison (3rd round)

The 1897 Lady Open Golf Champion Edith Orr (seated l.) with her sister, Theodora (seated r.) the silver medallist and Maud Titterton and Miss Kennedy (standing) the bronze medalists.

The Aftermath of the Orr Sisters' Triumph

After the Orr sisters' successes in the Open Championship, they were hailed as celebrities and any appearance Edith made on the links at North Berwick became a major story. The sisters were much in demand for a round of golf on the North Berwick course, among the great society figures who spent part of the 'season' in the town that summer. On Friday 18th June 1897, a few weeks after the Ladies' Championship, Edith was partnered with Sir Forbes Adam, against two of her sisters Theodora and Aimie. Sir Forbes, a well-respected Scots-born industrialist, with a fine record of public service in Manchester and Bombay, had learnt his golf during his school days at Loretto and would have been no match for any of the Misses Orr in a singles game. As it was, spectators were treated to some fine play and the match was halved.

It would seem that any appearance of Edith (or her sisters) on the links was turned into a newsworthy event, in the months following the Open. The foursome between Blanche Anderson and Edith Orr against Maud Aitken and Miss Whigham (Ayrshire), in July 1897, was described as 'interesting' and noted Blanche and Edith were in fine form, winning 6 up and 5 to play. In truth it was a very ordinary match between four friends, who were all excellent golfers and regular golfers at North Berwick.

In October, Margot Asquith, wife of the future Prime Minister Herbert Asquith and well-known socialite, fancied her chances when she teamed up with Ben Sayers for a friendly game against Miss Ethel and Miss Theodora. But she was to be disappointed:

> **"At the outset the Misses Orr assumed the lead with a splendid 4 at Pointgarry against a stiff wind.... The Misses Orr led by 2 at the turn. Showing splendid form the Champion and runner-up secured three holes successively. Mrs Asquith and the professional somewhat improved their position by winning Perfection, but a half at the Redan decided a capital match in favour of the Misses Orr here by 4 up and 3 to play."**
>
> (*Golf Illustrated*, October, 1898)

In July 1897, the Ladies' Club organised a tournament over the long course, under championship conditions for a Diamond Jubilee Gold Medal. There were eighteen competitors, but the focus of attention was on the Orr sisters, who were making a rare appearance in a medal contest. From the start, the expectation among the spectators was that Miss Edith Orr, the Champion, would win. There were other 'capital' players in the tournament, such as Madeline Campbell and Blanche Anderson. The Orr sisters dominated the final stages of the competition. Theodora was knocked out first and then Edith defeated her younger sister Aimie in the semi-finals and went on to win the medal in the final against another very splendid golfer Maud Aitken.

Given the enormous success of the Scottish ladies at the British Ladies' Championship at Gullane, in 1897, there were great expectations that a Scottish contingent would break their apparent reluctance to participate south of the border and compete at Great Yarmouth the following year. All the coaxing by the Ladies Golf Union fell on deaf ears: the only Scottish entrant was Maud Titterton from Musselburgh – and she was put out in the semi-final. Many golfing enthusiasts were particularly disappointed by the absence of the Orr sisters. The following year at Newcastle, Co. Down was no better and remarks were made of a 'puir show' by the Scottish players. Perhaps there were mitigating factors. North Berwick was not at that time affiliated to the LGU and so the cost of entry to the championship had to be borne by the individual. On top of that there was the cost of travel and accommodation for the best part of a week. On the other hand, there were murmurings in the tearooms of English Clubhouses that Scottish players were too lazy or arrogant to bother themselves unless the meeting was on their doorstep and worse, that they considered themselves, superior players to the English female golfers!

In August 1899, Mabel Stringer again visited North Berwick with an aunt for a month's golfing. The two women stayed at the Marine Hotel and Mabel later recorded the highlights of her holiday. At that time there were still uncompromising rules in operation with regard to ladies' play on the long course. Mabel's recollection that ladies were only allowed to start either before 9 o'clock in the morning or after 5 pm is an exaggeration, but the comments she makes about the determination of the Orr sisters, whom she observed frequently during her stay, are revealing. No matter how early Mabel and her aunt went out in the morning, the Orr sisters, were always there before them. Two of them usually started off and when they were well ahead with a clear green, another sister joined in – they never kept anyone back and they were far better players than any other of the women.

For many years, the sisters remained together at St Margaret's, according to their father's wishes, living quietly. Their golfing reputation remained legendary. Ethel and Ada eventually moved to the south of England. In July 1914, two of the sisters hit the headlines for an event entirely unconnected with golf. Theodora and Ethel were involved in an unpleasant accident in the centre of Edinburgh, on Saturday 11th July 1914. A pony, with a trap attached, was startled by a passing motor car and bolted. It charged along Princes Street towards Waverley Bridge, where it swerved suddenly, knocking Theodora and

Ethel to the ground. Before the animal was brought to a halt, the wheel of the trap hit the kerb, throwing two other pedestrians to the ground, seriously injuring both. All four casualties were taken to the Royal Infirmary in taxis! Ethel suffered cuts to her head and concussion, while Theodora broke several ribs. The women recovered, but a few months later, in October, Theodora was found to have cancer of the womb and died from heart failure during an operation to remove the growth. She was forty five.

Theodora Orr, the eldest of the famous Orr sisters and runner-up in the 1897 British Ladies' Championships, could take on and soundly beat many a male golfer.

Theodora's death must have caused the sisters great anguish, as they were each other's constant companions. But it was not the only great loss they suffered. On the very day that Theodora died, 22nd October 1914, their beloved brother Captain John Arthur Orr, 1st Bn. Cameron Highlanders, was killed in action at Ypres, in Belgium. His body was never recovered and he is commemorated on the Menin Gate.

The sisters' youngest brother Norman was killed on active service in 1923. He had joined 2nd Battalion Seaforth Highlanders in 1903 and had survived fighting in the Great War in France, in spite of being wounded twice. After the war, as a professional soldier, he was sent with the Seaforths to guard India's frontier with Afghanistan. There was little conflict at the time, apart from the usual inter-tribal feuds and the area was considered safe enough for a visit by the Prince of Wales who had been on a tour of India, the previous year. On the evening of 10th April 1923, Major Orr and a fellow officer Major Anderson had gone for a walk from their base at Landi Kotal, at the head of the Kyber Pass, when they were ambushed, shot and killed by a gang of rogue tribesmen. Both men are commemorated in Fort George memorial chapel at Ardesier, near Inverness.

~

In an extract from the minutes of the Extraordinary General Meeting of NBLGC held after the Spring Meeting on Wed 12th May 1971, there is the following entry:

> **"At the end of the meeting Mrs Burnett gave some interesting news. Miss Orr, of Dirleton Avenue, who had died recently, had been British Champion in 1897 having beaten her sister in the final."**

The Orr sisters had caused a sensation over their extraordinary success at the British Ladies' Open Championship played at Gullane Course in May 1897. But within several decades, memories had faded to such an extent that the 1971 North Berwick Ladies' Committee was unaware that the Miss Orr, who had 'died recently', was not in fact Edith Orr, the 1897 Ladies' Open Champion, but her younger sister, 99 year old Aimie Louise. Miss Edith Constance Orr, had died quietly on 19th February 1955, at the home she shared with her sisters at 18 Dirleton Avenue. She had had a fall and broken her leg, several weeks before, and then suffered a fatal thrombosis. She was 84.

The legend of the phenomenal golfing Orr sisters lives on.

CHAPTER FIVE

Kaleidoscopic North Berwick

"The kaleidoscopic North Berwick Society still changes. The newest arrivals are Mr and Mrs Asquith, Mrs Harry Stewart, Mr and Mrs Hambro and Miss Grahame. Mixed foursomes over the long links are the most popular matches and Mrs Asquith and Mrs Harry Stewart have continued the matches they played at St Andrews. The Misses Maxwell, Miss Langley and Miss Hope play every day. Miss Edith Orr and Mr Mansfield Hunter holed the long course in 84 against Miss Orr and Mr Hugh Brown. The terribly stormy weather seems over and a delightful calm reigns. Both long and short links are in perfect condition."

(*Golf Illustrated*, 20 October 1899 – On the Ladies Links)

The Ladies' Club held its final meeting of the 1899 season on 24th September in stormy weather. It was also their last meeting of the century. A new era was dawning. Queen Victoria had been on the throne for over sixty years and during this period Britain had forged ahead as a great economic and industrial power, with a vast Empire spread across the world. At home, Victoria's reign had been synonymous with authority, moral propriety and an established social order. When she died in 1901, her eldest son Edward, Prince of Wales, was crowned King Edward VII. He had an entirely different approach to life from his mother; he was frivolous and fun-loving and was a devotee of the art of enjoyment. He became King of the wealthiest society in the world and set the pace for the aristocracy and the new rich to follow. At its outset, the Edwardian era favoured wealth and privilege: it was a period of extraordinary brilliance, some of which radiated through North Berwick.

Margot Asquith (1864-1945), the sixth daughter of Charles Tennant and wife of Prime Minister H.H. Asquith, was a household name in the early 20th century. Stylish, witty, intelligent and outspoken, she had a passion for golf and was often to be seen on the North Berwick links, during the season. This photo of her was taken at Archerfield in 1926.

In October 1902, the new King graced North Berwick with his presence. It was already a popular summer retreat of the spectacularly rich and famous. Arthur James Balfour, who became Prime Minister in July 1902, following his uncle the Marquis of Salisbury into the post, made an annual pilgrimage to the town to golf. The Balfour's family seat was Whittinghame, in the East Lothian countryside and A.J.B. spent as much time as he could on various golf links in the county, when he was away from London and his political duties. The newspapers charted his movements during his visits north and *The Guardian* noted in September 1903 that "Mr Balfour has engaged rooms at the North Berwick hotel for a month for the purpose of golfing." Little evidence of the pressures of high office there! After Herbert Henry Asquith (Home Secretary in 1894 under Gladstone and Prime Minister from 1908 to 1916) married Margot Tennant, daughter of Sir Charles Tennant on 10th May 1894, he and Margot became frequent summer visitors to North Berwick:

> **"I hear that during the visit of the Home Secretary and his wife to Sir Charles Tennant, Mr H H Asquith was initiated by the fair Margot into the mysteries of golf, caught the usual fever and has never lost a chance of playing since."**
>
> (*Hearth & Home*, 1 November 1894)

It was rumoured that on occasions, after he became Prime Minister, Asquith was almost able to hold a Cabinet meeting in the town, so popular was it among the political classes. As long as North Berwick retained its reputation for its unrivalled golfing facilities and its esoteric charm as a seaside resort, key figures in society continued to flock to its doors.

In spite of the dreadful weather on that September day in 1899, a large crowd gathered on the ladies' links. They were there to watch the ladies play, but also to catch a glimpse of visiting royalty in the person of the Duke of Cambridge, a grandson of George III. The Duke made regular appearances during the golfing season, not because he was a golfer; it was simply fashionable to be there:

> **"The Duke of Cambridge intends paying a visit to North Berwick about the end of the present month, and to make a fortnight's stay there. On the occasion of his visit last year the Duke was taken by Sir Walter Hamilton-Dalrymple, the Lord of the Manor, to Tantallon Castle and his Royal Highness manifested the greatest interest in the historic fortress."**
>
> (*Golf: A Weekly Record*, 24 September 1897)

A.J. Balfour golfing at North Berwick in September 1905.

Tantallon Castle with a view of the Bass Rock in the distance.

The Duke was not the only focus of attention; taking part in the competition was a rising star, Dorothy Campbell, now seventeen. In the event, Dorothy won the principal scratch award, achieving two rounds of nine holes in 67 and carried off the prize for the lowest scoring single round of 32. The Duke presented the prizes and confidently voiced his opinions on the progress and virtues of golfing. He expressed regret that as golf was scarcely known outside Scotland in his youth, he had had no opportunity to play and at his present age of eighty, it was too late to learn. His audience hung on his words as he attributed 'the national character for enterprise' and 'manly undertakings' to Scotland's pre-eminence in golf: they cheered and applauded.

Possibly unfamiliar with the spectacle of a group of young, enterprising and sporting women, he seemed to struggle to make an appropriate comment on the ladies' riveting display of the game, which had undoubtedly brought him pleasure. He conceded that golf was 'an exceedingly suitable exercise for the fair sex' – but that the ladies should 'keep within their proper sphere'! (*Aberdeen Weekly Journal* 25 September 1899) The reactions of Miss Dorothy Campbell and the other competitors were not recorded: it is almost certain that the Duke's remarks would not have gone down well with the more forward-thinking young women, some of whom were beginning to strike out against the constant limitations imposed on their public activities, for which there seemed no basis in logic.

Dorothy Campbell, one of the greatest lady golfers of the day, learned her game at North Berwick. This photo of her was taken in about 1904.

The *Pall Mall Gazette* (23 September 1899) took a more sardonic, but equally patronising, view of his presentation at the ladies' course, commenting:

> **"His Royal Highness has not been induced, even by the Ladies of North Berwick, to learn the game at eighty years of age, although it is not to be doubted that all [the ladies] would have been delighted to take him round the links. One is inclined to think that it is a pity he has not succumbed to the mysterious fascination of the sport."**

Other 'royals' appeared with increasing regularity at North Berwick, generally in late September, to watch the golf, if not to play. Their arrivals were loudly heralded by the local press, but in reality, their connections to the British royal family were often somewhat distant and some could be described as hangers-on. The Duke of Teck, a minor German royal, whose wife was granddaughter of George III; Prince and Princess Edward of Saxe Weimar; Prince and Princess Herman of Saxe Weimar and Princess Olga of Russia, all made appearances in the little burgh, at the turn of the century. Apart from the town's Provost appearing on the station platform to carry out his civic duty in welcoming the royal guests, if called upon to do so, the ordinary North Berwick folk had little direct contact with these high-class visitors. Of course, for the local traders, their visits were a bonanza. Orders came flying in to supply quantities of meat, fish and a variety of other foodstuffs to the houses and hotels where they were lodged or entertained. It would be fair to say, the local community thrived on the rapid strides in popularity of North Berwick as a golfing mecca and fashionable resort.

Prince and Princess Edward of Saxe-Weimar leased The Knoll, from ophthalmic surgeon Dr George Berry (later Sir George Berry) in September and early October between 1899 and 1902, paying about £200 in rent. They had been regular summer visitors to North Berwick for some years before this, often as guests of Sir Charles Tennant or the Earl of Wemyss. The Knoll, with its four reception rooms, nine principal rooms and two bathrooms, excluding domestic quarters, was state of the art when it was designed by George Washington Browne in 1898 and built on the slope of the hill that rises immediately above the town to the south. It was here that the Saxe-Weimars hosted the newly crowned King Edward VII on his coronation visit to North Berwick in October1902. The house was subsequently renamed King's Knoll. Prince Edward belonged to the German royal family and his tenuous link to Edward VII was through his mother's sister Adelaide, the wife of William IV. His wife Lady Augusta Catherine Gordon-Lennox, daughter of 5th Duke of Richmond, was considered, in German royal circles, an unsuitable match as she was not of German royal blood. Fortunately for the couple, who lived in Britain, Queen Victoria stamped on such nonsense after their marriage in 1851 and Augusta was treated with the dignity accorded a Duke's daughter. The King's visit must have taxed the constitution of Prince Edward, who was seventy nine and in failing health; he died a few weeks later – and his Princess eighteen months after that. For a decade he and his wife had headed the list of celebrity visitors to North Berwick, but it was not long before other 'names' appeared on the links to fill their shoes.

Lady Augusta Katherine Gordon-Lennox, wife of Prince Edward of Saxe-Weimar.

George Berry's royal connections went further than renting The Knoll to Prince Edward of Saxe-Weimar; Sir George was Surgeon-Occulist in Scotland to King Edward VII and later to George V. He was knighted in 1916; became President of the Royal College of Surgeons; President of the Ophthalmic Society of Great Britain and was elected MP for the Scottish Universities in 1922, when that electoral anomaly still existed. He and his wife Agnes were part of the Edinburgh set (their house was in Drumsheugh Gardens) who holidayed every year in North Berwick. Agnes had a fascinating upbringing in India where she and her fourteen siblings were born. Her father was Sir William Muir, who had a distinguished career in the Indian Civil Service, rising to become Lieutenant Governor of the North Western Provinces and an influential member of the Viceroy's Council. Some years after the family's return to this country, Sir William was elected Principal of Edinburgh University, a post he held from 1884 to 1903. Before they built The Knoll, George and Agnes Berry rented the first floor of Westgate House, for their North Berwick holidays. Agnes and her three daughters Phyllis, Dorothy and Agnes Mary (known as Nancy) were keen golfers and members of the Ladies' Club. Agnes died at King's Knoll in July 1929, at the age of seventy two after a sudden heart attack, much loved for her gentle caring nature and respected for her intellect.

The Knoll, the home of Sir George Berry and his wife and golfing daughters. They sometimes rented the house out during August and September. It was renamed King's Knoll after Edward VII stayed there in 1902, as a guest of Prince Edward of Saxe-Weimar.

The upper classes were quick to adopt the ladies' links at North Berwick as something of their own territory. There was even a reference (mistaken!) to the 9-hole course being the private course of the Tennants. At certain periods of the year, it might as well have been. The Tennants, their extended family and distinguished friends, played golf most days during the season, while resident in North Berwick. Whether it was a deliberate ploy or not, Margot Asquith was always recognisable on the course wearing a bright red cap. She was a most enthusiastic golfer but it was once remarked: "Playing golf was the only thing Margot did badly!"

The taboos and constraints imposed on lady golfers, hardly applied to ladies of the aristocracy, who were a law unto themselves. They played whenever they wished and with whomsoever they wished. Grace Blackburn (1857-1946), the second wife of the Francis Charteris, 10th Earl of Wemyss and March, was one such lady. First and foremost, she was a brilliant golfer. She had married the widowed Lord Wemyss in 1899 when he was 81 and she was 42. The union caused a murmur of disapproval among friends and family who were left a little unsure of whether her lineage was sufficiently noble for such a noble Lord. Undeterred Grace swung into her role as the consort of one of Scotland's leading aristocrats, a gregarious man and one who had many valuable political connections at Westminster and who loved his family seat, Gosford in East Lothian. It meant they were regular visitors to the county and were frequently accompanied by their elite circle of friends and acquaintances – and not just in the summer months. The following extracts in Grace's diary, in December 1911, give a splendid flavour of the effortless superiority of the ruling elite and the extent to which golf was an important part of their leisurely routine.

Grace Blackburn, 2nd wife of the 10th Earl of Wemyss took a great interest in women's golf and was an excellent player. She is playing here at Kilspindie with Hugo Charteris and George Vernon in 1911.

December 20th, 1911 – Gosford

"Came up on Saturday and found the Duke of Rutland and Diana* in one of the carriages – Mr Asquith in another – had some conversation with the latter. I went and sat with Henry Rutland and Diana went to see PM – looking very pretty. Wemyss did not wish to see the PM & he went one way & me another at Longniddry."

**(Diana Manners the youngest daughter of the 8th Duke of Rutland, later famed for her beauty, would have been nineteen in December 1911.)*

Monday – meant to go to Edinburgh, but no motors ready – went to North Berwick in afternoon and saw Mrs Lubbock – she looks thinner and better.

Tuesday, a lovely morning went into Edinburgh to shop – went at 11 got back at 4.30 – lunched at club – saw Lucy Hope and Miss Graham Murray. [Both were members at NBLC.]

Wednesday pouring – no golf, which I was to have played with Mrs Lubbock.

Friday 22nd – Hugo (Charteris), George (Vernon) and I had a match at golf. George drove occasionally like Braid, but missed the simplest approaches. Hugo gave us a third and we beat him. I am bad with my wooden clubs."

Mrs Lubbock, the former Lady Tennant, who remarried after the death of her first husband Sir Charles Tennant. The photograph was taken in the 1920s, a decade after the events referred to in Grace Wemyss' diary.

On Christmas Day, Grace was out on the golf course with house guest Sir Edgar Vincent playing against Arthur Balfour and Mr Elves, and as usual was a harsh critic of her own game: "I played badly – they gave us four strokes & only beat us at the last hole". In April 1912, Grace and Elsie Grant-Suttie played together against Sir Maurice Bonham-Carter and Rita Grant-Suttie (Elsie's sister) on the ladies' course and won comfortably. On June 17th, Grace organised another match, in which she partnered James Braid against Elsie Grant-Suttie and Harry Vardon. Braid and Vardon were two of the greatest golf professionals of the day. Elsie and Vardon gave their opponents three strokes, only one of which came in, and won the match 2 up. While Grace commended Braid and Vardon's driving skills, she also wrote: "Their putting is not so good. They came back to tea." Also invited back to tea that day were J.H. Taylor and Ted Ray – completing Grace's scoop of the best golfers of the day in her drawing room: "Taylor was too good-mannered almost, but Ray over-did being at ones ease!"

Gosford House, East Lothian seat of the Earls of Wemyss and March.

In August, Grace was again golfing at North Berwick, on this occasion with Ben Sayers against Elsie Grant-Suttie. There is little doubt she was competent enough to hold her own against the most formidable opponents. The irony is that perhaps her position as wife of a high-profile Earl stymied any possibility of her taking golf more seriously and competing at the level of her great friend Elsie Grant-Suttie, who had the advantage of being merely the unmarried daughter of a younger son of a local laird, and therefore sufficiently wealthy and independent to pursue her love of the game.

Grace enjoyed the freedoms and privileges that her marriage had given her. She loved golf and she could play with whom she pleased, man or woman. During the early years of the twentieth century, Emmeline Pankhurst's Suffragette movement campaigned vociferously for the extension of women's rights and the right of women to vote in parliamentary elections. One might have assumed that it would have the support of forthright women, like Grace Wemyss, but this was not the case. On Tuesday 5th March 1912, Grace commented in her diary : "The Suffragettes are abominable, breaking windows and behaving like lunatics. Mrs Pankhurst got two months [jail sentence]."

During the golfing season, the Earl and Countess of Wemyss entertained a constant stream of guests at Gosford and after a few rounds of golf on their own course, Kilspindie, would bring their guests to North Berwick, either to take part in, or provide an audience for, the many matches that were taking place across both the long links and the ladies' course.

A regular guest at Gosford was Lady Charlotte Ribblesdale, the graceful and charming wife of Thomas Lister 4th Baron Ribblesdale and elder sister of Margot Asquith. She was an enthusiastic golfer and in 1900 her photo appeared in *Golf Illustrated* accompanied by a short article entitled 'Interesting Golfers':

> **"Lady Ribblesdale.... may often be seen on the links at St Andrews and North Berwick.....her husband Lord Ribblesdale is also a keen golfer.... Mrs Asquith, Lady Ribblesdale's sister, and Sir Charles Tennant of The Glen, her ladyship's father, are well-known golfers."**

Charlotte Ribblesdale, a sister of Margot Asquith, was featured in Golf Illustrated as an 'Interesting Golfer' in Feb 1900.

Charlotte Tennant (Charty) had married Thomas Lister in 1877, and had given birth to three daughters and two sons. Their eldest son Thomas was killed on active service in Somaliland in 1904 and their younger son Charles died from shell wounds in Gallipoli in August 1915, a few months after burying his friend and comrade, the poet Rupert Brooke, on the Greek island of Skyros. As neither Ribblesdale son was married, the title became extinct on the death of Lord Ribblesdale in 1927.

Charlotte's father Sir Charles Tennant (1823-1906), whose principal residence was The Glen in Peeblesshire, had been a member of the New Club from its formation in 1880. He and his first wife, Emma had twelve children, of whom eight survived to adulthood. Not long after Emma died in 1895, Charles met the young, vivacious Marguerite Agaranthe Miles, whilst golfing at Biarittz, whom he married in 1898. He was seventy five and she twenty nine, but in spite of the difference and his advanced years, they had four daughters: Peggy born in 1899, Jean born 1900, Katherine in 1903 and Nancy in 1904. Jean suffered poor health and died in 1911. It appears that almost all the Tennant children of both marriages learned to play golf and continued to do so as adults – often at North Berwick. In 1902, Charles Tennant purchased, for Marguerite, Buchanan Lodge from Dame Alicia Buchanan Riddell, widow of Sir Walter Buchanan Riddell of Riddell. The house was set in over an acre of ground between Dirleton Avenue and the Marine Hotel, in close proximity to the links and directly opposite Hyndford, which Charles Tennant had owned since 1886 and made over to his son Frank in 1895. Buchanan Lodge was re-named Glenconner and became a place family and friends could congregate and enjoy the delights of the golfing 'season' in the 'Brighton of the North'. Even after Charles Tennant died and Marguerite had married widower Major Geoffrey Lubbock, she continued to live part of every year at Glenconner, until her death there in 1943.

THE TENNANT WOMEN

Charles Tennant (1823–1906) married 1st Emma Winsloe (d. 1895) and 2ndly Marguerite Miles (1869–1943). He had 12 children by Emma and four by Marguerite.

Charlotte, Lucy and Margot, daughters of his first marriage, were well-known figures on North Berwick links during the summer months. Charlotte (1858–1911) married Thomas Lister, 4th Baron Ribblesdale in 1877 and became Lady Ribblesdale; Lucy (1860–1942) married Thomas Graham Smith, a banker, in 1879 and was widowed in 1908. Margot married Herbert Asquith MP in 1894 and became Mrs Asquith, later Countess of Oxford. Charles Tennant's son Frank was married to Anne Redmayne and she and her daughters Frances, Dinah and Kathleen were members of NBLGC.

Charles Tennant's 2nd wife Marguerite was a first-rate golfer and a lady member at North Berwick. Three daughters of this marriage, Peggy, who married John de Vere Loder and became Lady Wakehurst, Katherine, who became Baroness Elliot and Nancy, who became Lady Crathorne, continued their association with North Berwick and golfing for many years.

Although the North Berwick golfing community arrived in the town from all corners of Britain, they connected up to each other like a several-stranded graduated pearl necklace – it was possible to start from the clasp and work round through relatives, friends and acquaintances and move on to the next loop. There was undoubtedly a pecking order: qualification in one of the recognisable areas – a royal connection, a title, political involvement, land-ownership, a splendid house in the town, professional success, inherited wealth or money made through industry – would ensure the desired social inclusion beyond the golf course.

The Marine Hotel was often a centre for activities associated with the ladies' golf.

There were many golfing visitors to North Berwick who chose to stay in one of the town's hotels or guest houses, rather than buying a second house. Though he was a frequent visitor to the town, A. J. Balfour never bought a house there. There were several reasons: he was a bachelor; he was never short of invitations to private homes and he owned a large mansion house in the county. His favourite place to stay in North Berwick was Bradbury's, on the corner of York Road, where he could have his own suite of rooms and depend on the integrity and discretion of the hotel manager John Campbell. It had the advantage of rather select clientele such as Her Grace the Duchess of Montrose, also there for the golf. Besides, it was convenient for the links; a five minute stroll would take Balfour to the clubhouse, where he had his own locker and could quickly be on the course.

The Marine Hotel was the first port of call for several golfing families, before they decided to invest in a permanent holiday home in the town. Harry and Kate Armitage took a suite at the Marine over several seasons, before purchasing the Grange, from law lord and golfer Lord Trayner in 1902.

The drawing room of the Marine Hotel c.1900.

> **"The Marine Hotel, North Berwick... is now one of the best in the kingdom, and well-known to golfers... 'If a stranger', says a recent description, 'happened by chance to look into any of the private sitting-rooms of the Marine, ten to one he would find some golf clubs lying about. These implements pervade the place. In the height of the season no room is too sacred for them. It is doubtful whether they do not even find their way to church.' The Patent Church-Attender is the newest development in the evolution of the golf club."**
>
> (*Golf*, April 14, 1893)

The Armitages had a slightly different profile to many members of the golfing community, but infiltrated it very successfully; they were neither London, Edinburgh or Glasgow based and neither did they appear to have any Scottish roots. It is not clear what first brought them to North Berwick, possibly a friendship with Charles and Mary Hemingway, who lived in the Yorkshire village, Ecclesall Bierlow where Kate had been brought up. Mary Hemingway was born in Scotland and had golfed at North Berwick for many years. She continued to golf here after her marriage and encouraged all six of her daughters to play a decent game of golf.

Whatever the connection, once the Armitages had visited North Berwick, they were smitten and both took out a membership of the Ladies' Club – Harry Armitage as an honorary member. In addition Harry Arnold Armitage, retired Captain of XV Hussars, was able to convince the elite camarilla of the Old North Berwick Club that he had the correct pedigree to become a member. He also enjoyed membership of the New Club, Tantallon and the Royal and Ancient at St Andrews.

Their house, the Grange, designed by Sir Robert Lorimer, one of Scotland's pre-eminent architects, in 1893, for Lord Trayner, stood in a commanding position in thirteen acres of ground, on the brow of the hill above the burgh. For Armitage, who had inherited a good deal of money from his father Joseph, a Huddersfield woollen manufacturer, the small mansion house wasn't sufficiently grand. He commissioned Lorimer to extend it and his extravagance stretched to a fifteen metre high castellated tower, a defining feature, which gave many clues as to the character of the man. He was short in stature, but in personality as expansive as his wife was restrained: he fished and hunted; he was a gentleman jockey, riding his own horse, Tame Vixen; he was an artist of considerable talent, exhibiting in the Royal Academy; he annoyed his wife, by inviting young women from the town to model for him in his studio; he not only played a good game of golf, he also made many of his own clubs. Kate on the other hand, after suffering several miscarriages and the agony of a still-born daughter, seemed to content herself with playing golf on the ladies' course, not terribly well, and act as a society hostess in her fine house. There was even a ballroom on the first floor with a high-vaulted ceiling and external stone steps led from here to ground level where a 'ladies' walk' followed the boundary of the formal garden. A smoking room led off the dining room and a billiard room was situated beyond that. On sunny afternoons croquet matches were played on one of the lawns. The wing of the Grange laid out as a nursery, remained empty.

The Rev. William Houldsworth and his family (ref. chapter 3) continued to make North Berwick central to their golfing plans each summer. As the years passed, they favoured North Berwick over Nairn, but retained the habit of visiting Nairn first and arriving in North Berwick at the end of September.

They had created a large circle of friends among the summer golfers and instantly upon arrival they were caught up in the social activities prevailing amongst their set.

On Friday 27th September 1907, the Rev. William, his wife Eulalie, daughter Dossie (Dorothy) and son Gil (William Gilbert) arrived in North Berwick, by train from Nairn, in time for dinner at Westbrook, the house they had taken for the season. By now, the two elder Houldsworth girls were married; Lillie in 1905 and Marion in June 1907. Gilbert was fifteen and Dossie thirteen and both avid golfers. As soon as dinner was over, the Rev. Houldsworth took a brisk walk to Wellbent in York Road, to arrange a game of golf for the following day at Muirfield with his friend Lord Moncreiff. It seems that the golfing programme was still initiated and led by the man of the house and so what of the ladies? Aged fifty, Eulalie was playing less and more typically would meet friends for tea or go for a carriage drive into the countryside. One Saturday, Houldsworth and a group of his pals went for a round at Muirfield and Eulalie and Marion drove out in a fly to have tea with them after the game, only to be told that 'ladies could not take tea at Muirfield on Saturdays'! A hundred years down the line, ladies are not yet welcome at Muirfield on a par with the men!

The youngsters were golfing at every opportunity - Dossie was soon on the ladies' links with her contemporary and great chum, Faith Laidlay, who in spite of her youth was playing off two, in club matches. She looked like a rising star and perhaps it was the intervening war years that removed opportunities for her to compete and improve her game; she was never quite in the championship league. She won the ladies' gold badge in the North Berwick Coronation Competition in June 1911. In June 1914, she played in the successful North Berwick B team in the Eglinton Quaich competition and was playing well enough to take part in the Scottish Ladies' Championship at Muirfield in the same month, but didn't reach the final stages. She was, however, sought after as a reliable golfing partner and in September 1911 appeared on the links with the prime minister's son Raymond Asquith in a game against Elizabeth Asquith (the PM's daughter) and James Braid, the professional golfer, who had won the Open Championship a record five times. In September 1919, she married Captain Frank Stobart, 18th Hussars, who had survived the war, in one piece. A. J. Balfour attended the wedding, but more importantly it was conducted by her dear friend Dossie's father, the Rev. Houldsworth, who had taken time out from his incessant golfing to perform the ceremony.

Faith Laidlay (Stobart) on North Berwick Links in the 1920s.

Most of the Rev. Houldsworth's golfing activities involved his wide circle of male friends, for example, on one occasion he golfed with Walter Powell in the morning and Horace Peel and Crum-Ewing in the afternoon. His conscience must have pricked as afterwards he took, his daughter Dossie for a round over the long course. As they didn't start until 4.15, they had to stop at the 11th and walk in, as it was getting quite dark – perhaps Dossie could be justified in feeling a little side-lined!

The men, however, didn't call all the shots. When the Rev. Houldsworth invited his friend's wife, Emily Mure, to a round one morning, he recorded ruefully in his diary: "A very high wind and she won". Mrs Mure had a handicap of 4 from the Ladies' Club – and so perhaps her success was an indication of the high standard set by the club. Sunday was the day for church and visiting: there was no golf played on the Sabbath. The Rev. Houldsworth, who was a parish priest in London, often assisted at Holy Communion in St Baldred's or gave the sermon at evensong. They were almost sociable occasions; the pews were filled with golfing families. Among the permanent pewholders were the Laidlays, the Adam's, the Armitages, the Maxwells, Teachers, Tennants and Grant-Sutties.

In September 1909, the Houldsworth's travelled from their golfing holiday in Nairn to their golfing holiday in North Berwick by 'motor car' and ferry, instead of by train. It was not completely straight forward. The party was in three cars and one burst a tyre south of Perth and arrived at Burntisland to find the ferry was full. On this occasion the Houldsworth party had rented Glendalough, owned by Sir William Baird. To their annoyance the house was not ready on their arrival and so they dined at the Marine and had a 'rather stiff interview with Lady Baird on the telephone' the following day, whereupon 'the things required came in'!

The following autumn, the Houldsworths, perhaps weary of the uncertainties attached to renting, took the plunge and bought a house in North Berwick – Anchor Villa, in West Bay Road, almost on the edge of the 18th green. The economics of house buying in this high end Edwardian 'watering place' were interesting. The house was perfectly situated for golfing and a perfect size for purpose; there was space for family and guests with three principal rooms, eight principal bedrooms, two bathrooms and six servants' bedrooms. The initial asking price was £3700, but "the solicitors evidently expected much less and asked for an offer". William Houldsworth hesitated as the property next door, Tantallon House appeared on the market for a similar asking price. Spoilt for choice, Houldsworth was able to offer £2000 for Anchor Villa and was successful. It was then renamed Cranston.

The Houldsworths arrived in North Berwick with their small retinue of household servants in early October 1912, in high winds and driving rain and moved into the newly refurbished Cranston. The following day, the Houldsworth girls and Faith Laidlay preferred the Musselburgh Races to the wind-swept links of North Berwick. The weather improved and the ladies were soon back on the golf course and the usual matches and contests took place, before the season came to an end for another year.

Muriel, Hilda, Ethel and their younger brother Archie Grant-Suttie on the rocks at North Berwick c.1910. They were first cousins of famous golfer Elsie Grant-Suttie and members of the Ladies' Club.

The old East Lothian county families continued to have a close involvement in golf, alongside the newcomers. The three Grant-Suttie girls, Hilda, Muriel and Ethel, daughters of Robert and Edith Grant-Suttie of Balgone (an estate on the outskirts of North Berwick), joined the Ladies' Club as each of them turned fourteen. Hilda joined in 1901, Muriel in 1902 and Ethel in 1907. They were good golfers but not in the same class as their famous cousin, Elsie, the daughter of their father's brother Francis. In June 1911, Hilda and Muriel Grant-Suttie were staying in London with relatives for the Coronation of King George V. Their mother Edith wrote with all the North Berwick news and of Elsie's victory in the Scottish Ladies' Championship at St Andrews:

Balgone House home of the Grant-Suttie family.

My Dearest Muriel
You must not expect a long letter as we are going to be very busy this morning putting away the china, but I will scribble you a line first. It has been raining this morning and is still going on which will do a world of good and save both garden and the poor birds who are pretty

Elsie Grant-Suttie in action c.1911.

hard up….. Daddy wants you to send round to 33 Eaton Place to say what time the Olympia business begins and what time we ought to be there. Wasn't it a splendid triumph Elsie winning the Championship? I am so glad, she certainly deserved to win. She and Rita are coming up the day after tomorrow, so we shall hear all about it. Ever your most loving Mother"

What the family would hear about was that Elsie had come up against Dorothy Campbell in the second round and in a close-fought match, beat her by one hole and knocked her out of the competition. In the final Elsie had an easy run for the trophy and the £25 prize against Miss Maitland of Elie, defeating her by 7 and 5.

In December 1913, tragedy struck the Grant-Suttie family; Muriel suffered a perforated stomach caused by complications from an appendicitis and died a few days before Christmas: the family were devastated. Cousin Elsie's continued success in competitive golf brought some distraction. In May 1914, in a letter to his daughter Hilda, Robert Grant-Suttie comments: "I see Elsie and Rita both play for the championship and are today playing for Scotland. I should like them both to get into the final and Rita, for choice, win. Much love, yours affectionately R G Suttie". Elsie's younger sister Rita, mentioned in both letters, also enjoyed considerable success as a golfer.

Competitions, Competitors and Control of the Club

Whatever was happening elsewhere in the golfing world, the North Berwick Ladies' Club regular competitions continued throughout the early years of the twentieth century. The scratch players were out in force for the annual meeting of the Ladies' Club in early September 1904 - a total of nine scratch players were among the forty four competitors: Mrs Couper (formerly Elsie Hall Blyth), Miss Janet Blair, Miss Adelaide Gillies Smith, Miss Coventry Gillies Smith, Miss Lucy Cochrane, Miss Margaret Gillies Smith, Mrs Nicholas, Miss Annie Dalziel and Miss Hilda Sant. There was a splendid array of handicap prizes, a silver clock, a gold bracelet set with turquoises, a leather writing case set with silver mounting and a silver pin box, but of course, the most coveted prize was the Club gold medal. Lucy Cochrane was a favourite to win, as she had lifted the trophy the previous year. But there were so many first class golfers on the links, competition was intense.

Hilda Sant, who had won the medal in 1902, got off to a cracking start with a three at the first hole and a two at the second, which she achieved with the aid of a 'long steal'. A five at the third, marred an otherwise perfect performance. The experts in the crowd reckoned her mistake was to use a mashie for her tee shot, which fell short. She then got a two at the fifth and finished with 30 after the first nine holes. She did even better on the second round with a final score for the two rounds of 59. It was a record for the double round in the medal competition and she easily secured the gold medal.

Glasclune, the house designed for Lord and Lady Kinross in North Berwick.

A large crowd followed the progress of the match throughout the afternoon. Among the spectators were Annie Maxwell (a sister of great Amateur Champion golfer Robert Maxwell), who watched her sister Isabel compete and Ethel Orr, a younger sister of the 1897 British Lady Champion Edith. Lady Howard Vincent, Mrs Dalziel, Mrs Mary Hemingway and Mrs Blackwood Porter were there to support their respective daughters.

A heavy shower in the middle of the afternoon had sent the officiating

Robert Maxwell (1877-1949) painted by Spy, for Vanity Fair, after his celebrated win in the Amateur Championship at Muirfield in 1903. Unfortunately, there are no similar images of his sister Annie, excellent golfer though she was!

party scurrying into the Marine. They reappeared to watch the ladies coming in at the end of their second round and for the prize-giving ceremony. Lady Kinross presented the prizes. She was the wife of John Blair Balfour, Lord President of the Court of Session, who had been elevated to the peerage in 1902 and took the name Lord Kinross of Glasclune. Glasclune was the name of the Queen Anne style mansion designed for them by Kinnear & Peddie in 1889, to the east of the town, overlooking the Coo's Green and sitting between two other great houses of the town's golfing fraternity, St Baldred's Tower and Redholm. Lady Kinross' own daughter, the Hon. Gwendolen Balfour, won the fourth handicap prize of the contest. In September 1908, Gwendolen's marriage to Lieut. Percy Henry Havelock Bailey, at St Baldred's Church in North Berwick was not quite the society wedding of her brother Patrick, to Miss Johnstone-Douglas, five years earlier, every perfect detail of which was covered in the press. The marriage was disastrous and ended in an annulment after an unpleasant court case in 1917. Gwendolen never remarried and settled in England where she died at the age of 75 in 1961.

Among the competitors that September afternoon in 1904, Isabella Maxwell, playing off a handicap of 10, was further down the field than might be expected. She and her eight siblings had been playing golf at North Berwick for as long as any of them could remember. Their father Captain Francis Maxwell was a prominent landowner in Dumfriesshire and their mother Adelaide Louisa was a daughter of Rear Admiral James Hay of Belton and almost before it was fashionable, the Maxwell's had rented a house at North Berwick for the summer season and golfed. The children had lessons from Bob Miller, one of the best-known and well-respected 'fisherman golfers' in the town, who played to a professional standard. He used to say that while Robert Maxwell was his ideal of a perfect gentleman golfer, Annie Maxwell was his ideal as a lady golfer. Annie was an excellent player and better than any of her sisters, but like Blanche Anderson never won a big title.

Francis Maxwell died in 1892, when Robert was on the cusp of his extraordinary golfing successes. Adelaide Louisa died suddenly in January 1900, a few weeks ahead of her daughter Adelaide's wedding to John Campbell Kennedy of Dalquharan (Ayrshire). The wedding went ahead at St Baldred's, but was scaled down. Annie, Isabella, Ethel, Mary and Robert, none of whom married, shared a house in the town, situated in West Bay, a short step from the first green. It was named it East Gribton – a nod to the family estate, Gribton, in Dumfriesshire, much of which was sold off in about 1880. Isabella survived into her eighties – a tall, fearsome lady – who perhaps was uncomfortable with the notion of the new classless society of the 1960s and looked back on her younger days, when all her needs were attended to by a household of servants and long summers were filled with the pleasures of a daily round of golf.

At the September meeting in 1905, the scratch award went to the beautiful and talented sixteen year old Winifred Martin Smith, daughter of Martin and Cecilia Ridley Smith, with a score of 59 for the two rounds. Martin Smith was an immensely wealthy London financier, enterprising horticulturist and golfer. The family had a London house in Cadogan Square, but also a mansion house, The Warren in Hayes, Kent, which Martin Smith had bought from another great London financier and North Berwick golfer Walter Maximillian de Zoete. Both families came to North Berwick every year for the golfing season. Winifred was the youngest of Martin Smith's nine children and was seen as a potential lady champion. She came closest to achieving that coveted prize, the Ladies' Championship at St Anne's, in June 1913 when she was fancied to win after some splendid play in the early rounds of the competition. She reached the final eight, before she was defeated by the eventual runner-up, Miss E. Chubb. At North Berwick, in September 1905 she caused a stir, with her charming style and 'delightful swing' and her undeniably pretty looks. Although she was an active summer member at North Berwick, she was more involved at Princes Ladies' Club near her home in Kent and when selected for international competition played for England rather than her mother's native Scotland.

No matter how many glamorous society ladies graced the links or talented young women impressed the spectators with their fine play, contributing to the fame and prosperity of the town, the gentlemen maintained their control over the Ladies' Club, the lady golfers, and the composition of the Committee of the Ladies' Club continued to be all male. When the New Club Committee met on the 5th April 1900, it was decided that during the main golfing season – 'the crowded season' – which ran from July to October, the ladies' starting times on the long course should be limited to before 9.00am, between 11.00am and 1.00pm and between 4.00 & 5.00pm In this way the men would have left the starter's box by 11 o'clock and 'the links would then be free for the ladies and it would be more convenient for all concerned'. If the ladies' views had been sought they might have questioned the assumption of convenience: 'ladies' were unlikely to be found golfing before breakfast; they certainly would not appreciate a round which interfered with lunch; and teeing off after 4.00pm – afternoon tea time – was quite unacceptable. Of course, the men's aim was to keep the ladies on their own short course, where they were free to play at any time that suited them.

Benjamin and Millicent Hall Blyth with their grandchildren, Ian, Millicent and Angela Couper c.1910.

The matter was re-visited two years later, on 14th March 1902, at a joint meeting of the Green Committee of the New Club and the Committee of the

North Berwick Ladies' Golf Club. The ladies were represented by three of their Committee members, Charles Blaikie Esq, David Stevenson Esq and James Cree Esq. The meeting was held at 23 Thistle Street Edinburgh. A letter was read stating that if the morning hour for ladies in summer was extended to 9.30am in place of 9.00am, the ladies would be satisfied with the hours as adjusted. The meeting however didn't see its way to making this modification and the Secretary was instructed to answer to that effect!

The membership continued to increase and by 1906 had reached an agreed maximum of 300. New names appeared, yet many of the stalwarts of the early days continued to play and compete: Millicent Hall Blyth wife of founder Benjamin Hall Blyth was still a member and the family still lived at Kaimend, as close as one could get to the ladies' links. Her daughter Elsie Winifred married solicitor John Charles Couper of 15 Rutland Square in 1899 and settled in the newly fashionable Murrayfield district, to the west of Edinburgh, where large detached houses seemed to ape the grand North Berwick residences –or vice versa. Elsie continued to golf at North Berwick and after the death of her parents inherited Kaimend.

On 13th May 1917, the larger-than-life Benjamin Hall Blyth died at Kaimend, after struggling against an invasive cancer of the tongue. In his sixty seven years, it seemed he had filled every day with some constructive achievement. His obituary in the Scotsman lists his colossal engineering achievements – the construction of Edinburgh's North Bridge connecting the historic Old Town with Princes' Street and the new Town; Edinburgh's iconic Waverley Station and Glasgow Central Station; and bridges which spanned some of Scotland's principal rivers, the Clyde, the Dee and the Tay. His strong physique contributed to his prowess as an all-round sportsman, but perhaps golf was his greatest love. He didn't simply play the game, he made it possible for other people to play. He should be remembered as one of the men who succeeded in the acquisition of the Braid Hills as a recreation area for the citizens of Edinburgh and the laying out of a golf course there. After initial reservations, Benjamin Hall Blyth helped to establish ladies' golf in North Berwick, and became one of its most ardent supporters. Although he could never contemplate the woman running their own club and insisted on the all-male committee, nevertheless, his was a great gift to the furtherance of women's golf.

His wife Millicent had predeceased him in 1914. She became very ill early in 1914 with a recurrence of breast cancer which was first diagnosed ten years earlier. She was determined to spend the summer in her beloved North Berwick, as she had done all her married life. Although very unwell, she sat out in the garden at Kaimend, which was full of the flowers she loved and she was able to look out over the ladies' links, the creation and enjoyment of which had been so much part of her family.

War was declared in August and the sons of many of Millicent's friends and acquaintances marched off to Belgium and France, with the British Expeditionary Force, to halt the advance of the German army on Paris. Millicent's practical response was to take out her knitting needles and make a variety of 'comforts' for the young soldiers and encourage other ladies to do the same. It was typical of her to focus on other people's problems rather than her own:

> **"She was warm-hearted and generous and no organiser of any movement calculated to relieve genuine suffering who approached her was ever sent empty away."**
>
> (*Haddingtonshire Advertiser*, September 1914)

She succumbed to the cancer on 12th September, at the age of sixty two. On the day of her funeral, the Edinburgh trams stopped running for 15 minutes as a mark of respect. (Benjamin Hall Blyth was chairman of the Tramway Company.) The golfing fraternity turned out in force at the two services held in her memory – one at St Baldred's, where she worshipped at North Berwick and the other at St Mary' Episcopal Cathedral, where she worshipped in Edinburgh. She was buried in Edinburgh's Dean Cemetery among the great and the good of that city.

Her legacy to ladies' golf is difficult to define. To what extent did she influence her husband to promote golfing for women by establishing the Ladies' Club? Her strongly held view was that a woman's place was either by her husband's side, supporting his endeavours, or in the home. While she encouraged her only child Elsie to participate in the club matches from a young age, she held back from joining until August 1890, by which time she was confident that it was socially acceptable for a married woman to do so. She must have taken a pride in Elsie's successes on the golf course, winning the coveted club gold medal two years running in 1894 and 1895. However, she was probably just as content to see Elsie suitably married off at the age of twenty two to a successful solicitor, a pillar of society, from a respectable Edinburgh family. Did she live long enough to recognise the exceptional golfing talent in her granddaughter and namesake Millicent Couper and what would she have made of the path that Millicent followed? Her death coincided with the end of an era – she could not have foreseen how society would change and become more liberal post war.

The twentieth century, which had opened with confidence and optimism, especially among the middle and upper classes, had moved almost imperceptibly, in just over a decade, towards an unforeseen and unthinkable catastrophe. Young women certain that they were on the threshold of greater independence and lifestyle choices, suddenly found that the men who had dominated and to a large extent controlled their lives were marching off to a dreadful war, from which many would not return. During the First World War, about half the members of the Ladies' Club lost a close family member – Eliza Cree, Mary Hemingway, Mary Macfie, Mary Blackwood Porter and Isabella Lyon, Emma Asher, Arabella Gardiner-Baird – all lost sons; Hilda and Ethel Grant-Suttie lost a brother, as did the five surviving Orr sisters. Marion, Lillie and Dorothy Houldsworth lost their only brother Gil. Mansfield Hunter who partnered Edith Orr over the long course, in the match highlighted at the start of this chapter, suffered the loss of his younger brother Norman at Ypres in 1915. There were many more: it must have seemed that life would never be quite what it had once promised.

Faith Laidlay, who was travelling in Germany with her brother John when war broke out, expressed in a letter she wrote to *The Scotsman*, how the outbreak of hostilities had taken them by surprise. On the 31st July 1914, the pair had planned to travel from Hamburg to Berlin. There was no indication of trouble, but Faith decided to check with the British Consul in Hamburg, who advised them to stay put. That evening, ugly rioting unsettled them and the following morning, advice from the Consul was to leave immediately and speak to no-one in English. They fought for a place on an overcrowded train and after hours of chaos arrived at the Hook of Holland, ravenously hungry, cold and minus their luggage. Faith confessed to smoking 35 cigarettes on the journey to calm her nerves, although she had never smoked in her life!

CHAPTER SIX

Shots of the 1906 Membership

"The membership is 300 and the club is in a flourishing condition."

By 1906 the North Berwick Ladies' Golf Club was well-established and had its full complement of 300 members, plus 20 extra, such was its popularity. The list of names and addresses of the members confirms the social character of the club; less than a third had North Berwick addresses and those that did were the wives and daughters of the wealthy owners of the massive multi-roomed dwellings to the west of the town, such as the Laidlay's at Invereil, the Tennant's at Hyndford and the Craig's at Carlekemp, many of which were summer residences. The rest came from all points between Aberdeen and Kent, but most often from London and Edinburgh. There were few local townswomen among the membership. The Club was not for the likes of such respectable souls as the postman's wife Elizabeth Campbell, whose husband was Verger at St Baldred's and whose sons sang in the choir on Sundays. Nor was it for her daughters, 24 year old Ann, who worked as an assistant in the Bass Rock cycle shop and 21 year old Margaret, who worked as a general domestic servant, probably in one of the houses owned by the golfing fraternity. They were not to be found on the ladies' links competing against the Honourable Miss Violet Meysey-Thomson of Kirkby Hall, York and Miss Vera Vincent of Grosvenor Square, London.

Mary Queen of Scots at prayer, by Patrick Adam RSA. It was thought at one time that his wife, Alice, a member at North Berwick, was the model for the painting.

The process of qualifying for membership was little different to that of most golf clubs today – every candidate had to be proposed and seconded by an existing member. There was, however, an unwritten rule as to whom would be considered 'suitable' to propose and a 'class ceiling' to break through, before reaching that stage. The cost of membership was prohibitive to most ordinary working families – ten shillings entry fee and ten shillings annual subscription. It followed that the common factor among the membership was that they all either belonged to, or were closely connected to, the 'moneyed classes'.

Many of the 320 ladies listed in the 1906 Club Membership, who in spite of their assured middle-class status in 1906, have disappeared from view, leaving few clues as to who they were, or what they contributed to society. There follows a glimpse into the lives of those, who by virtue of their fathers, their husbands or in a few cases on their own account left more than a faint impression of their lives on and beyond the ladies' links at North Berwick.

The list is roughly alphabetical, but mothers, daughters and sisters appear together regardless of surname. Their biographical details are given according to any facts that are known. There are few contemporary images of the women in public collections.

Alice Adam photographed on the links (3rd left) with her husband Patrick (1st left) in the early 1920s.

Mrs Adam (1866–1951)
Miss Adam (1890–1965)

Alice Adam was married to Patrick Adam (1852–1929), the artist. She was born Theodora Alice D'Olier near Dublin on 9th November 1866, into a wealthy Irish Protestant family. The D'Oliers were originally French Huguenots who came to Ireland in the early 18th century to escape religious persecution. One of Alice's forebears was Jeremiah D'Olier (1745–1817) a goldsmith and founder of the Bank of Ireland and after whom is named one of Dublin's principal streets D'Olier Street. Her father Edmund D'Olier was involved in the wine trade, a business often associated with the Huguenots in Ireland.

Alice met her future husband Patrick in Italy in 1888, while both were doing the 'European tour', still a cultural requirement of the wealthier classes. Patrick was pursuing his interest in landscape painting and produced some stunning images of Venice, where he and Alice spent their honeymoon in 1889. Patrick was a competent portrait painter and Alice soon became the subject of some of his most delicately handled work. She was remembered in North Berwick as a very beautiful and elegant woman and this is how she appears in his paintings of her. It is often thought that she was the model for Patrick's painting of Mary Queen of Scots at Prayer, but that was painted in 1883, some years before he met Alice. It would have been a nice touch, as Queen Mary is so closely associated with women's early forays into golf and it is claimed she played in the grounds of Seton Palace, in East Lothian.

Alice and Patrick Adam moved to North Berwick in about 1902, with their only child, a daughter, Beatrice, who was aged eleven at the time. They

Ardilea by Patrick Adam.
A painting of the interior of the home of Patrick and Alice Adam in Dirleton Avenue.

bought Ardilea, a large detached house in Dirleton Road and mother and daughter joined the Ladies' Club. Both women played well enough to have a club handicap, but Beatrix was a much better player than her mother and was soon playing off eight. In December 1915, Beatrice married Lt. Walter Stuart Wingate Gray of Nunraw, who was on active service with the Royal Horse Artillery. He was twice wounded, but survived and was awarded the Military Cross. After the war, Walter continued his military career, which included a posting to India, where Beatrice joined him. Beatrix died in England in 1965.

Patrick Adam probably spent more time in his studio than on the golf course and became renowned for his paintings of interiors – many of them the houses of the Adam's social circle and golfing friends in North Berwick. Patrick painted two beautiful interiors of Ardilea where he died at in 1929 and Alice, some years later, in 1951.

Miss J Aitchison (1869–1948)
Miss N Aitchison (1879–1940)

The Aitchison sisters Jane and Helen (Neta) were two of five children of James Aitchison (1838–1921), an Edinburgh goldsmith and jeweller, and his wife Jane Begbie (1846–1926). There were four daughters and one son. By 1906, the two older girls were married. James Aitchison had joined the family firm in Bank Street in Edinburgh's Old Town, as a young man, but by the 1880s he had successfully expanded the business and had opened a top-class jewellers at 80 Princes Street, in one of Britain's most exclusive shopping centres. He held a Royal Warrant and advertised himself as Court Jeweller in Scotland. The children were brought up at the family home, 7 Regent Terrace, in Edinburgh. Their neighbours were William and Emily Campbell and their large brood of nine children, at 1 Carlton Terrace. Both families spent summers in North Berwick, the Campbells at Inchgarry and the Aitchison's at Rockend, their holiday house on Marine Parade. In 1898, the eldest Aitchison daughter, Agnes, married Thomas Campbell. Thomas' youngest sister grew up to be the world famous golfer Dorothy Campbell. At the time Dorothy was cutting her golfing teeth on the ladies' links. The Aitchison girls were active members of the Ladies' Club, during their teens and twenties, but Jane and her younger sister Helen continued to golf at North Berwick until the 1930s. Jane is recorded as winning the principal award in the annual stroke competition in September 1911, over the corporation links, to the east of the town, going out in 65 and coming home in 45. Helen came second. In 1915, Jane was a good enough golfer to have a club handicap of 4, while her younger sister played off 8. When Helen married in 1918, she and her husband Arthur Rickards made

Agnes Aitchison (1865–1949), who married Dorothy Campbell's brother Thomas in 1898.

North Berwick their permanent home, at Glenburn, further along Marine Parade. Jane never married and died at North Berwick in 1943.

Mrs Kate Armitage (1865–1932)

Kate Armitage joined the Club when she moved to North Berwick from Yorkshire. Her husband Harry Armitage was by far the keener golfer of the two, but both enjoyed mixed foursomes and he was one of a couple of dozen gentlemen who were honorary members of the Ladies' Club in 1906.

Mrs AGG Asher (1863–1942)

Emma (neé Barclay) Asher was a member of the Ladies' Club in the years before the First World War. Her husband Augustus, an Edinburgh solicitor, whom she married in 1895, was well-known for his sporting prowess. He was one of the early brilliant Scottish internationalists and an excellent cricketer. The Ashers lost their only son Ronald in October 1917, aged 19, when he was killed in action in France. There is little record of them in North Berwick after the war.

The Hon. Lady Gardiner Baird (1855–1916)
Miss Gardiner Baird (1881–1955)

Arabella Rose Evelyn Hozier was the daughter of William Wallace Hozier Ist Baronet Newlands. Her father was fabulously wealthy and influential in political circles. Her brother James was private secretary to the Prime Minister, Lord Salisbury, uncle of A J Balfour. In 1879, Arabella married William James Gardiner Baird, whose father Sir James Gardiner Baird was a close political ally of her father. The wedding took place at her family home Maudslie Castle in Lanarkshire and after a lavish reception, and "amidst a shower of slippers and rice", the couple set off to Paris for their honeymoon. William became 8th Baronet Baird of Saughtonhall in 1896 on the death of his father and inherited a valuable estate to the west of Edinburgh. There was controversy over his father's will, as the life-rents of the estate were left to his mother. Sir James' will stated: "My reason for leaving the said life-rents to (my wife) is not for any want of affection towards my son, but from my wish that my wife may continue to enjoy after my death, the same comforts and luxuries which she has enjoyed during my life." Perhaps Sir James felt that Arabella's wealth would support his son's life-style. Sir William and Lady Gardiner Baird regularly came to North Berwick for golf. For several years they rented Leuchie, seat of Sir Walter Hamilton-Dalrymple, but bought Glendalough in Fidra Terrace in about 1908. The whole family enjoyed golf, but neither Arabella nor her daughter Frances were particularly good golfers. In 1910 Frances married John Edulph Blagrave Swinton. He was in charge of the Lothian Borders Horse and at 49 was too old for active service when war came in 1914. Both Frances' brothers were commissioned officers – James was wounded and awarded the Military Cross for bravery and William was killed in action in 1914. Arabella's health deteriorated and she died at North Berwick on 18th June 1916, in the Bradbury Hotel.

The Hon. Gwendolen Balfour (1886–1961)

Gwendolen Balfour, born and brought up in Edinburgh at 6 Rothesay Terrace, daughter of John Blair Balfour and Marianne Moncrieff (Lord and Lady Kinross). The family's North Berwick home was Glasclune. She played golf from a young age and in 1907 competed in the Scottish Ladies' Open Championship at Troon. She had a rather chequered personal life, to which there is reference in Chapter 5.

Miss Barclay (1855–1937)

Elizabeth Caroline Edith Barclay owned Inchdura, in Hamilton Road a step away from the Ladies' Club House. Her younger sisters had married, but she stayed at Inchdura with her widowed mother Jessie. The house was named after the family home Dura, near Cupar in Fife.

Miss Bell (1858–1932)
Miss J A Bell (1864–1939)

Eleanora and Janet were two of three daughters of Sheriff Benjamin Bell, who lived in Grosvenor Crescent in Edinburgh's West End, most of their lives. Their older sister Margaret married Hugh Blair and lived close by in Randolph Crescent. The Bells and Blairs were archetypal Edinburgh professional families who rented a house in North Berwick (not always the same one) and spent their summers there for decades. Both women were active members of the Ladies' Club from its inception in 1888 and excellent golfers.

Miss Janet Agnes Blair (1884–1951)

Janet never married and lived most of her life at her parents' home, 15 Randolph Crescent, Edinburgh. She was the only daughter and eldest child of Hugh and Margaret Blair and niece of Eleanora and Janet Bell. The family was steeped in golfing at North Berwick. Janet was an accomplished golfer, a scratch player in the club and had an LGU handicap of 7. She competed in the Scottish Ladies' Open Championship, from 1905 to 1911. During the Ladies'

Open at Muirfield in 1914, Mabel Stringer the well-known English golfer and journalist stayed with the Blairs, who had rented Ben Sayers' house in Dirleton Avenue for the event.

Mrs Agnes Berry (1857–1929)
Miss Phyllis Berry (1885–?)
Miss Dorothy Berry (1888–1970)
Miss Agnes Mary Berry (1890–1983)

Agnes Muir, daughter of Sir William Muir, renowned administrator in India and later Principal of Edinburgh University, married George Berry in Edinburgh in 1884. It was she who was rather more interested in golf than her husband and after years of renting holiday accommodation in North Berwick, she possibly persuaded her husband to commission their house, the Knoll in 1898 as a more permanent residence in the town. When her three daughters were old enough, she encouraged them to golf and they became members of the NBLGC. Mary, the youngest, married Ivan Boyd Sprot, 2nd Lt. Cameron Highlanders on 24th March 1914, but he was killed in action in Flanders just seven months later on 23rd October. It must have been a very difficult experience for a young woman. However, in 1919, she met and married Denis Sanders. The wedding was held at St Baldred's, in North Berwick and the couple subsequently moved south of the border. Neither of her sisters married.

Mrs C L Blaikie (1874–1962)

Isabel Steaines the daughter of a prosperous London-based tea merchant visited North Berwick one summer and met Charles Blaikie, an Edinburgh Chartered Accountant and Secretary of the Ladies' Club. Charles was a bachelor of 38 and Isabel was 27. They were married in London, in July 1899, and moved into St Catherine's, a substantial 6 bedroom house on Dirleton Avenue, which Charles had been in the throes of refurbishing for several months. Ten years later, on the evening of 15th October 1909, Charles Blaikie died from a massive heart attack. Within a short time, Isabel, widowed and with two young children, returned to London.

Mrs Hall Blyth (1852–1914)

Millicent Blyth (nee Taylor) was the wife of one of the Ladies' Club founders, Benjamin Hall Blyth and mother of Elsie Couper. Although she chose not to participate in competitions, she was present at almost every club tournament, lending support or presenting prizes.

Mrs E L Ireland Blyth (1863–1929)
Adria Susan Josephine Rose married Edward Lawrence Ireland Blyth in London in 1885. She had married into a large influential Edinburgh engineering family, several of whom made North Berwick their HQ during the summer months. Her husband bought Inchgarry, formerly the property of Dorothy Campbell's grandfather, the huge Victorian House in a prime location on West Bay, on the edge of the golf course. Her parents-in-law, Edward and Kathleen lived there in their later years. When her husband went to the north of Scotland shooting and fishing, she headed down south to visit her English friends.

Mrs WP Brodie
Miss Alison Brodie
Miss Betty Brodie
Chartered accountant William Brodie, who lived at Rosebery Crescent in Edinburgh's West End, started to bring his family down to North Berwick in 1899, after he became a member of the New Club. They generally took accommodation in one of the small hotels/boarding houses in the town, but later bought a house, Ardvulin, in Clifford Road. Brodie's wife Agnes joined the Ladies' Club and by 1906, their two daughters Alison, aged 15, and Betty, aged 12, were also enrolled as members.

Miss Burke (1847–1914)
Georgina Burke was one of the first members of the Ladies' Club and maintained her membership until her death in 1914. She was born at the family home, 40 York Place, Edinburgh on 1st June 1847. Two weeks later, on 16th June, her 43 year old mother, also Georgina, died – one would presume from complications associated with giving birth, though no cause appeared on the death certificate. The sad coincidence for baby Georgina and her two older siblings, was that their father Francis suffered a fatal heart attack within days of Georgina's birth and died on 4th June 1847. The orphaned children were split up – Georgina was brought up by her mother's sister, Elizabeth, wife of engineer David Stevenson and her brother and sister were taken in by her mother's brother, Robert. The Stevenson household was big and boisterous – there were eight children, though two of the boys had died from whooping cough and measles by 1861. Summers were spent at North Berwick, where the children played with their cousins from their father's side, including a young Robert Louis Stevenson. It was during this period that Georgina developed a love of golf, which she shared with the Stevenson family, though she was never an outstanding golfer. In the Club competition held on Thursday 27th

September 1906, and with an allowance of 15, she returned a score of 78, but was well down the field of 36 contestants. (See Stevensons below)

Mrs H F Cadell (1871–1935)

In 1897, Fairley Charlotte Blair married Hew Francis Cadell, son of Thomas Cadell of Cockenzie House in East Lothian. Thomas Cadell was hailed as the 'bravest man in India' after he won the Victoria Cross for his actions in saving a wounded bugler from his regiment, in fierce fighting in Dehli, during the Indian Mutiny in 1857. Hew pursued a much less adventurous career as an Edinburgh solicitor and he and his wife lived in Rothesay Place in Edinburgh, close to Fairley's Blair cousins.

Miss Muriel Campbell (1879–?)
Miss Dorothy Campbell (1883–1945)
Mrs Madeline Swanston neé Campbell (1877–?)

At 3.00 am on the morning of Saturday 24th March 1883, Emily Mary Campbell gave birth to her ninth child a daughter at 1 Carlton Terrace, Edinburgh. The baby was named Gladys Iona Emily and was soon the focus of attention of her two brothers Thomas Buchanan and Edward and six sisters, Constance, Louise, Eveline, Edith, Madeline and Muriel, who ranged in age from 4 to 21. This was the beginning of the life of one of the greatest Scottish golfing talents, a young woman who learnt her skill on the links at North Berwick. Of course, no-one has ever heard of the great lady golfer Gladys Campbell, simply because, by the day of the baby's baptism on 29th May, the name Gladys had been substituted for Dorothy. Although Dorothy continues to attract attention as a great golfer, the other Campbell sisters were also gifted golfers, particularly Muriel and Madeline. Madeline continued her membership of the Ladies' Club, and participated in club matches, as Mrs Swanston, after she married and moved to Newcastle. (There are further references to the Campbell sisters throughout the book.)

Dorothy Campbell playing in the British Ladies Open at St Andrews, in 1908, where she was runner-up.

Miss J A Channing (1874–1948)

Julia Allen Channing was part of the London set who golfed in North Berwick during the season. Her father, Lord Channing of Wellingborough, was a well-respected Liberal politician. In 1906 Julia was living in the family's London home at 40 Eaton Place. Julia never married and died in a home in Eastbourne in May 1948.

Miss Ada Clark (1872–1946)

Ada was the youngest of five siblings who lived together in Learmonth Terrace in Edinburgh. Their father had a printing business. None of them married. After Ada's brother Edward and sister Minnie died in 1926, she and her other two sisters moved to North Berwick, to a large house, Glenfuir, in Hamilton Road.

Miss Cochrane (1876–1959)
Miss Joy Cochrane (1878–1960)
Miss Lucy Cochrane (1880–1965)
Miss Anna Cochrane (1883–1955)

The four Cochrane sisters were all good golfers, especially Lucy and Anna, who both played off scratch. They became Club members in about 1899, when their father, a Galashiels woollen manufacturer, bought a house, Balwearie, in Dirleton Avenue, next door to the renowned pro golfer Ben Sayers, from whom they may have had golf lessons. In 1903, Lucy won the Club scratch gold medal with a score of 63.

Mrs John C Couper (1877–1954)

Elsie Winifred Couper (nee Blyth), the daughter of Benjamin and Millicent Hall Blyth, married John Couper at St Mary's Episcopal Cathedral in Edinburgh in 1899. She was a first-class golfer, winning the Club scratch medal on two occasions, but playing during North Berwick's golden era of the 'golfing ladies' there was always a lot of competition. The fact that she married relatively young and had four children in quick succession would have halted any golfing ambitions she may have held. Motherhood certainly put her out of contention for the Scottish Ladies' Championship, in the early 1900s, however, she competed in the September meeting of the Ladies' Club in 1904, tying for the scratch award with Lucy Cochrane and Ada Gillies Smith. A report in *The Scotsman*, recounted the play off:

> **"In playing off the tie, Mrs Couper (who as Miss Elsie Blyth was frequently prominent in the Ladies' club contests at North Berwick) gave a capital display – her game throughout being of a strong and steady character – and she carried off the first scratch prize with a 30 for the nine holes."**
>
> (*The Scotsman*, 28 September 1904)

In 1912, Elsie had a fifth baby, another daughter, Priscilla. In the 1920s she could comfortably outplay her three older daughters, but that didn't last. All the girls were excellent golfers, particularly Millicent, who won the Scottish Ladies' Championship in 1933. Even though the 1920s saw an increase in female emancipation in politics and education, Elsie's husband John virtually ran the Ladies' Club, as one of five male Trustees, after the death of her father in 1917. Elsie died at the family home Kaimend, in North Berwick, on 4 th January 1954, the same day as her great golfing contemporary and adversary, Elsie Grant Suttie.

Mrs Addie (1843–1931)

Mary Dundas Addie (ms Jardine) was married to John Addie, a member of the family of Lanarkshire colliery owners Robert Addie & Sons. The Addies had four sons, one of whom Robert Jardine later married Eleanor Turnbull (See below, Mrs James Craig) and settled in North Berwick.

Mrs James Craig (1877–1969)

Eleanor Turnbull had golfed on North Berwick Ladies' Course with her two sisters, since she was a teenager. The girls first joined the Club in 1894. Eleanor's father David Turnbull, an Edinburgh solicitor, started golfing seriously in North Berwick around 1890. Whatever his motives, he rented rather grand houses outside North Berwick, during the golfing season, but always within striking distance of the coast and the links. Initially he settled on Gilmerton, the ancient mansion of the Kinlochs, but in 1894 plumped for the Hamilton-Dalrymple's seat, Leuchie, which was rented out during the summer, as the family stayed in the less grand Lodge House in the town! In 1902, Eleanor's holiday association led to greater things; she married James Craig, a member of the wealthy Penicuik paper manufacturing company. James was a bachelor and fifty eight years old: Eleanor was young and twenty six. In 1898, James had commissioned John Kinross, the renowned Arts and Crafts architect, to build an elaborate Tudor-style mansion situated on raised ground looking over the golf course, on the western edge of the town. Did he build Carlekemp with Eleanor in mind or once it was built, did he reckon it would work better with a gracious hostess at its heart? For most of his life, James had lived with his parents (and siblings) and perhaps their influence had stifled any thought of independence. In 1910, James's younger brother, Robert, commissioned Robert Lorimer to build him a house, Bunkerhill, just along the road from Carlekemp. Lorimer admired Carlekemp, but noted its extravagant style and commented: "God help the man who has to pay for it." But Carlekemp pleased Eleanor. She could golf to her heart's content without having to make the tiresome journey from Edinburgh.

Eleanor was widowed in 1917, but in 1923 married Robert Addie, son of Mrs Addie (see above). They lived at Greyholm (later called Teviotdale) a

Lorimer house in Abbotsford Road, close to Carlekemp. Eleanor was appointed Lady Captain in 1933 at the same time as her husband was appointed Captain of the New Club. It was during the period of their Captaincies that the subject of the amalgamation of the Ladies' Club with the New Club was raised. Eleanor died in 1969, aged 92.

Miss A F Craig (1856–1928)

Annie Florence Craig was the younger sister of James and Robert Craig (see above). In 1906, she was fifty years old and had remained at home with her parents and consequently never married. She was brought up at the family home, Craigesk House, near Penicuik. The family golfed at North Berwick for many years. Later Annie moved with her parents when they retired to Drumsheugh Gardens in Edinburgh. In her younger days, she was an accomplished Gaelic singer. After her parents died, she bought a house at 6 Murrayfield Drive, where she lived until her death in May 1928.

Mrs Eliza Mabel Cree (1872–1925)

Miss Irene Cree (1894–1974)

Eliza Mabel Fleming, daughter of an Edinburgh doctor, played golf at North Berwick as a youngster before she met and married James Edward Cree in Edinburgh in 1893. James had spent much of his childhood on his father's cattle ranch, the VV Angus Ranch in New Mexico, in the days before New Mexico was integrated as an American state. Years later James passed on tales of his father's encounters with legendary 'wild west' characters, such as Billy the Kid and 'Apache Indians'. If the stories were embellished, they would not be far from the truth – it took some courage to forge a living there, over a century ago. James and Eliza went out to the ranch after their marriage, and three of their five children were born there. They returned to Scotland and in about 1902 came to live at 'Tusculum', in North Berwick, which had been built by James' parents in 1860, overlooking the links and with a fine view out to

Tusculum in 1860 and after the 1902 extension.

the Bass Rock. James doubled its size and turned it into a great rambling 40-roomed house. Eliza took up her golf again and encouraged her children to play, signing up the girls as members of the Ladies' Club. The Cree's eldest son, James Fleming, was killed in September 1918, towards the end of the Great War, at the age of 23. He had been on patrol duty, with a small group. When two of his men failed to return, he went out to look for them and was shot by a German sniper. Eliza Cree never fully recovered from her loss and suffered indifferent health for the remainder of her life, dying in 1925.

Eliza's daughter Irene continued to live at Tusculum, and was a member of the Ladies' Club until her death in 1974. She and her younger sister Norma were often seen on the golf course in the 1920s and 30s. In the early 1950s, Irene divided the house into six manageable apartments and retained one. The family donated the Cree Medal to encourage young golfers. It was first competed for in 1904 and continues to be played for today.

Miss F L Crombie (1887–1982)

Frances Liddle Crombie was the fourth child and only daughter of the North Berwick' answer to Dr Finlay – Dr John Liddle Crombie. He attended births, sicknesses and deaths of probably three generations of North Berwick families. His wife inherited Park House in Westgate, which had superseded Quality Street as being the smart end of the High Street by the 1880s. Frances belonged to that generation of women for whom the possibilities of marriage were reduced through the casualty of war. She retained her membership for a few years, but never displayed any real talent for the game.

Miss M H Cunningham (1887–1945)

Miss Cunningham gave her address as 83 Eaton Place, London. She was possibly Mary Harriet daughter of Sir Henry Stewart & the Hon. Lady Harriet Cunningham. Several lady members had exclusive addresses in and around what is now SW1.

Miss Blair-Cunyngham (1878–1966)

Eleanor Blair-Cunyngham was the younger daughter of Edinburgh surgeon Robert Blair-Cunyngham. The family lived in Walker Street and later Rothesay Place in the Edinburgh's West End and golfed at North Berwick. Her older sister Mabel, who was married with two young daughters, died in 1903, aged 32, from complications caused by diabetes. In 1907 Eleanor married a doctor, David Halliday Croom.

Miss Dalyell
Miss L Dalyell
Miss M Dalyell (1879–1953)
Mrs Horace Peel

The Dalyell sisters Ruth, Jane, Lillias and Magdalen were regular visitors to North Berwick during the season. They lived in Onslow Gardens in Kensington and their father Ralph, a high-ranking civil servant, was a member of the New Club. In London, they were neighbours and friends of the Houldsworths. In 1899, Jane Violet Dalyell married Horace Peel, who also lived nearby in London, and had golfed in North Berwick since the 1880s.

Mrs Dalziel (1848–1923)
Miss Annie Dalziel (1872–1933)

Annie Dalziel joined the newly founded NBLGC in 1888 at the age of 16. Her mother Mary Lyall joined the club later. Annie's father George Dalziel, a solicitor, was a founding member of the Ladies' Club and as a committee member helped to run the club for many years. Annie was an excellent golfer and a scratch player. In 1909, she was locked in fierce competition in the semi-final of the Ladies' hole-and-handicap tournament, but was defeated 3 up and 2 to play by another prominent lady golfer Rita Gillies Smith. Annie was brought up in the family home at 25 Drumsheugh Gardens, Edinburgh, but passed many summers first at the Dalziels' North Berwick house in West Bay Road and later at Redholm, which George Dalziel bought from the Shaw-Stewarts, another golfing family, in about 1905. Annie never married and had moved to Edzell in Angus at the time of her death in 1933. She was 61.

Mrs Dewhurst (1870-1942)

Maud Heugh Dewhurst (neé Aitken) travelled from Oundle, Northamptonshire, where she lived with her husband, William and children, to play golf during the season in North Berwick. She had played golf at North Berwick from early childhood and in her time had been tipped as a potential Open Champion. (Maud Aitken features in more detail in Chapter 7.)

Miss Lucy Duncan (1865–1944)
Mrs J C Dunlop (1863–?)
Miss M Dunlop

Lucy Duncan was one of the original members of the Ladies' Club in 1888 and continued her membership at least until 1920. In 1891, Lucy's sister Mary married a young Edinburgh doctor James Crawford Dunlop. Mary continued her golfing activities after her marriage and probably encouraged her husband's sister, Mary Dunlop, to join the club.

Mrs T S Esson (1864–?)
Miss Esson

Elizabeth Reid Fleming, like so many other club members had golfed at North Berwick since childhood and joined the NBLGC within months of its opening. In September 1889, she married Thomas Skene Esson, a wealthy solicitor who built Windygates, one of the mansions built on the ridge to the south of the town. Frances was their only child, who after she married, remained a member of the Ladies' Club as Mrs Cook.

Mrs J Ferguson (1852–1912)

Annie Gillespie Ferguson was the wife of James Ferguson, a retired army officer, born in India in 1841. They lived at the Nether Abbey, in Dirleton Avenue and had no children. Mary died at Newark in 1912 and James at North Berwick in July 1917.

Mrs Herbert Haldane

Helen Alston, who lived in Coates Gardens in Edinburgh, married chartered accountant Herbert Haldane in 1902. Until then, he had lived around the corner from Helen in Grosvenor Crescent. After their marriage they moved to a house nearby at 21 Palmerston Place. It is very likely Helen was friendly with several of the other golfing ladies, who lived in the same smart Victorian residential area in Edinburgh's West end.

Mrs G. W. Hartley (1867–1950)

Mary Laurie Hartley was the wife of Gilfred Hartley. They bought a house in Cromwell Road, North Berwick, from the brewer Robert Younger in about 1903 and named it Moresby, after their home in Carlisle. Mary was a keen golfer and a member of the Ladies' Club for many years.

Miss Evelyn Harvey (1880–1953)
Mrs Adeline Buchanan, neé Harvey (1878–1961)

Evelyn and Adeline were the daughters of a wealthy London merchant Richard Harvey, whose business was based on trading with the West Indies. They had a house in Eaton Terrace, one of the most expensive residential areas in London. From 1889, the family travelled to North Berwick during the summer in order to golf, each year taking a rented property. In 1902 they stayed at Westfield, in Links Road, a stone built house with a southern aspect. It had a drawing room on the first floor and 8 bedrooms, in addition to 4 maids' rooms. There was a stable and a garage with accommodation for a chauffeur above and a good-sized garden. Evelyn and Adeline both joined the Club in 1890 as young girls of 10 and 12. By 1892 they were competing in the mixed doubles tournament, Evelyn partnered by her father and Adeline by her brother Gerald. In the 1894 autumn meeting, Evelyn was an easy winner of the first handicap award and in fact missed the scratch award by being beaten on the play off by a single stroke. By happy coincidence her father had been invited to present the prizes! In 1903, Adeline married Henry Buchanan a Dumfriesshire landowner. In 1910, Evelyn married a Norfolk farmer Harry Buxton, and although her sister and brothers continued their association with North Berwick, Evelyn's membership lapsed.

Miss Marion Houldsworth (1884–1976)

Marion Edith Houldsworth was one of three daughters of the Rev. W. and Mrs Houldsworth (see Chapters 3 & 5) and an accomplished golfer. The family were London-based but kept up the tradition of golfing in North Berwick during the season. Neither of Marion's sisters were members in 1906, although they were both golfers. Her older sister Lillie had married in 1905, while her younger sister Dorothy, at 12 years old, wasn't ready to play in the ladies' medals. Marion was probably the best golfer of the three. In June 1907, Marion married Hugh Wyld, son of a family friend. The wedding took place at her father's church, St Andrews, Marylebone. Her father recorded the occasion in his diary: "Bay's (Marion's) wedding at 2.30 – Bishop of London married her – choir sang very well – crowded church and crowded reception after. Bay and Hugh left at 4.30." There was no mention of the beautiful bride! On Saturday 28th September 1907, Marion and Hugh travelled from London and joined the rest of the family, on their annual visit to North Berwick. Early on the Monday (there was no golfing on Sundays), Houldsworth played a round of golf with his new son-in-law, Hugh, on the west links. In the afternoon, Houldsworth, Hugh and Marion drove to Muirfield and while the men had a round of golf, Marion "had tea"!

Mrs J E Laidlay (1868–1948)
Miss Faith Laidlay (1896–?)
Mrs Theophila Laidlay (1862–1935)

Jane Eileen Redmayne married John Ernest Laidlay in 1889. It is possible their romance blossomed on the golf course at North Berwick, where Laidlay was a member. Jane's older sister Annie and her husband Frank Tennant owned Hyndford and both were fanatical golfers. Jane was a frequent visitor. She was a brilliant golfer, but has never had the attention she deserves, as the focus has always been on her golfing champion husband. Their daughter Faith was introduced to golf at an early age – she too was a first-rate golfer but possibly not as talented as her mother. Faith's great friend was Dorothy Houldsworth and in September 1919, the Rev. Houldsworth conducted Faith's marriage to Captain Frank Stobart, 18th Hussars, at St Baldred's Church.

Theophila was the sister-in-law of Jane Laidlay through her marriage to Andrew Laidlay, John Laidlay's brother. (Chapters 3 & 5 give more details on the Laidlay ladies.)

Mrs Isabella Lyon with her boys at Tantallon Lodge c.1900, (l. to r. standing, William, Isabella, John, Walter; sitting Patrick, a friend, Charles).

Mrs Walter Lyon (1860–1933)

Isabella Lyon moved from London back to her native Scotland in 1894 after the death of her husband, architect Walter Lyon. She enjoyed golf and settled in a large detached house, Tantallon Lodge, in York Road, North Berwick. She was the mother of six sons and although she lost one in infancy, one could reasonably expect that most of the others would outlive their mother. An almost unbearable tragedy unfolded, as Isabella lost all her sons one by one. John died at school in Haileybury in 1907, aged 14, from TB. Walter, Patrick and Charles were killed in action in the opening months of the First World War. To compound the tragedy, her one surviving son William died suddenly of heart failure in April 1922, aged 37, weeks after she had attended the official dedication of the North Berwick war memorial to her sons and the other men from the town killed in the War.

Miss Mabel Malet (1859–1932)
Miss Ethel Malet (1861–1938)

The Malet sisters were neighbours of the Dalyell sisters in Kensington, and on that basis, it is likely that they found their way to North Berwick for golf. They had been born in India where their father Octavius Warre Malet was a judge in the Indian Civil Service. The family returned to England in about 1870. Their father was one of eight sons of Sir Charles Warre Malet, an important figure in the East India Company, and Susanna Wales. The family was well-connected. In spite of this, however, Octavius was not a wealthy man and after his death in 1891, the sisters opened up an antiques business to make ends meet. They lived in a house in what was then called Trafalgar Square, but was renamed Chelsea Square in 1937, to avoid confusion with its more famous namesake. Their house would be worth several millions at today's values.

Miss M H Maxwell (1870–1935)
Miss I A Maxwell (1879–1961)
Miss Annie Maxwell (1875–1922)

Mary, Isabella and Annie were three of the sisters of Robert Maxwell, their celebrated brother who was twice Amateur Golf Champion in 1903 and 1909. Golf appeared to be the main focus of their lives. The siblings lived together at East Gribton, a house on West Bay Road, North Berwick, overlooking the 18th fairway. (Annie is featured in Chapter 7)

Mrs G F Melville

Mrs Melville and her husband Sheriff George Fisher Melville lived in Springbank House in Fidra Terrace. Mrs Melville was a friend of Mrs Houldsworth's – it would appear from the Rev. Houldsworth diaries that these ladies enjoyed having tea with each with each other more than a game of golf.

Miss I Menzies (1860–1918)

Isobel Menzies was the unmarried sister of John Menzies the Edinburgh stationer and the youngest child of John Menzies, the firm's founder. At this time, Menzies was the largest newspaper distributor, book wholesaler and stationers in Scotland. Isobel was brought up in Edinburgh. The family golfed regularly at North Berwick and owned Westlands, (later West Links House) on West Bay Road, overlooking the 18th green. They also rented Darnhall House, in Peeblesshire, where Isabella died suddenly in July 1918.

Mrs W J Mure (1860–1944)

Emily May Innes married William Mure in 1878 and they lived at 39 Heriot Row in Edinburgh. William Mure became a member of the North Berwick

Mrs Emily Mure (2nd l.) attending the Old Club Meeting in the 1930s. Also in the photo are Lord and Lady Kinross (centre) and Violet and Murray St. Clair (to left & rt.).

New Club in 1882. Emily golfed but didn't join the Ladies' Club until the couple took the tenancy of St Ann's in York Road, in about 1900. In the early 1920s, they bought the Corner House in Fidra Road, where William died in 1924 and Emily in 1944. Their daughter Sybil (Steele), who had married in 1903 and was living in London, later became a great stalwart of the Ladies' Club. The Mures were friends of the Houldsworths and they often golfed together.

Mrs T M Murray (1867–1943)

Thomasina Maude (neé Shearer) was the wife of Harry Smith Murray, a member of the well-known Galashiels wool trading family. She was brought up in Edinburgh and spent holidays in North Berwick as a young girl and was one of the first members of the Ladies' Club in 1888. She continued her membership after her marriage in 1893, but it had probably lapsed by the time of her husband's death in 1924.

Miss M L Macandrew (1854–1935)
Miss I M Macandrew (1858–?)

Margaret and Isabella had joined the Ladies' Club in August 1888 and took part in the competition for the Club medal. Neither sister made a return. It would appear that this put them off entering Club tournaments. Despite this, they remained members for many years, travelling to North Berwick from their Edinburgh home at 16 York Place, staying sometimes in a house in Westgate, sometimes in the Marine Hotel.

Mrs Mary Juliana Orphoot (1850–1928)
Miss Mary Joan Orphoot (1868–1950)

Mary Juliana and Mary Joan, mother and daughter, were active members of the Ladies' Club for many years. Mary Juliana continued to play until she was about seventy – quite unusual for the time. Mary Joan was a sufficiently expert golfer to have an official Ladies' Golf Union handicap.

Mrs A M Renton (1861–1929)
Miss H S Renton (1864–1956)
Miss M C Renton (1859–1942)

The Misses Renton were granddaughters of a prosperous and respectable Edinburgh medical man Dr Robert Renton and his wife Christina. Their father, also Robert, had carved out a career in the Indian Army, where met his wife Jane. Their daughters, Agnes Madeline, Harriet Stewart and Mary Christina were born in Mysore in India. After Robert died in about 1895, Jane and her daughters would come to Baltrenon, a house in Dirleton Avenue, certainly for the golfing season and for a time it was their permanent home. Jane's two spinster sisters-in-law lived in Invervar, further along Dirleton Avenue. In May, before they arrived, Jane would engage William Auld & Son, to freshen up the house, by lifting out the carpets and beating them. In May 1899, Jane paid 12s 2½d for 14 hours of carpet beating and re-laying!

William Auld's men beating carpets on the green. It was a common practice when houses were being opened up for the season, as part of a spring-cleaning.

Miss Beatrice Birnie Rhind (1889–1975)
Miss Kate Birnie Rhind (1892–?)

There were four Rhind sisters, but in 1906, only Beatrice and Kate were old enough to be members of the Ladies' Club. The two younger sisters were Primrose and Noel. Their father William Birnie Rhind was a talented architectural sculptor. In 1906, he had just completed what has become one of his most famous pieces, the Boer War Memorial in Edinburgh, which depicts a group of Royal Scots soldiers. The family lived in Cambridge Street in Edinburgh's West End, but also had a house in North Berwick, Norham in Marmion Road, designed by their uncle Thomas Rhind. In 1915, both women went as volunteers with the Scottish Women's Hospital to Serbia. Beatrice married Zerub Baillie Anderson, son of clothier, William Kinloch Anderson, in 1916.

Miss Hilda Sant (1870–1943)

Although Hilda Sant lived in London, she visited North Berwick every year and was a Ladies' Club member. She was one of the most talented golfers of the day. (She is profiled in Chapter 7.)

Miss Primrose Rhind photographed in the 1920s at North Berwick.

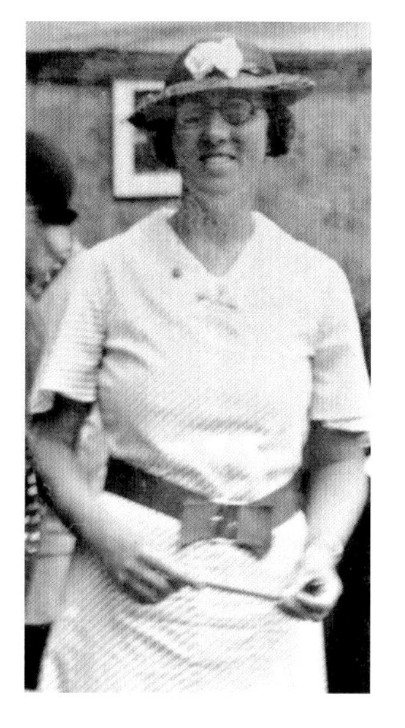

Mrs Schafer
Miss Geraldine Schafer (1887–1979)

Geraldine Schafer was daughter of eminent physiologist Edward Sharpey Schafer. Geraldine had two brothers, Jack and Thomas, and a younger sister Margaret who had died. After their mother Maud Dixey died in 1896, Edward Schafer remarried. His new wife was Ethel Roberts. With his appointment to the Chair of Physiology at Edinburgh University, Schafer moved his family north from London. The family enjoyed golfing and after renting Cromwell Lodge in the summer of 1900, Edward Schafer commissioned Robert Lorimer to build him a house in North Berwick. It was an impressive long rectangular three-gabled arts and crafts house called Marly Knowe, set on the ridge of the hill looking out over the Firth of Forth. Ethel and Geraldine signed up for the Ladies' Club. The war years brought tragedy as both Jack and Thomas were killed in the conflict. Thomas left a widow and young son, Edward. After her father's death in 1935, Geraldine, who remained single, moved south. She died in Winchester in 1979 aged 92, a much-loved aunt and great aunt.

Mrs J H Scott (1869–1946)

Mina Maria Scott was the wife of James Henry Scott (1845-1912), of the shipping family Scott's of Greenock. They lived at 5 Princes Gate, London and travelled to North Berwick in late August for golf. Mina Maria was also sister-in-law of Mary Dunlop (née Duncan), a long-time member of the Ladies' Club.

Mrs Gillies Smith (1841–1903)
Miss Margaret Gillies Smith (1871–1951)
Miss Coventry B Gillies Smith (1874–1953)
Miss Ada Gillies Smith (1875–1961)

The Gillies Smiths are featured in Chapters 1, 2, 3 & 7.

Mrs Martin Smith
Miss Winifred Martin Smith (1891–1932)

Cecilia Martin Smith and her daughter Winifred were regular visitors to North Berwick during the season. They were part of a prominent set of wealthy stockbrokers and bankers from London and the south, who appeared in force on the links during September. Winifred was a brilliant golfer and showed exceptional promise as a teenager. She enjoyed many golfing successes in the Ladies' Club matches. By 1914, she was considered to be 'one of the best 8 or 10 lady golfers in the country' and was selected to play for the English home international team. (Winifred is referred to in greater detail in Chapter 10.)

Studio portrait of Winifred Martin Smith, at the time of her marriage to Roland Olaf Hambro in 1917.

Miss Janet A Spens (1873–1951)
Miss Ariana Spens (1877–1954)

The two sisters had been golfing with their family at North Berwick since they were very young and Janet had been one of the very first members of the Club. By 1906, they were no longer such keen competitors as they had been in the early days of the club, but like the majority of members played for enjoyment. In 1917, Janet married a widowed clergyman. (See Spens Chapter 2.)

Miss Mary Isabel Shaw-Stewart (1865–?)
Miss Agnes Ethel Shaw-Stewart (1867–1959)
Miss Olive Margaret Shaw-Stewart (1876–?)

Mary Isabel, Agnes Ethel and Olive Margaret Shaw-Stewart were the three daughters of Robert Farquhar Shaw-Stewart and his wife Isabella Jane. Their

father was the second son of Sir Michael Shaw-Stewart Bt. of Greenhall and Blackhall and apart from holding a commission in Scots Fusilier Guards, Robert lived comfortably from private means. In 1892, he commissioned architects Dick Peddie, Mackay to build a splendid house, Redholm, at the east end of North Berwick, over-looking the Coo's Green and alongside Glasclune and St Baldred's Tower. There were seven Shaw-Stewart children, but four, all boys, had died relatively young. The result of such loss, was that Isabel became over-protective and possessive of her daughters, all three of whom were still living at home in their forties. Their father died in 1911 and their mother in September 1916. Within weeks of her mother's death Olive, at the age of 40, announced her engagement to the Rev. Thomas John Hardy, Warden of St Mary House and was married in April 1917. One might speculate Olive had kept her romance secret for fear of parental disapproval.

Hilda seated and Muriel standing in the garden at Balgone c.1906.

Miss Hilda Grant-Suttie (1886–1978)
Miss Muriel Grant-Suttie (1888–1913)

Hilda and Muriel Grant-Suttie were the two older daughters of Robert and the Hon. Edith Grant-Suttie. There were five siblings, three girls and two boys and they were cousins of the renowned golfer Elsie Grant-Suttie. Their father Robert was a well-known golfer and member of both the old North Berwick Club and the New Club. Tragedy struck the family when Muriel became ill with an appendicitis and died on 19th December 1913, after complications. Their younger brother Archie was killed in action on the Western Front in 1917.

Mrs Teacher
Miss Frances Teacher (1885–1955)
Miss Helen Teacher (1884–?)

Bertha Teacher was step-mother to Frances and Helen Teacher. Although she was a member in 1906, Bertha would not have been playing much golf as she gave birth to a baby girl, Olivia in November. Meanwhile Frances and Helen were attracting attention in the golfing world, both competing in the Scottish Ladies' Open for the first time in 1907. Frances caused a stir by beating Dorothy Campbell in the final and winning the championship, while Helen reached the semi-final. Frances and Helen's younger sister Muriel probably joined the Club the following year and their half-sister Olivia was an active member of the club in the 1920s.

Frances Teacher out for a stroll, c.1915.

Mrs Frank J Tennant (née Redmayne) (1864–1956)
Miss Dinah (Geraldine) Tennant (1890–1974)
Miss Frances Tennant (1888–1925)

Annie Tennant was the wife of Frank Tennant, son of Sir Charles Tennant, a Scot, whose fortune came from his father's enterprise in developing a chemical process to aid the bleaching of linen. The Tennant family were among the wealthiest in Britain and by 1906 were at the centre of the North Berwick golfing society. Frank and Annie owned Hyndford House in North Berwick, where they came to golf in the summer months. Annie died at Hyndford in July 1956. Two of their three daughters were members of the Ladies' Club in 1906. In 1912, Frances married Guy Charteris, a younger son of the Earl of Wemyss, but died from tuberculosis in 1925. Dinah was regarded as a society beauty. In 1915 she married Ian Colquhoun of Luss. Their younger sister Kathleen, would have been twelve in 1906. She became the Duchess of Rutland as the result of her marriage in 1916.

The Hon Violet Meysey-Thomson (1886–1960)
The Hon Helen Meysey-Thomson (18?–1958)

The Meysey-Thomson sisters were daughters of an aristocratic and privileged family who owned Kirkby Hall in Yorkshire. Their father Sir Henry Meysey-Thomson was created Baron Knaresborough in 1905, allowing them the title 'honourable'. He had had a long political career and at one time had been the private secretary of the then Prime Minister, William Gladstone. The family were regular visitors to North Berwick from the late 1890s, when it became absolutely the height of fashion to golf there in September. Lady Knaresborough was a good golfer and often played a round with her daughters. In 1912, she presented the prizes at the Autumn Meeting, in which she and her daughters had taken part. The Meysey-Thomson women also enjoyed salmon fishing – 'the thrill of the pull' – on the Tweed, which took place in October and November. In 1910, Violet married an army officer Charles Vandaleur, who was killed in the first weeks of the war in the first battle of Ypres. Her only brother Claude was killed in action in June 1915.

Miss Georgina A R Veitch (1867–1942)
Miss Florence Haswell Veitch (1880–1960)
Miss Frances C S Veitch (1874–?)
Mrs P H Coats (1871–1951)

Georgina and Florence were two of five Veitch sisters who lived at Friarshall, in Paisley, where their father was a Banker. The older sisters had joined the

NBLGC in 1894, when their parents started to bring them to North Berwick during the summer. Florence, the youngest, enjoyed the greatest golfing success; she competed in the Scottish Ladies' Championships, though never finished in the first four. She was, however, in the North Berwick team when it won the Eglinton Quaich for the first time at St Andrews in 1911.

In 1896, the eldest Veitch sister, Catherine Evelyn had married Peter Coats, a member of the famous thread firm, J & P Coats (Ltd), of which he became a director. They owned Kilrie, a large Victorian house on Dirleton Avenue. Legend had it that they brought their own cow to North Berwick, so they could have fresh milk! In fact, they owned a small dairy and henhouse at Smiley Knowe, on the south side of Dirleton Avenue. So fresh eggs as well as milk before golf! Various members of the Coats' family golfed at North Berwick over several decades.

Miss Margaret Coats, daughter of Sir Stuart Auchincloss Coats golfing at North Berwick, in 1928, with Edward Tyrwhitt, 2nd Viscount Knollys, shortly before their marriage.

Lady Howard Vincent (1861–1952)
Miss Vera Vincent (1884–1967)

Ethel Gwendoline Moffat, heiress to her parents' fortune built on the brokerage of a valuable 19th century commodity tea, married Charles Howard Vincent, soldier, journalist, barrister, police administrator, politician, in 1882. After an active career in several fields, Howard Vincent, knighted in 1896, became Conservative MP for central Sheffield. Although never part of the administration, he was a popular figure in political circles during the premiership of Lord Salisbury and then A.J. Balfour. Sir Howard was a keen enough golfer – his younger brother Edgar had a golf course laid out at his home Esher Park in Surrey, where he entertained royalty and politicians – but he was so often preoccupied with other interests that his wife and daughter golfed at North Berwick without him. The Vincent's owned a fabulous house, 1 Grosvenor Square, in London, but generally rented Cromwell Lodge in York Road, which was comparatively small, with only 2 public rooms and 4 bedrooms. In August 1904, Vera took part in the annual meeting for the club medal, while her mother looked on. Hilda Sant won the medal and Vera finished with a reasonable round of 80. Her allowance of 18 gave her a final score of 62. In January 1908, Vera married Bernard Hutton Croft, Grenadier Guards, just weeks before her father died suddenly of heart failure at the family property at Menton, in the south of France.

Miss C M Macfie (1897–1980)

Catherine Macfie was brought up in the large mansion, Gogarburn House, to the west of Edinburgh. She and her brother Claud were the children of their father's second marriage to Mary Young in 1891. Catherine's father had a share in a Glasgow sugar refining business and when he died in 1903 at the age of 81, he left his young wife and family well-provided. Golfing at North Berwick in the summer became a regular activity for Mary and her children, at first staying in the hotels such as the Warrender and later renting Warrix (now the White House) in Dirleton Road. Catherine showed promise as a young golfer and would only have been aged 9 in 1906. There were a clutch of girls of a similar age, Kathleen Stevenson, daughter of engineer David A. Stevenson, Marjorie and Lucy Kinloch of Gilmerton and Muriel Teacher, who were equally good golfers. The coveted prize for these youngsters was the Cree medal, played for each year, by the under 14s. In 1909, it was won by Catherine.

> **"Miss C. M. Macfie proved winner of the Cree Trophy with a card of 76 and she also gained the accompanying prize of a silver box. She had also the lowest net score, but was ineligible to win the handicap award, as being the merit winner."**
>
> (*The Scotsman*, 28 May 1909)

The carefree summers ended with the outbreak of war and Catherine's brother Claud was killed in action in France in June 1915. At the end of the war, Catherine married Charles Reid Peploe, who had seen active service in the Royal Navy at the Battle of Jutland and had been decorated with the DSO. Charles was later appointed Commander of the Royal Navy base at Portsmouth and Catherine moved south. There was, however, another Mrs Peploe in the North Berwick Ladies' Club – that was Dorothy Stevenson, (sister of Catherine's friend and golfing companion, Kathleen) who had married Charles' brother James Peploe in 1915.

In 1934 Catherine Macfie, by then Mrs Charles Peploe, was still producing splendid golf. She was runner-up in the Scottish Women's Golf Foursomes, played at North Berwick. She is photographed here (far left) outside Tantallon Clubhouse with the partner, Mrs Clarke (far right) and winners Eileen Tweedie (North Berwick) and Mrs Alex Stuart (centre).

Miss Lucy Hope (1856–1946)

Lucy Hope, a member of the Ladies' Club since the 1890s, was a great champion of the caddies. She was the youngest daughter of George Hope of Luffness M.P. and Caroline Montagu Scott and had spent part of her childhood in England. Her father died when she was seven. She was presented to Queen Victoria at the age of seventeen and attended society balls in London, dancing till three in the morning. She was bridesmaid at most of her brothers' weddings, but never made it down the aisle for her own wedding, possibly as she had taken on the role of companion to her widowed mother. After her mother's death in 1891, she acquired Angus House on West Bay in North Berwick, played golf and took up the cause of the young caddies from the town.

Most of the lads were from local families and took up caddying when they left school at the age of twelve. Miss Hope was concerned at the lack of educational and recreational opportunities for them, beyond what had been on offer at the Burgh school. Some were hardly able to read and write. Her solution was to set up a reading and games room for them. She raised over £1000 for a purpose-built hall in Forth Street, which was opened to great acclaim in October 1899: "Mr Robert Grant-Suttie [who formally opened the Hope Rooms] spoke in high praise of Miss Hope's efforts to improve the condition of caddies and other young men in the neighbourhood... all young men up to 21 years of age are eligible, and for a small payment can have the advantages of refreshments, reading and amusement provided on the premises." She organised activities in the hall: billiards, recitals and concerts and, in 1907, 'a cinematograph representation', which was given by Lizars of Edinburgh – an early style of film club! The initiative was successful; it kept young lads off the streets and out of mischief.

Lucy was a well-respected figure in the town. She was renowned for her hospitality; for her political activities as a member of the East Lothian Women's Unionist Association; as Convener of the District Nursing Association; as a member of the old School Board; but of all her work for the welfare of the community, her devotion to the young caddies stands out. In 1937, the Freedom of the Burgh was conferred on her, 'in recognition of her services to the cause of education'. The Hope Rooms, now owned by the council, are regularly used for fund-raising events for local charities.

Mrs David Alan Stevenson (1862–1945)
Miss Dorothy Stevenson (1892–1974)
Miss Kathleen Stevenson (1899–1978)

In January 1892, Dorothy Annie Roberts, daughter of East India merchant William Roberts, married David Alan Stevenson, grandson of the famous lighthouse engineer Robert Stevenson and cousin to Robert Louis Stevenson. David was by then a partner in the Stevenson engineering firm and business was booming. In November that year, their first child Dorothy Elizabeth was born at 45 Melville Street Edinburgh, the family home David inherited from his father. A second daughter, Kathleen was born a few years later – but no sons. By 1906, David Stevenson had bought a property in North Berwick, Westfield in Links Road, for the family's use in the summer and at weekends. Mother and daughters were great golfers and the girls regularly carried off the prizes in the North Berwick Ladies' tournaments. Kathleen won the Cree Medal in 1912. Later, Dorothy was invited to join the Scottish Ladies' International team, but turned down the invitation as by then she was married and pregnant. But Dorothy had another talent: from an early age she wrote stories and went on to publish over forty novels. Perhaps there was too much focus on her cousin, Robert Louis Stevenson's literary success, for anyone to take notice of Dorothy's progression as a writer and she never received the critical acclaim she deserved. She was clever and ambitious and, aged 17, she won a place at Oxford University. However, she had made the application without her parents' knowledge and they were adamant that university was no place for a young woman and refused to allow her to go.

In 1906, the majority of lady members were still defined through the dominant male family member, although some did achieve success in their own right in the developing world of golf. The experience of Dorothy Stevenson, however, highlights that by the early 20th century, although attitudes towards women may have progressed, particularly in terms of participation in sport and other outdoor activities, they had hardly moved forward in respect of a woman's right to higher education and pursuit of a career, if she so wished.

CHAPTER SEVEN

Swinging to Perfection: North Berwick's 'crack' lady golfers (c.1880-1920)

"As one of the younger members of the club, Miss Dorothy Campbell gives exceptional promise for her future success in golfing contests."
(Extract report on the Annual Meetingof he NBLGC, June 1899)

From the start, North Berwick seemed to attract and encourage excellent golfers. Although there were able players in the rest of the country, it is doubtful they were anything like the standard of the best of the North Berwick players, who could comfortably see off challenges from most of their rivals. In the first two decades of the twentieth century, several of Britain's top lady golfers were members of the North Berwick Ladies' Club – Dorothy Campbell, Elsie Grant-Suttie and Frances Teacher were all champion golfers. All three had sisters, most of whom also played exceptional golf, but not quite as exceptional as their more successful siblings. Madge Neill Fraser must be counted among the North Berwick lady cracks, though her tragic death during the First World War took away the chance of further renown on the golf course. These women were continuing a tradition of powerful play that had started in the 1880s, at North Berwick, with the Anderson sisters, the Gillies Smith sisters and the Orr sisters; of these Margaret Gillies Smith, Blanche Anderson and Edith Orr were among the most gifted golfers of their day.

Dorothy Campbell (1883-1945), Lady Champion extraordinary.

"The North Berwick (Ladies') Club has produced some of the best players. In its competitions have appeared the Misses Orr, Campbell, and Gillies Smith, one of the latter securing the handsome scratch medal no fewer than five consecutive times. Last season the sisters, Miss Madeline and Miss Dorothy Campbell were the heroines, and this year, at the opening contest, Miss Madeline carried off first prize. Miss Blanch Anderson, Miss Maxwell and Miss Aitken are also well known North Berwick players."

This homage to the North Berwick lady golfers was written by Amy Bennet Pascoe in 1899 – she had won the fourth Ladies' Golf Championship at Royal Liverpool in 1896, and her position as one of the better-known recorders of the contemporary ladies' golfing scene gives her testimony authority. In the early days of club golf, it seems the North Berwick ladies could knock spots off many of their rivals and the club had more than its fair share of members whose superior skills on the course were acknowledged in the golfing world. The Club has continued to produce star players right up to the present time – from Millicent Couper in the 1930s, Jean Donald in the 1940s, Marjory Fowler in the 1970s and 80s and in the twenty first century, Catriona Matthew, MBE.

It is worth reflecting that the early outstanding golfers were able to excel because they belonged to the upper strata of society. Such opportunities for daughters of 'ordinary folk' hardly existed. Membership of a ladies' golf club would be out of the question, both on the grounds of cost and lack of the correct social credentials. If a woman wished to take part in a match away from home, or enter a county or national championship, she had to fund it herself. It explains why talented women golfers such as Amy Pascoe, essentially from an ordinary middle class background, took up writing about golfing issues in periodicals of the day; it earned her about £100 a year. In reality golf was only possible for ladies with private means or an indulgent father or husband.

The first Ladies' British Championship, organised by the newly established Ladies' Golf Union, took place in June 1893 at Lytham St Anne's in Lancashire and was won by Lady Margaret Scott. There was disappointment among the organisers that there was not a single entry from Scotland. The contest inspired passionately argued correspondence in the *Golf* magazine: one side pointing out how misleading the title was, as there were several lady golfers in Scotland who were stronger players than the new champion, and the other pointing out that ladies' golf in England was overtaking that in Scotland, and it was time the Scots woke up to this fact or they may have to 'woo instead of being wooed'. In spite of the criticism of their non-participation, the Scottish women golfers were slow to respond to the challenge. They didn't compete in any number until the 1897 Championship, which was held at Gullane, a few miles along the coast from North Berwick and was won by the North Berwick player Edith Orr.

The general lack of interest shown by Scottish ladies in participating in the Ladies' Championships became an ongoing bone of contention with the Ladies' Golf Union, the regulating body, set up in 1893. The feeling was that the Scottish ladies only appeared when the meeting was at their own door, although excuses were made on their behalf that it was as much to do with the expense. The cost of entry was high for an individual if her club was not affiliated to the LGU. In addition there was the travel and accommodation to pay for. Harold Hilton, one of the great Amateur golfers of the day, entered the debate, perhaps rather unhelpfully, by suggesting that the Scottish ladies were "a class above" the English players.

The absence of Scottish ladies from these tournaments possibly enhanced the awesome reputation of clubs like the NBLGC and it became a talking point in golfing circles, particularly south of the border. Some of the English ladies developed a dread of facing the North Berwick players in competitions, particularly those held on the Scottish players' home territory. In August 1900, *Golf Illustrated* reported that Miss Rhona Adair, the1900 British Ladies' Champion found the North Berwick ladies a somewhat 'difficult handful'. In her first game there, over two rounds of the ladies' course, she was defeated by Madeline Campbell, one of Dorothy Campbell's older sisters: in her second game, she met the same fate pitted against Edith Orr, the 1897 champion.

Rhona Adair, championship golfer, was in awe of the North Berwick 'cracks'.

The discomfort, however, didn't prevent Rhona Adair, who had just won the Irish Ladies' Open for the second consecutive year, from returning to North Berwick the following year. On Tuesday 6th August 1901, a match between Rhona Adair and Dorothy Campbell proved very exciting. It was played over the long course. At the 15th, the Redan, Dorothy Campbell was dormy, but won the game by one hole. Shortly after this, Rhona Adair changed her technique, playing with a shorter swing. Was this in response to her consecutive defeats at the hands of the formidable North Berwick lady cracks? We shall never know. She did, however, go on to win the Irish Open for the third time in 1902 and again in 1903 and was British Open Champion for a second time in 1903 and in spite of her earlier anxiety in playing at North Berwick, she continued to enjoy the challenge of these links. In September 1903, in a match at North Berwick against Miss Glover, the Scottish Champion, Rhona Adair seemed to overcome the 'northern jinx' and tied up the game at the seventeenth green, winning by two holes. Her final match at North Berwick that September was with the town's great professional, Ben Sayers, who, after conceding a half at the sixteenth, won the match by three up and one to play. Perhaps Miss Adair was more affected by the windy conditions that day than Sayers, or perhaps Sayers was always going to be the better player, but Rhona Adair won respect for her ability to 'stand up to the ball, in a manner quite worthy of any of the sterner sex'.

The Gillies Smith girls

> **"Letters from North Berwick are full of the annual meeting there of the Ladies' Golf Club and of the competitions for the gold medal and the gold bracelet given by the Marchioness of Tweeddale, both these prizes falling to the prowess of the Misses Gillies Smith."**
>
> (*Pall Mall Gazette*, Wednesday 3 September 1890)

By 1894, the golfing press was hailing the Gillies Smith sisters' record of golfing success as unique within one family. Every year since it was first introduced, one or other of the sisters had won the Ladies' Club Gold Medal - with Margaret winning it on five consecutive occasions. When Margaret didn't win it, her youngest sister Ada did. Coventry was a scratch player, but, frustratingly for her, was almost always left in the wake of her siblings. In the annual July meeting at North Berwick, in 1903, Ada triumphed over a field of nearly forty players, by winning the scratch award with a score of 62. Coventry was four strokes behind with a score of 66! The *Pall Mall Gazette* (July 1896) recorded Margaret Gillies Smith's triumph in the club's midsummer scratch competition, when she came in with 60, commenting that even the Men's Open Champion, Harry Vardon, would find her score difficult to beat!

These were great accolades and recognition of the Gillies Smith sisters' golfing talents. In many respects they were ahead of their time. They were all excellent sportswomen, and Margaret at least could have found success on a wider stage had the opportunities been there, but in the early days of club golf, there were few inter-club matches and fewer international championship opportunities.

By the turn of the twentieth century, even though new talent was emerging among the lady members, the Gillies Smith sisters were still putting up a good fight against the younger players. In June 1901, when Ada and Coventry entered the club contest, the smart money was still on them to carry off the prizes. After the first round of nine holes, Ada Gillies Smith was leading the field with a score of 30. She was renowned for her short game, but on this

Ladies' Links c.1890, with the Marine Hotel in the background.

occasion she was also on good form with her drives. She kept up the pace in the second round and finished with a total of 61, well ahead of her main rival Madeline Campbell, another of Dorothy's sisters, whose actual score was 64. The Gillies Smith sisters were stalwarts of the North Berwick Ladies' Club; they were its first members in 1888 and remained its loyal supporters for the rest of their lives. Their contribution in helping to establish the high reputation of the NBLGC should not be forgotten.

Blanche Anderson at the wheel – c.1904, when few women were sufficiently liberated to drive.

Blanche Anderson (1871–1933)

All the Anderson sisters, daughters of the Rector of St Baldred's Church, Fortesque Anderson, could be described as golf 'cracks', but Blanche was the best of a brilliant bunch. By the time she was nineteen, Blanche was playing off scratch and working her way steadily up the results board. At the Club's July gathering in 1892 she won her first scratch award, with a return of 61 for two rounds of the ladies' course. Blanche and her brother Stuart won the popular annual mixed doubles tournament in August 1894, defeating Ada Gillies Smith who was partnered with George Gordon Robertson – husband of Blanche's sister Helen Maud. That year, Blanche set the record for North Berwick long links in a foursome, completing two consecutive rounds in 76. In spite of her singular golfing skills, Blanche failed to carry off a major ladies' golfing award beyond club level. At the 1896 July meeting, Blanche won the scratch prize at North Berwick with an excellent score of 63 for the double round. In September 1897, the magazine *Golf: A Weekly Record* commented:

> **"Miss Blanche Anderson bids fair to emulate the feats of the Misses Gillies Smith in connection with the meetings of the Ladies' Club at North Berwick. At the (July) competition Miss Anderson carried off the scratch gold medal and at the September meeting on Friday last, she was again to the front securing premier merit honours with the splendid score of 58 for the double round."**

Her score of 58 was unusually good, yet she bettered it when she established a new record for a single round of the nine-hole ladies' course with the amazing score of 26, knocking a stroke off the previous record of 27, which was held by Jane Laidlay, another great North Berwick lady golfer. With 29 already under her belt for the first round, Blanche achieved a new record of 55 for the double round and success in the gold medal competition.

Blanche was showing splendid form in late 1897, but unfortunately, at the time of the Ladies' Championship at Gullane in May, she was suffering from a virus which sapped her energy. In spite of her illness she got into the final eight, where she was perhaps unlucky to come up against Edith Orr, who defeated her and went on to win the championship.

It was Blanche's fate that she was contemporary with the Orr sisters. When the annual meeting of the NBLGC was held on Friday 27th August 1897, it was noted with regret that Edith Orr and her sisters were absent. Blanche, who could sometimes be more than a match for most of the Orr sisters, was regarded as second fiddle, but with all eyes fixed on her, she won the medal with a score of 63 for the double round.

Blanche's oldest sister, Maud, had moved to Wimbledon with her husband and young family and in 1898, Blanche moved south too. Both women became members at Prince's Ladies' Club, Mitcham where Blanche was soon establishing yet another course record, beating the 1896 British Champion, Amy Bennet Pascoe's 81 by one stroke. Her achievement was heralded by 'Lady Di', in The World of Sportswomen column in *Hearth and Home* in March 1899:

> **"Miss Blanche Anderson, who holds a high position among golfers, has the distinction of being a plus 2 player at Prince's, and holds the record of 80 for that club, having taken it by 1 from Miss Pascoe in January this year."**

This wasn't enough for the ultra-competitive Blanche and she could be observed practising on the links, day in and day out, in an attempt to bring her own record down to the seventies. At one point her handicap at Prince's was plus 7! She was admired as a self -taught golfer; she had only ever received three or four lessons as a young woman, from Davie Grant, the North Berwick professional. In her North Berwick days, she was renowned for playing the long links, which she adored, at a time when most of her contemporaries contented themselves with the less challenging elements of the ladies' course. Her skills as a golfer were well enough known for golf expert Molly Boys to profile her as one of the most brilliant lady golfers of the day, in *Our Lady of the Green* an early book on ladies' golf, published in 1899.

> **"She does not use a full swing when driving, but gets away a fairly long ball; the strongest point of her game is however, her iron play, which is considered magnificent, more especially her approach shots which she pitches with deadly accuracy. If hardly a player of such uniform steadiness as the Misses Orr, she is a golfer of great dash and brilliancy and has a thorough command over her clubs."**

Theodora Orr (1869–1914) and Edith Orr (1871–1955)

Two other young North Berwick ladies were identified in *Our Lady of the Green* among Britain's best scratch players – Theodora and Edith Orr. In the British Ladies' Amateur Championships held at Gullane in May 1897, Edith Constance Orr became the first ever Scottish winner. Her elder sister Theodora was the silver medallist. It was a great coup for Scottish ladies' golf and for the North Berwick Ladies' Club in particular, where the sisters were members.

Theodora and Edith Orr photographed with their caddies – the North Berwick professionals Davie Grant and Ben Sayers – after their triumph at the Ladies' Open Championship played at Gullane, in 1897.

Amy Bennet Pascoe, the Ladies' Open Champion at Royal Liverpool in 1896, wrote enthusiastically about them. "First among the best exponents of the women's game are the Misses Orr. They grew up with clubs in their hands. David Grant of North Berwick links trained hand and eye. They possess an unobtrusive, easy style, natural, accurate, scientific play and a high reputation, which is but the shadow of their brilliant game. The best players in Scotland have made North Berwick famous."

The prodigious golfing talents of the Orr sisters were fully recognised at the 1897 Open, but there was a note of frustration among golfing journalists who recorded the sisters' triumph, that they couldn't build on any prior assessment of their skills or make any meaningful predictions about their future, as they hardly ever took part in golfing competitions. They did in fact occasionally compete at North Berwick, for example in the Diamond Jubilee Medal at NBLGC in July 1897, which Edith won. Edith didn't always do better than Theodora; at a golfing competition at Nairn in 1894, consisting of 36 holes (four rounds of the ladies' course) Theodora won the first prize with a score of 114, while Aimie Orr came second with 122 and Edith third with 123.

There was really very little to choose between Theodora and Edith in terms of their golfing skills. Theodora's almost full swing carried great power. Her approach game was accurate and according to golf writer Miriam Boys, she played "in a thoroughly accomplished and business-like manner". Edith was said to have a "full round swing which gives the impression of ease, although the downward part of the swing exhibits something of an effort, which has aptly been described as a push forward". She was always able to maintain a perfectly graceful style and at the same time "drive an exceptionally long ball" and her approach play was "extraordinarily accurate". It was said that once she was on the putting green, she appeared to be able to "hole out in one from almost all parts of it".

In 1902, Frances Griscom, an American champion golfer included Edith Orr in a selection of the ten top women golfers. According to Griscom, Edith had the best half-swing she had ever seen. The pity of it was that Edith Orr never allowed herself the opportunity to win another championship.

Maud Aitken.

Maud Aitken (1870–1942)

Maud Aitken deserves to be included as one of the North Berwick 'lady cracks', although like several other promising golfing contemporaries she never lifted a championship trophy. She first came to the attention of the golfing world at the Ladies' Open Championship at Hoylake in 1896, where, in the third round, she played one of the best matches in the tournament against Issette Pearson, who was one of the leading English golfers at the time. She was winning the match until she was bunkered at the last hole. She was one of only a handful of Scots who played in the Open before 1897. At the Open at Gullane, she was beaten in the fourth round by Musselburgh player, Maud Titterton.

Mary (Maud) Heugh Aitken was one of six children of John Aitken of Gartcows, near Falkirk, the owner of James Aitken& Co. Brewers and his wife Elizabeth. Her father was a keen golfer and built a house at Gullane, to pursue his sport and where the family could come in the summer months. In 1897, John Aitken was Captain at Gullane. Maud and her siblings played a lot of golf, but were entirely self-taught. Their father apparently did not see the need to spend money on lessons for his daughters. In spite of this Maud had a wonderful talent for the game. She was a member of several ladies' golf clubs other than North Berwick – Gullane, Falkirk Tryst, St Rules (St Andrews), Murrayfield and the Edinburgh Ladies' Golf Club. Of all the courses she played, she used to say her favourite was the long course at North Berwick.

Maud was an enthusiastic and successful participant in the NBLC matches. In 1896 she won the North Berwick Gold Medal and the Edinburgh Ladies Silver Bowl. Both Maud and her sister Agnes played in the Ladies' Open at Gullane, in May 1897, where Agnes was defeated in the 3rd round and Maud in round four. At the time Maud was undoubtedly one of the clutch of outstanding players at North Berwick. She was one of the fancied players for the Open, but was recovering from typhoid fever which she had contracted while on holiday with her family in the South of France, earlier in the year. By the time of the September meeting at North Berwick, Maud was back on form, and, competing against a strong field, won the medal.

Amy Pascoe, champion golfer and sports writer, identified her as a promising golfer, who she was sure would one day win the championship.

> **"Miss Maud Aitken who began her golfing career with a half-swing, recently exchanged for a full one, has done a good deal in a short time. A constant player at North Berwick and other centres which afford the best practices and example, with a natural turn for golf, she has every facility for reaching perfection. Only it requires time to make a champion."**

In April 1901, Maud Aitken married William Dewhurst, the son of a prosperous cotton thread manufacturer from Skipton in Yorkshire. William didn't follow his father into the textile business, but instead he bought a farm near Stamford in Lincolnshire and Mary was soon preoccupied with bringing up their young family. The time for her to be a champion golfer had passed.

Annie Maxwell (1875–1922)

Annie Maxwell and her siblings spent their summers, from early childhood, golfing at North Berwick. She and her older sisters became members of the Ladies' Club in 1889 – just a year after it had started up – the younger ones joined later. Annie was regarded as a crack golfer, though her public golfing successes are few. Perhaps it was Annie Maxwell's misfortune that she was golfing at North Berwick at a time when there were a clutch of excellent lady golfers, who were all members of the same club, and therefore making it extremely difficult to outshine them. On the other hand, she may have been over-shadowed by the golfing successes of her brother Robert, who became revered as a great amateur champion, winning at Muirfield in 1903 and 1909. Whenever she achieved any success, she was generally referred to as the sister of the distinguished player, Robert Maxwell. However, by the time Annie was in her twenties she was regarded as a possible future champion. Before the 1897 Ladies' Open at Gullane she was tipped as the 'first favourite' to win: "Miss Maxwell drives splendidly, plays a steady game, knows how to use her iron to advantage and extricates herself from a dilemma with adorable neatness." She did achieve the best overall results in the pre-Open competitions, and survived in the championship until the 5th round when she was defeated by Theodora Orr. After that, rather like the Orr sisters, she confined herself to friendly matches rather than competitions, even though it was reckoned both her long and short game got better and better. It became something of a challenge for the gentleman to pit themselves against the top lady golfers. In September 1899, Sir Archibald Buchan-Hepburn found he was outclassed when Annie defeated him over 2 rounds by 9 holes. Annie died unexpectedly, at the age of 47, at East Gribton, in June 1922, after a nasty bout of bronchitis turned to pneumonia. (Annie Maxwell is also referred to in chapters 5 & 6.)

Hilda Sant in a very striking golf outfit, c.1900.

Hilda Sant (1871–1943)

North Berwick Ladies' Club can claim Hilda Sant as one of its crack players, although she generally considered Wimbledon her home club. In September 1900, she won the North Berwick gold medal with a score of 64 for two rounds of the ladies' course. Her chief opponents were Madeline and Dorothy Campbell - at the time Madeleine, who tied for second place with 67, was considered the strongest player in the club. Muriel Campbell, another sister, who also offered some serious competition, finished fourth. *The Scotsman*, commenting on Hilda Sant's win, reported that she was one of the best players in the Wimbledon Club and that her victory was as popular as it was well-deserved and not unexpected by people who followed her play.

Hilda Sant was a member of NBLGC over many years. She was born in London, in 1871, the youngest by several years of seven children of the celebrated portrait painter and Royal Academician James Sant and his wife Eliza. Her father became painter in Ordinary to Queen Victoria, but was best known for portraits of children, often based on his own five daughters and two sons. After her mother died, Hilda stayed at home to be a companion for her elderly father who died in 1914 at the age of 94. Golfing does not appear to have been a family activity, yet Hilda took an immediate liking to the game when she first visited North Berwick in 1891 and engaged Ben Sayers to give her a few initial lessons. Beyond that she learned her considerable skill from observing other good players.

She played for the Middlesex county team, where she had a reputation as an excellent driver: "She drives a good ball, with an uncommonly pretty swing and plays well through the green, but is especially good with short approaches." She was widely renowned for her approach play and 'her deadly prowess in laying the ball dead'. After she carried off the gold medal at North Berwick in September 1900, her handicap at the club was reduced to scratch. The medal was only one of many prizes she scooped up as she played round various clubs – Prince's, Raneleagh and Wimbledon. She visited North Berwick every year and used to say the long links there was her favourite course. She continued to live in her childhood home at New Cavendish Street off Portland Place in London, where she died on Christmas Day 1943.

Madge Neill Fraser (1880–1915)

Madge (Margaret) Neill Fraser, who was born in Edinburgh on 4th June 1880, was the youngest of five children of Patrick and Margaret Neill Fraser. Her father was a partner in a long-established printing firm Neill & Company Limited and the family lived in a splendid house, Rockville, in the Murrayfield district on what was then the western edge of the city. When the Murrayfield Golf Club opened in 1896 it welcomed ladies as well as men and Madge emerged as a talented member, playing regularly for the club in inter-club matches. She also became a member at North Berwick and Dornoch. However, it was not until after the death of her father in February 1905 that Madge participated beyond club level and from that time she played for Scotland for nine consecutive years until war broke out in 1914. It is possible her father did not sanction her involvement in national competitive golf, where she could not be properly chaperoned.

Every year from 1906, Madge entered both the British Ladies' Open Championship and the Scottish Ladies' Championship. In June 1906, the

Madge Neill Fraser, a young Edinburgh woman, member at North Berwick, died in Serbia in 1915, working for the Scottish Women's Hospital organisation, helping wounded soldiers.

Scottish Ladies' Championship took place at Cruden Bay and Madge Fraser stole the headlines, at least in the early stages, with her extraordinary long drives. In an exciting semi-final Madge was defeated by the young North Berwick golfer Dorothy Campbell, who took the title. In May 1910, Madge pushed her way into the semi-finals of the Ladies' Open, at Westward Ho!, only to be defeated by a relative new-comer, 19 year-old Lily Moore (Olton), to whom Elsie Grant-Suttie (another North Berwick crack golfer) gave short shrift in the final. Madge was a familiar figure on the North Berwick Links. In the 1911, she was one of the six-member North Berwick team, which won the Eglinton Quaich at St Andrews. Her most glorious golfing moment was as runner up in the Scottish Ladies' Championship, played at Lossiemouth in 1912. Madge had entered from North Berwick. She was pitted against Dora Jenkins (Troon) in the final and although she had beaten her in round five of the Ladies' Open Championship at Turnberry a few weeks earlier, Dora had the upper hand and won the match by 4 and 2.

Madge Neill Fraser was renowned for her powerful drives and was always there in the leading group, although she never won a championship match. When war came in 1914, she didn't hesitate to join Elsie Inglis' pioneering Scottish Women's Hospital organisation, which established medical centres in key areas of conflict in France and Eastern Europe. Madge Neill Fraser went out to help set up a unit in Kraguievatz, in Serbia, after completing a brief but intensive training course in basic nursing, leaving behind her comfortable middle-class surroundings and her golf clubs. The women were working in makeshift huts with an inadequate water supply and few medical resources to deal with soldiers, who were suffering from a range of injuries. Madge contracted typhus and died there on 7th March 1915. Her funeral in Serbia was an elaborate affair, conducted with great solemnity according to the rites of the Greek Orthodox Church. She was laid to rest at Chela Kula military cemetery. One of her comrades sent home a detailed account, published in *The Scotsman* 2 April 1915, which concluded with these observations:

> **"The regret and distress expressed on all hands was genuine and touching in the extreme; one little Serbian lady was overwhelmed. She kept murmuring in her foreign accent during all the procession – 'It's so noble – so noble. To give one's life for la Patrie is fine, but to give it for the country of another, that is incredible.'"**

Agnes Grainger, the President of the Scottish Ladies' Golf Association paid

Madge a great tribute, quoted in *The Scotsman* 16 March 1915:

> **"She has given her life in a noble cause and we Scottish golfers are very proud of her. Her place in the team will be hard to fill. Those associated with her, at golf meetings and in golf work, will always remember her lovable personality and her thoroughness in everything she undertook."**

A fund in her memory was subscribed to by golfers from all parts of the world, as a result of which a new hospital unit was fitted out at Kragijevatz. The First World War affected the golfing community as it affected every other area of British society. Just over a year later, one of Madge's brothers, Patrick was killed in action on 1st July 1916, the first day of the battle of the Somme. He was one of 20,000 men killed that day.

NORTH BERWICK LADIES AND THE EGLINTON QUAICH

The silver Quaich was presented to the Scottish Ladies' Golfing Association in 1906 and was played for annually at the Scottish Ladies' Championship. The competition was open to any clubs affiliated to the SLGA, who could enter a team of four, five or six players drawn from entrants to the Championship. Between its inception in 1906 and 1928, North Berwick won the Quaich at St Andrews in 1911 and at Muirfield in 1914. On both occasions Elsie Grant-Suttie was awarded the 'Baby' Quaich for the lowest scratch score in the competition. Her score of 85 set a record for a women playing a full round at Muirfield.

The 1906 North Berwick team:

- Elsie Grant-Suttie (82)
- Dorothy Campbell (94)
- Madge Neill-Fraser (94)
- Miss F Veitch (96)
- Miss F. Harvey (104)
- Miss Janet Blair (101)

The 1914 North Berwick team:

- Elsie Grant Suttie (85)
- Rita Grant-Suttie (97)
- Frances Teacher (90)
- Helen Shand (neé Teacher) (99)
- Muriel Teacher
- Dorothy Stevenson

Frances Teacher (1885–1955)

Frances Teacher and her two sisters Helen and Muriel were gifted golfers. Frances' bigger reputation stems largely from her unexpected success in the Scottish Ladies' Open Championship at Troon in June 1907. It was the first foray into the championship for both Frances and her sister Helen. They both reached the semi-final, in which Helen was defeated by the holder Dorothy Campbell. Frances went on to win the title from Dorothy in a nail-biting final that finished at the 21st hole. A few weeks earlier Muriel, who was several years younger than her sisters, won the Cree Medal, at North Berwick.

Frances Teacher, Scottish Ladies' Open Champion, 1907.

The girls and their brother Murray were brought up in Edinburgh, where their father Charles Teacher, a medical practitioner, worked at the University. Their mother Frances became ill shortly after the birth of Muriel and died in February 1895, aged 35. The older girls went to St Leonard's School in St Andrews, where there were opportunities to play golf. In April 1903, Charles Teacher married Bertha Salomons (and in 1906 they had a daughter Olivia). He had retired by then (aged 48!) and as a keen and regular golfer at North Berwick, he had rented Angus House, in West Bay Road, for the summer months. He was also in the process of buying the newly-built Craigend, in Cromwell Road. In September that year, 16 year old Murray, also a promising young golfer, called on his friend Alex Ross, whose father Sandy was a well-known amateur golfer. The boys were looking at their father's shotgun, when the younger Ross brother pulled the trigger, completely unaware the gun was loaded. Murray was hit in the neck and the bullet lodged in his spine. He never recovered from his injuries and died at Craigend eight months later on 27th May 1904, to the heartbreak and despair of all concerned.

Frances took part in the 1909 British Ladies' Open at Birkdale, which became one of Dorothy Campbell's great victories. The previous year, when the Open was held at St Andrews, Frances was disqualified as her entry got lost in the post! She had little better luck at Birkdale, as she was defeated by a young, inexperienced player. In fact, she was unwell at the start of the championship and probably should have pulled out. She recovered in time, however, to travel to the United States with a group of six Scottish ladies, including Dorothy Campbell, to take part in the US Women's Open. The Scots ladies were feted wherever they went, on account of Dorothy's victory in the championship.

The 1914 Scottish Ladies' Amateur Championship was held at Muirfield – the first time a ladies' competition had been held there. The local clubs were well-represented, but of the last eight, five were North Berwick players. The odds were certainly on another North Berwick champion. There was excitement at the progress of Frances and her sister Muriel, entering the competition for the first time. Muriel upset the bookies by defeating the title-holder Jean McCulloch (West Kilbride) to reach the semi-final, raising the prospect of a family interest in the final. There was a second set of North Berwick sisters in the running, Elsie and Rita Grant-Suttie. Frances dispensed with Elsie during the morning of 10th June and defeated Rita in the next round in the afternoon. At that stage Muriel was knocked out by Eva Anderson (Macrahanish), who then met Frances in the final. It was compelling spectating; at the 18th they were all square and again at the 19th. The huge crowd hardly noticed the lashing rain, so intent were they on the outcome. At the 20th the drama was complete as Frances knocked her opponent's ball into the hole and Miss Anderson took the match.

Although Frances Teacher only won one major title, she was a great match player, who could hold a crowd. Many observers regarded her as the outstanding golfer of the day, with her free and graceful style and astonishing ability to hole a ball from the edge of the green. After her marriage to Edmund Mather in 1924, she moved to England. Helen remained an enthusiastic club competitor. Muriel was just making a name for herself in the championship stakes when the outbreak of the First World War interrupted her progress. She married in 1919, not long after the war ended and brought to a close a promising golfing career, almost before it had begun.

Dorothy Campbell (1883–1945)

> **"Dorothy Campbell was at that time the rising star. She was only a 'flapper' but her golf was amazingly fine and she had done wonderful scores on the little ladies' course."**
>
> (English golfer Mabel Stringer's description of Dorothy Campbell, after a visit to North Berwick in 1899.)

The layout of the Muirfield course for the 1914 Ladies' Championships.

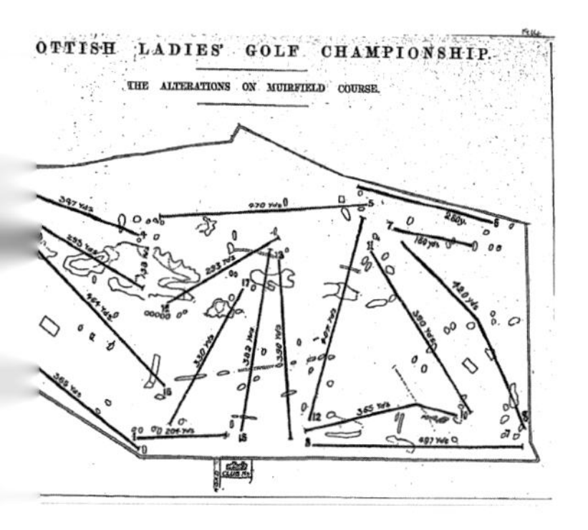

Dorothy Campbell was simply one of the best lady golfers of her era and it was on the links at North Berwick that she had her first experiences of the game. She was born on the morning of Saturday 24th March 1883, at the family home, 1 Carlton Terrace, Edinburgh. She was the youngest of nine children of William and Emily Campbell. Her mother was 48 when Dorothy was born. Her eldest sister was twenty one. All the children were living at home. The new baby was registered by her father as Gladys Iona Emily on Friday 13th April. Perhaps she just didn't look like a Gladys – though there might have been mileage in the name Gladys, old Welsh for 'nation' - or perhaps Mrs Campbell hadn't had time to settle on a name, but by the end of May, Gladys had been re-registered as Dorothy.

There were indications of Dorothy's prodigious golfing talent in the records of the NBLGC matches from quite early on. As all her older sisters were members of the club, Dorothy joined as soon as she was old enough, but the rules stated: "Members under age 14 shall not be eligible to play in competitions unless otherwise authorised by the Committee". In a far-sighted or simply liberal-minded move, the Committee sanctioned Dorothy's entry into Club competition. At the annual autumn meeting of the NBLGC in September 1895, Dorothy, aged 12, was the winner of the first handicap prize. With a generous allowance of 16, her score for two rounds of the ladies' course was 58. By 1897, Dorothy was regularly performing well in the club matches. In the August meeting that year, her sister Madeline came second in the scratch contest with a score of 65. There was a tie for the first three handicap places, but the fourth handicap prize went to young Dorothy. She had played two rounds of the ladies' course in 68, and with a handicap of 7, the result was a net score of 61. From this time, Dorothy began edging her way up the ranks of good players and it soon became clear that, even among so many fine golfers at North Berwick, she had a quite extraordinary gift for the game.

Dorothy Campbell (far right) reached the semi-finals in the first Scottish Open Championship at St Andrews, in 1903.

Dorothy competed in the very first Scottish Ladies' Open Championship at St. Andrews in 1903, aged 20. There was an entry of 46 and Dorothy reached the semi-final. This would seem an excellent result, but she was singled out by the Scotsman reporter for her weak putting: "Oh! Hamlet, what a falling off was there when [Miss Campbell] came to the putting-green." Apart from this short-coming, she "drove a long ball and used her iron clubs with good judgement and effect" (*The Scotsman*, 23 June 1903). Dorothy's dramas aside, the Open was hailed a success.

Dorothy entered the second Ladies' Scottish Championship, which took place on 17th May 1904, at St Nicholas Links, Prestwick. It was open to all lady golfers who were members of Scottish golf clubs, but in spite of the enthusiastic response to the first Open, there were only thirty five entries. However, the previous year's champion Miss Glover and the runner-up Molly Graham were there and another North Berwick player, Mrs Swanston. Mrs Swanston was one of Dorothy's older sisters, Madeline Campbell. She had married William Swanston, a Tyneside ship owner in January that year. It would appear that the responsibilities of marriage affected Madeline's enthusiasm for competitive golf, as she failed to put in an appearance, on the opening day of the championship. Further no shows and mishaps reduced the field even more. The previous champion Miss Glover, had the misfortune to slip and fall in her hotel lobby on the evening of the first day. She recovered well enough to play in the second round, in which she was drawn against Dorothy. It was the match which brought out the crowds, but in the event, it was a lack-lustre performance from both women. Dorothy never got on top of the game and it ended at the 12th with a victory for Miss Glover, who was 7 up and 6 to play. The title was won by the very talented Molly Graham (Nairn), British Ladies' Champion in 1901. Dorothy Campbell had to console herself with winning the prize for the best scratch score of 86 in the pre-competition event.

Up until that time, Madeline had been regarded as the better player between the two Campbell sisters and certainly the one with the more graceful style. A retrospective piece in the *Sunday Post* of 2nd October 1927, pin-pointed the reason for Madeline's failure to realise her potential as a great golfer:

> **"Dorothy Campbell and her elder sister Madeline, were two of the prettiest girls in North Berwick. Madeline was a beautiful golfer, much more attractive to watch than Dorothy, but she married early and settled in England."**

Marriage often sounded a death knell for success in many fields for women, before the First World War. Once married, many women were swallowed up by a convention that meant they addressed their husband's priorities rather than pursuing their own interests and activities. Of the great golfing women who came out of North Berwick in those early years, those who continued competitive golf beyond club level for the most part remained spinsters. Dorothy Campbell was unusual in that, after she married in 1913, she did not allow the constraints of marriage to draw her away from her golfing ambitions and she succeeded in becoming one of the first internationally recognised female golfers. For the next decade, from 1904 to 1914, Dorothy's star was in the ascendancy on the golf course and she became the person everyone aspired to beat.

Within twelve months of her defeat at Prestwick, Dorothy was able to demonstrate her talents on the golf course in front of a home crowd. In June 1905, the Scottish Ladies' Championship was held at North Berwick. There was a noticeable press presence and pages of coverage in the newspapers over several days, particularly in *The Scotsman*. Miss Hamilton Campbell, the Hon. Sec. of the Scottish Ladies Golfing Association was in charge of the arrangements. In addition, the Secretary of the NBLGC, Charles Blaikie, and Robert Maxwell, trustee, made themselves available – just to ensure the event ran smoothly!

On Monday 19th June there was a stroke competition open to all championship entrants, organised by the Scottish Ladies' Golfing Association. The Town Council and the North Berwick Ladies' Club donated the prizes.

Summer had been particularly warm and dry and the ladies were hoping the good conditions would continue for the duration of the championships. The draw for the main event was held in the evening, in the Marine Hotel, where the SLGA had taken over a room as a clubroom. There were 43 entries of whom four were members at North Berwick– Miss Janet Blair (niece of the Misses Bell), Miss Helen Teacher and two of the Campbell sisters, Muriel and Dorothy. There was a great deal of interest in Dorothy's play as she had done so well at the British Ladies' Open at Cromer earlier in the year, reaching the semi-final.

The competition kicked off on Tuesday 20th at 10.30 in the morning. Crowds of people gathered to watch:

> **"The large company of ladies and gentlemen who went down to the course were treated to some very fine play, for although the scoring on average was high, it has to be borne in mind that the course stretched to the full medal round, this having been done at the request of the ladies themselves."**
>
> (*The Scotsman*, 21 June 1905)

The run of fine weather ended and the competitors had to contend with driving rain and high winds. Dorothy's early experiences on the North Berwick links no doubt helped her to hit long straight balls from the tee and through the green, in spite of the gale force wind. She had taken on board the criticism of her game at St Andrews and putted with great accuracy. The final day of the contest brought sunshine and a crowd of about 2000 spectators. Dorothy pleased the home crowd with her win over Molly Graham, British Champion in 1901 and Scottish Champion in 1904, though Molly had also first learned to play golf at North Berwick in 1889, at about the same time as Dorothy. On 23rd June, *The Scotsman* headline announced VICTORY FOR NORTH BERWICK LADY and alluded to her "magnificent driving under trying conditions that had marked her out from all her opponents". A year later, in 1906, over the Cruden's Bay Course, Dorothy had a second consecutive victory in the Scottish Open, beating Miss Glover, by three holes up and one to play. 1908, brought further accolades for Dorothy, when she was runner-up in the British Ladies' Open at St Andrews in May and won the Scottish Open at Gullane in June.

The Ladies' Championship at Birkdale, in May 1909, was a triumph for Dorothy Campbell. She had already won the Scottish Ladies' Championship three times. She had been both silver and bronze medallist in the same event. Success at Birkdale meant she had achieved Gold, Silver and 3 Bronze

Dorothy Campbell after her victory at Birkdale in 1909.

medals in the British Championships. A note of caution for the good folk of North Berwick who wish to portray Dorothy's sensational win at Birkdale as a feather in the Burgh's cap: Dorothy had entered the 1909 championship from Musselburgh and not North Berwick!

The Scottish press was thrilled, regardless of inter-club politics, and reported extensively on her victory, although a small matter of bureaucracy almost robbed Dorothy of her title. By this time, official entry forms had been introduced for championship competitions and with them the rule that the winner of the match should personally report the result to an LGU official. In the 3rd round Dorothy Campbell had won her match by 9 to 7 and, in the excitement of the moment, forgot to give in her result. There was a strong possibility she might be disqualified. Cecil Leitch, making her own début at a championship match, later wrote about the incident in *Golf for Girls*:

> **"Never shall I forget the excitement this omission caused. Anyway she went out in the afternoon with the sword of Damocles over her head, not knowing what was the decision of the Championship Committee who had been called together to decide her fate. This must have affected her game, as at the 16th she was down one. At this point the gods came to her assistance, for her opponent had to take a brassy off a tempting-looking lie on blown sand; she fluffed the shot and lost the hole. Dorothy Campbell was not yet out of the woods, for on the home green she had to negotiate one of the deadliest stymies I have ever seen, to save the match. The crowd left their tea to gather round the home green; not a sound was heard; not a sneeze or a cough as Dorothy Campbell took her mashie, studied the shot from every point, played the most perfect chip – and holed out, winning the match. Then a great shout went up from us all, friends crowded round to congratulate her, for there had been much feeling about the morning incident and had the Committee decided other than they did, several competitors had announced they would retire from the contest in protest."**

Soon after the championship Dorothy travelled to the USA and in 1909 amazed the golfing world by triumphing in the US championship and then the Canadian championship in the following year. She returned to Britain to take part in the Ladies' Open at Portrush in May 1911 and in 'steady form' took the title for the second time. It was the high point of her golfing career and she was widely acknowledged as the greatest lady golfer ever. In 1911, at the time when she was holder of three championships – US, Canadian and British –

(the only woman in her lifetime to do so), Dorothy accepted the captaincy of the Hamilton Ladies' Club, in Ontario and a position as joint editor of a golf magazine. It was clear that she would not be returning to Scotland in the foreseeable future.

Dorothy's golfing career in the US and Canada is well-documented. She was made an honorary member at Merion, Philadelphia, where she was the first non-American to win the U S Women's Amateur Championship. They now have a cup, the Dorothy Campbell Howe Cup, named after her. She was also made an honorary member at Rosedale, Toronto in response to her triumph there in 1912, when she carried off the Duchess of Connaught Gold Cup, the trophy presented to the winner of the Canadian Amateur Ladies' Championship.

By the late 1920s, although Dorothy was still winning trophies, she was no longer winning the big titles. In September 1927, she was put out in the first round of the US Ladies' Championship on the Cherry Valley Course, Long Island, New York: "Mrs Hurd of Ottawa, who as Dorothy Campbell of Edinburgh won the British and Scottish Championships several years ago, was unexpectedly beaten by Mrs Pressler, the Western Champion, by one hole". Her reputation was such, however, that whenever she took part in a tournament, she was still able to pull in the crowds.

Dorothy's first marriage to J.V. Hurd of Pittsburgh, which took place in 1913, ended in divorce in 1921 and in March 1937, she quietly let it be known that she had married Edward Howe, a 66 year old American banker, who had just taken up golf! Dorothy would have required a great deal of patience to enjoy a round of golf with her new husband, but in any case, the marriage didn't survive long. Dorothy's life came to a tragic end in March 1945, when she was struck by a train in Yemassee, South Carolina, four days before her 62nd birthday.

DOROTHY CAMPBELL'S GOLFING ACHIEVEMENTS

Scottish Ladies' Champion
1905, 1906, 1908

British Ladies Champion
1909, 1911

Canadian Champion
1910, 1911, 1912

American (US) Women's Champion
1909, 1910, 1924

Western Pennsylvania Championship
1914

North & South Champion
1918, 1920, 1921

Boston Champion
1922

Florida West Coast Champion
1923

Philadelphia Champion
1925, 1926, 1927, 1929, 1934

Bermuda Champion
1931, 1934

Elsie Grant-Suttie (1879–1954)

Elsie Margaret Hew Grant-Suttie belonged to one of the old East Lothian landowning families. Her father, Captain Francis Grant-Suttie R.N. was the second son of Sir George Grant-Suttie of Balgone, and Lady Harriet Charteris, daughter of the 8th Earl of Wemyss. Francis was brought up at the family home, Preston Grange, an old Scottish baronial mansion. While he followed a career in the navy, his older brother inherited the title and Preston Grange and his younger brother Robert inherited the Balgone estate, two miles south of North Berwick.

Francis Grant-Suttie's naval career took him to Australia where he

Elsie Grant-Suttie in full swing to victory, after her win at Westward Ho!

met and married Elizabeth McIntyre in Sydney on January 15th 1877. At the time, Francis was 45 and Elizabeth 26. The couple returned to London and when Francis retired from the navy in 1880, he built a house in North Berwick, to the west of the town, on an acre of ground feued by Sir Hew Dalrymple. He named the house Hyndford, after his grandmother, the Countess of Hyndford. The house stood on slightly raised ground to the south of the recently opened Marine Hotel and had excellent views across the links to the sea. The four Grant-Suttie children were born in quick succession, George in 1877, Sheila in 1878, Elsie in 1879 and Harriet in 1880. Francis died at Hyndford, on February 28th 1884, at the age of 52, from kidney disease, before Elsie or her siblings had had much experience of golfing. Hyndford was subsequently bought by Sir Charles Tennant for his son Frank and for many years was associated with the Tennant family rather than Elsie Grant-Suttie.

Elsie and her sisters attended a small private girls' boarding school in Folkstone and opportunities for playing golf were restricted to the holidays in North Berwick. But the sport must have been in her blood. The Grant-Sutties were an integral part of the history of the old North Berwick Club and Elsie's father was the second Captain of the New Club, from 1882-83. Elsie and her siblings golfed with their Balgone cousins, Hugh, Hilda, Muriel, Edith and Archie who were much younger. It was clear early on, that both Elsie and her sister Harriet (Rita) had extraordinary golfing talents. Rita moved in her older sister's shadow and has not received the attention she deserves as a first-class golfer. In the 1914 Scottish Championships at Muirfield, for example, both women reached the final eight, at which point, both were defeated.

Elsie represented Scotland in Home Internationals on many occasions – in 1908, 1910 & 11, 1914, 1922 & 23. She achieved her greatest triumph, in 1910, when she won the 18th British Ladies' Open Championship, played at Westward Ho! The critics commented on her full swing and her ability to drive a long ball, but it was generally agreed that her iron play was the strongest part of her game. The following year, she came up against her arch-rival, Dorothy Campbell, in the fifth round of the Ladies' Championship, at Portrush, Northern Ireland, and was defeated by 2 up and 1 to play. A few weeks later in June 1911, she won the Scottish Ladies' Championship, at St Andrews. First, she took her revenge on Dorothy, beating her in the second round and in the final defeated Ida Kyle, the St Rule golfer, by one hole, in a brilliant finish. This championship marked a turning point in women's golf, as it attracted more high calibre golfers than in previous years, thus raising the standard of play. The ladies were generally hitting the ball longer and faster and seemed less constrained by etiquette. The event brought out an enormous crowd, estimated at over 4000. Five of the last eight were North Berwick members! In 1914, Elsie reached the semi-final of the British Ladies' Open, at Hunstanton, but was put out by the eventual winner Cecil Leitch.

After the interruption of the Great War, Elsie continued competing. In 1920, the Ladies' Championship was scheduled to take place at Newcastle, County Down. Elsie, unhappy at the turbulent political situation in Ireland which had virtually turned into a war over Irish independence, led a protest against the chosen venue. She raised a moderate amount of support, but ultimately the protest failed and the championship went ahead without her. In 1924, her LGU handicap was plus one. She was the runner-up in the Scottish Ladies' Championship, at Gullane in 1925.

Elsie Grant-Suttie's life did, however, extend beyond competitive golf. She was a member of the Red Cross for many years and during both wars volunteered as an ambulance driver. Between the wars, she was concerned at the lack of an ambulance to serve the local community in East Lothian and by 1939 had raised sufficient funds to buy one. She became part of a voluntary team of drivers, responding to emergency calls and providing transport to ferry patients to hospital. After 1945, enthusiasm and public spiritedness waned, yet Elsie carried on virtually single-handed. She often drove to Edinburgh and back, twice in one day. She was rewarded with the British Empire Medal in 1949.

Elsie retired to the picturesque, but small, Garage House, in the grounds of Marly Knowe, on the southern edge of North Berwick. She continued to

Cecil Leitch photographed on a visit to the links at North Berwick.

Elsie Grant-Suttie in relaxed mood resting on the links, in the 1930s, with her cousin Hubert Grant-Suttie – and smoking a cigarette!

enjoy competing in the NBLGC matches, winning the Club Gold Medal in 1927, 1930 and 1931, but was beginning to be eclipsed by the next generation of North Berwick golfers, Millicent Couper, Violet Grahame, Eileen Tweedie and school girl, Jean Donald, who was creating a stir on the green. In 1948, at the age of 68, Elsie won the Hunnewell Bowl and the first handicap prize at the Club's Spring Meeting. It was her swansong in competitive golf.

Elsie did not always endear herself to people in the community. She became a rather forbidding and intolerant lady as she grew older. She didn't suffer fools and became inflexible in regard to the views of others. She was, however, a brilliant golfer – one of the best to ever come out of North Berwick. Collective memories can afford to be generous, in remembering a women who played for love of the game, but was always ready to put her principles first. Elsie was found dead at her home on 4th January 1954. The heart problems that had dogged her for years had taken their toll and she had suffered a coronary thrombosis. Elsie was a legend in the town and sixty years later, anecdotes of her splendid play and sturdy character are still recalled by those who remember her swinging to perfection on the North Berwick links!

CHAPTER EIGHT

Fashion on the Fairway

> **"Though women are recommended, indeed requested to wear low flat heels when golfing, the majority do not and it is these sharp pointed heels which do such incalculable harm."**
>
> (*Golf Illustrated*, 16 March 1900)

The question of what ladies ought to wear on the golf course became a talking point early on in the development of women's golf. Opinions were freely expressed in newspaper columns and periodicals. In those days of male hegemony, it was often the men who were making the loudest comments and attempting to set the standards of what was and was not acceptable. In the *Girls' Own Paper*, 14 April 1894, Garden G. Smith, a Scots born journalist, ventured his opinions:

> **"The question of what ladies ought to wear in playing golf is one of such profound difficulty and to the male mind beset with so many impenetrable considerations that a positive finding is impossible."**

This seems to suggest a lamentable lack of male confidence in women's ability to dress appropriately for the occasion. Reading on, it becomes clear that the choice of a well-tailored, fitted and consequently flattering outfit for ladies was an anathema to many male golfers: "There are certain varieties of dress which ought not to be worn". Of what were the men afraid? Were they really concerned that high-heeled boots, close-fitting skirts and jackets with tight sleeves were not conducive to a correct stance and free-swinging arm movements, so vital to an acceptable standard of play? Were they jealous that

Frances Jessie Turnbull, 'beautifully attired' for golf. She is pictured on the Braid Hills in 1902.

beautifully attired, the ladies may draw too much attention away from the men's game, and anxious that other men may find their wives too attractive? Or was the Victorian male still hidebound by a misplaced belief that he must continue to exert control over his wife or his daughters, beyond the confines of home, so that, Canute-like, he could stem the tide of female emancipation that was sweeping towards the shore? It would, of course, be unfair to suppose all men shared the same views.

It was often women who were the worst detractors of their own sex. Mabel Stringer, the English golfer turned golfing journalist, had much to say on how ladies dressed on the golf course and she was suitably critical of women who, instead of establishing a feminine touch in their golf attire, turned up dressed like men. She believed such women made their sex a laughing stock by wearing mannish clothes – shapeless red coats and narrow and ungainly cycling skirts. They tied their hair in a knot on top of their head and pinned a man's cap on top. They allowed their faces to get 'tanned' from constant exposure to sun and they wore thick clumsy boots. Stringer much preferred a more feminine appearance, achieved by wearing a small sailor hat, perched neatly on beautifully coiffed hair; a smart red coat; spotless white blouse and tie; an ordinary tailor-made skirt and well-made walking boots.

It wasn't only about dressing carelessly for golf, it was important to know what was acceptable to wear, and the Victorian fashion gurus were ready to shoot down in flames any woman who turned up on the links inappropriately clad for golf:

> **"Unfortunately, all women do not realise the fact that good dressing means suitable dressing. Anything out of place, however good in itself, is bad taste; hence a woman donning London silks on the links is as much a fish out of water as a riverside maiden's costume in Regent Street."**

The ladies' pages of golf magazines had to work hard to promote the idea that just because a lady was keen on golf it didn't mean she wasn't interested in fashion. The *Pot Pouri* column in *Golf Illustrated* gave suggestions on how to dress correctly. The nub of the advice was that the simpler and plainer the style the better – a thick tweed, or warm lightweight woollen suit in 'useful colours' were deemed suitable. In addition, a corduroy jacket was recommended for winter on the grounds that it never tore and never wore. Cold hands could be a problem in cold weather and woollen cuffs were recommended rather than gloves which could get in the way and created problems with gripping the club. One famous exception to that idea was Champion golfer, Dorothy Campbell, who always wore gloves.

Attention to hair-style was equally important and it was observed that ladies engaging in sporting activities might overlook the necessity of well-coiffed hair, which, "for participation in any form of sport, should be coiled as neatly, firmly and simply as possible". The weather, however, often intervened to the detriment of a tidy head of hair and hats on a windy day could bring their own problems. Cecil Leitch in *Golf for Girls* recommended wearing a hat in windy weather:

> **"Tight caps fitting to the head like a man's and made to match the dress always look well....Wind and golf go together marvellously often and everything fly-away in a woman's attire should be carefully eschewed."**

Cecil Leitch believed it was practical for a girl golfer to carry an umbrella in her 'caddie-bag', though her rationale seems quaint with no mention of the more obvious discomforts of a soaking wet clinging top!

> **"I would just add how fatal it is for a girl to get her shoulders wet, as a wet and clinging blouse binds the shoulders and seriously interferes with the swing."**

Sensible footwear was highly recommended, although it was acknowledged it could look ungainly:

> **"Thick sensible shoes with broad toes and flat heels are indispensable – of course they make the feet look larger than their wont and ankles thicker. But appearance to the winds! Women must be practical to participate in any form of sport and keep their silken hose and patent leather shoes for other occasions."**
>
> (From *Womens' Dress on the Links, Golf Illustrated*, 24 March 1893)

Propriety and the shorter skirt

It was plainly difficult to wear a conventional full-length skirt for golfing, as the ideal for playing was for a skirt to be 8 to 10 inches (20-25cms) off the ground, so the length of ladies' golfing skirts became a matter of intense scrutiny and debate. Full-length skirts and golf were never going to work together, but how seemly was it for a lady to wear a shorter skirt, once she had stepped off the green? The Victorians came up with an ingenious solution – the New Forest skirt. In length it was about 12 inches (30cms) from the ground. A deep tuck over the hem hid several buttons sewn around it at intervals. The idea was that at the end of a game of golf the wearer would button on an extra length of skirt, giving it a conventional appearance and the lady could make her way home with her modesty unquestioned.

For many women golfers the shorter skirt was a fashion too far. To get around the problem of ruining a long skirt on the golf course, one lady came up with the bright idea of protecting the bottom of her skirt, by tacking on a length of leather to the hem. It was done in such a way that it didn't show, but gave protection to the skirt. The innovative lady was keen to share her tip with other lady golfers: "My dressmaker purchases this at Evan's in Oxford Street and a dress length costs only 2s 6d". The idea caught on, but some women attached a leather piece to the bottom of a shorter skirt while playing and replaced it in the clubhouse after the game with another matching piece. In this way a woman could maintain her desire for propriety and keep her 'long' skirt or gown clean to travel home. Another popular idea was an all-purpose skirt with a double hem – so the skirt could be easily lengthened when the season was over.

In Scotland it was not unusual for women to wear kilts to play golf, but a cheap imitation wouldn't do. In order to allow free movement as well as look good, the kilts had to be properly made. There were plenty of tartan tailors in Edinburgh's High Street. It was the norm in the late Victorian era for skirts to have linings and layers of petticoats, but for golf, these had no place – an unlined skirt was more practical and more comfortable.

Cecil Leitch's skirt was a fashionable 12 inches from the ground.

Stereotypes and straightjackets

Most women enjoyed the fashion of the tight-fitting bodice, which could be flattering to the figure, but they found themselves in a real straightjacket when it came to golfing. Tight fitting garments limited a woman's ability to swing a club above shoulder level – the result was that it was considered unseemly and the men were quick to have their say on that topic:

> **"We venture to suggest seventy or eighty yards as the average limit of a drive advisedly; not because we doubt a lady's power to make a longer drive, but because that cannot well be done without raising the club above the shoulder….the posture and gestures required for a full swing are not particularly graceful when the player is clad in female dress."**
>
> (Lord Moncrieff, *Golf*, Badminton Library, 1902.)

Loose blouses became *de rigeur* on the ladies' links. They had a high neck-line with a turned down collar, under which a tie with club colours was often worn.

There was even a 'North Berwick' skirt marketed and sold in John Wight, Princes Street, Edinburgh, in 1910. Its special features – it was tartan and reversible!

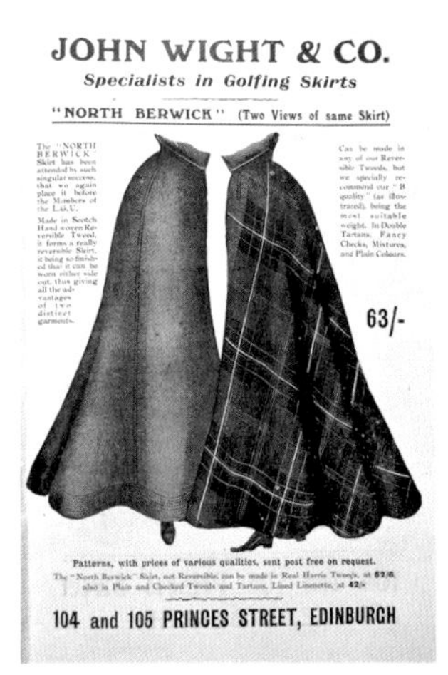

They were made of cotton or flannel and tucked in at the waist. This fashion didn't suit some menfolk either. In October 1900, an article appeared in *Golf Illustrated* by a contributor who signed himself 'a mere man' and proceeded to hurl ferocious insults across the page at women golfers whose choice of golf attire did not coincide with his:

> **"Golfing Gorgons! They are a class by themselves. Female yet scarcely feminine, lacking as they do, all or a large part of those qualities, graces and attributes which so endear the softer to the sterner sex. To begin with, their dress ......approximates as nearly to that of the man golfer as they can get their 'tailor' to produce: a stand-up collar, a man's tie, a loose golfing jacket, a 'figure' absolutely free from any encasement which might tend to make the best of the situation."**

He curiously finds fault with the fact that their skirts are so short that their feet are displayed, their stride ungainly and, from a distance, they look like men! If they wear a cap it's like a man's and if they are bare-headed their hair looks sun-bleached and straw-like, and their "complexion utterly ruined and weather-beaten". How perceptions of beauty have changed!

This particular outfit was described in the *Standard* in 1899:

"It has a brown serge skirt, with a double hem which reaches only to the ankles. The full blouse is of buff-coloured cambric, with white spots and is made with comfortable bishop sleeves, drawn into turned-back cuffs, a deep turn down collar, with brown silk tie and a draped silk wide waistband, sailor hat of buff straw, with brown band. If particular colours are worn by the golf club it is easy to have the dress made in such colours. A golfing costume, like one for tennis or cricket, should allow plenty of room for freedom of action; the skirt and blouse form is therefore best. An extra coat or cape is a necessity."

Changing standards of dress

Part of the problem was that sportswear for women was an entirely alien concept, but as golfing became more popular for women, the designs in golfing clothes improved and became more flattering. In 1891, Messrs Hogg and Sons, military tailors and outfitters in London, patented a new Norfolk jacket. The

A silk knitted golf coat allowed freedom of movement.

coat was designed with golfers in mind, to give the wearer a greater degree of freedom of movement and flexibility, but remain comfortable when, for example, driving off the tee. It was noted in *Golf: A Weekly Record*, 18 Sept 1891:

> **"We have recently tried one of these coats and found that with the swinging of the club there was a delightful feeling of ease and absence of constraint attaching to the whole movement of the body."**

Messrs Hogg & Sons were already confident of the success of their new coat as they proudly announced that no lesser person than the Chief Secretary for Ireland had bought one – in other words A. J. Balfour, who, of course, was a regular visitor to the North Berwick links. One other vital selling point – the style could equally well be applied to ladies' clothing! At about the same time, Messrs. Davis, Blake and Farr, Army and Navy tailors, in London's Portman Square, brought out a waterproof coat which was particularly serviceable to golfers. The sleeves were not attached to the coat, but joined together by a stockinette vest of very light and elastic material. These were put on first, and then the coat, which covered the entire body to well below the knees. The idea was that in wet weather, while using clubs, the arms were not constrained by the waterproof. The modern light-weight material made it easy to fold up small enough for the caddie to carry it around in case of a downpour! Burberry, which, in the 1890s, had a well-established reputation for outdoor garments, was soon on the golfing band waggon, promoting ladies' 'free-stroke' coats, with a newly patented pivot sleeve, which gave plenty of freedom to swing a club, without feeling constrained by the more usual firmly-structured garments, which were the norm.

Details of new designs of costume for golfing women filled every newspaper and magazine fashion page. Golf capes were designed to look neat and feminine and not completely envelop the wearer. Checked tweeds capes were in, with plain coloured silk linings picking up the colours of the tweed. Discussions continued on the subject of the most practical gloves to wear. Washed leather gloves were popular, as they allowed a firm grip on the leather handles of the golf clubs.

'Mrs Aria', giving fashion advice, in a weekly column, in *Hearth & Home*, recommended the Norfolk jacket to one correspondent in February 1894.

> **"...Have a Norfolk jacket with full blouse sleeves. This, as you doubtless know, is made with three box pleats at the front and three at the back, and has a belt round the waist. You will find it quite comfortable and very nice for playing golf."**

As a new market developed in women's golfing fashions, Burberry were quick to take a lead.

In April 1906, 'The Asquith', 'Ribblesdale' & 'Cadogan' golf coats were launched. Smart and business-like, they were made from hand-woven Irish tweed and promoted by the Irish Industries Association, which was heavily patronised by the Royal family and the aristocracy. They became the garment of fashion on the golf course. Naturally, they caught on pretty quickly in North Berwick where both Margot Asquith and her sister Charlotte Ribblesdale were frequent visitors. The Irish textile industry, which produced hand-made lace, linen and woollens and which depended on poorly paid Irish weavers, was at the forefront in making high-quality golf clothing:

> **"The Countess of Cadogan, one of the latest recruits to golf, has recently shown her interest both in the game and in Irish industries by ordering a "Ribblesdale" golfing blouse, with toque en suite (matching close-fitting hat) to be made for her at Miss Mahaffy's Industry, Howth, close to the famous Portmarnock links."**

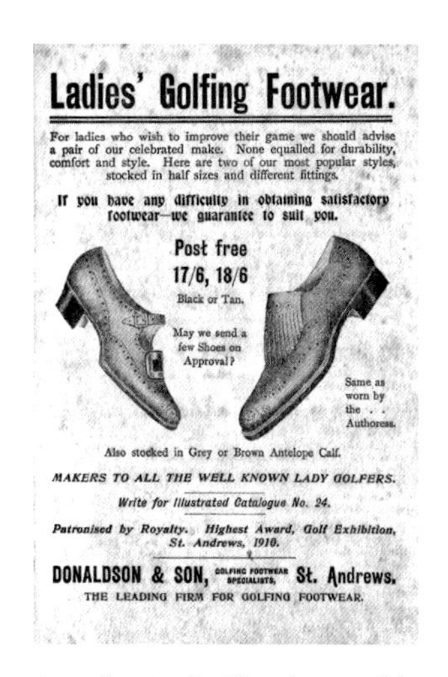

A good pair of golfing shoes could improve a ladies' game!

The society ladies regarded their patronage of the Irish textile industry as a charitable gesture, by giving the Irish peasants some employment!

The better local dress shops, in North Berwick and nearby Haddington, advertised tweed suits and overcoats as suitable for golfing and the pricing was competitive. At George Spark in Haddington's Market Street, Scotch tweed suits would cost between 50/- and 60/- (£3), while at Inglis in the High Street, they were retailing for slightly more at 3 guineas (£3 3s). As more ladies' links opened across the country, drapers started to stock clothing and footwear suitable for golfing. As early as July 1888, the month the ladies' links opened at North Berwick, the firm C. Donaldson & Sons, St Andrews, was advertising ladies' golfing brogues – ladies were invited to send a pair of worn shoes to get the measurements for a replacement pair! Aware that a lot of these fashions could stretch a lady's clothing allowance, shops often stocked similar garments of differing quality and price. *Hearth & Home* ran adverts for Garrard's great summer sale of ladies' golf blouses – two qualities 3/11d and 4/11d.

Spin offs and branding

It wasn't just clothes that were marketed to attract lady golfers – food manufacturers quickly cottoned on to the endless marketing opportunities for their products through the growing popularity of ladies' golf. Cadbury's was soon pushing its 'sustaining cocoa', not just as a delicious hot drink, but as a 'food possessed of staying power' and 'a necessity for those upon the links'. The advertising suggested that a cup of cocoa before going out on the links

FASHIONS OF THE DAY 1908

"The latest style for golfing ladies may be of interest. A tall lady was observed a few days ago, cigarette in mouth and a caddie by her side, proceeding to play on the old course at St Andrews. Her dress consisted of a soft green slouch hat, carelessly pinned well over her hair. A long sweater of grey knitted Shetland wool covered her body, round which was encircled a glazed yellow belt. The skirt was short and green. Her feet were encased in shoes which at the first glance looked as if they had not been brushed for weeks. However, on closer inspection they were discovered to be made of green leather to match the skirt". (*Telegraph and Post*)

would be an excellent preparation for the physical activity that was to follow! Cadbury's milk chocolate was recommended for its nutritional properties, on the basis that it contained a large range of types of food – fat, carbohydrate and protein – because it had been made with cocoa, sugar and full cream milk. Of course, it was so deliciously sweet, it was not a difficult task to sell the proposition that it was perfectly sensible to have a bar of chocolate tucked away in a skirt pocket, to recharge the batteries around the half-way mark in a match.

By the time Mabel Stringer published her *Golfing Reminiscences* in 1924, times had changed and she had modified her ideas accordingly: "The golfing girl of today should indeed be grateful that she need not play golf in a sailor hat, a high stiff collar, a voluminous shirt and petticoats, a motor veil or a wide skirt, bound with leather so that the mud collected could easily be sponged off". She reflects on how it was ever possible to hit a ball or "get along at all in the outrageous garments which fashion decreed we wear to cover ourselves," and comes to the conclusion that it is "one of the great unsolved mysteries of that or any age".

Mabel Stringer's remarks resonate eerily with the criticisms which appear in the media today about the potential harm to young woman of the pressures on them to aspire to having the apparently flawless bodies of models whose images fill the pages of glossy magazines and appear on screen. It is difficult to conclude that we have progressed much beyond the attitudes of the late Victorians to women and fashion, when, "every self-respecting woman had to have a waist and the more it was drawn in, the more it was admired. This was a terrible drawback for golf."

USE
FRY'S
PURE CONCENTRATED
COCOA.
Ask your Grocer for a Sample, Gratis.
" It is especially adapted to those whose digestive organs are weak."—*Sir Charles A. Cameron, M.D.*
[65-12

Mabel Stringer in 1924 – although she was free with her advice regarding appropriate golf wear for women, she was not the snappiest dresser on the green.

The biggest upset to what was an acceptable form of dress for women came in 1933, when American Gloria Minoprio appeared at the English Women's Golf Championships at Westward Ho! in trousers. There were remarks of regret from competition officials that Miss Minoprio had flouted convention. She was unfazed and firmly pointed out that trousers were more convenient than a skirt for playing golf.

At least one lady was brave enough to wear trousers at the Deuchar Foursomes at North Berwick c.1934.

Footnote

In 1899, inspired by the nation's patriotic response to the Boer War and support of the British Army in the field, some lady golfers took to wearing khaki hats and jackets on the golf course. It was a fleeting fashion and shortly after the war ended in 1902, the khaki outfits were handed down to the ladies' maids!

CHAPTER NINE

Changing Attitudes

"Ladies have now taken to the game in droves. They have donned short-skirted frocks and bewitching gaiters and vie with the men in their devotion of the game."

(*Golf Illustrated*, 1893)

On Wednesday February 18th 1914, nearly seven years after her victory in the Scottish Championships, Frances Teacher was spotted playing golf on the North Berwick links and described in the *Haddingtonshire Courier* as the 'Scottish ex-Champion'. It was winter and out of season and perhaps the reporter was short of a better story. However, the headline is telling; it is an indication of the value society placed on golfing achievement – it doesn't have to mention the word 'golf', it's understood, but just as important is the implication that attitudes to women were changing. A few decades earlier, women who 'disported themselves on the green' – i.e. played golf or indeed participated in any sport in public – were often treated with disapproval and found themselves the butt of unflattering jokes, sarcasm or condescending remarks that appeared in periodicals and magazines of the day. A comment in *Punch* magazine of Saturday May 10th 1873 was a direct snipe at women's efforts to get involved in sport of any description:

After the First World War (1914–18) attitudes towards women golfing had completely changed and, as this photo taken on the West Links in the 1930s demonstrates, a mixed foursome was a very relaxed affair.

"Irrepressible Woman is again in the field. 'Ladies cricket' is advertised, to be followed, there is every reason to apprehend, by Ladies' Fives, Ladies Football, Ladies Golf etc. It is all over with Men. They had better make up their minds to rest contented with croquet, and afternoon tea and sewing-machines, and perhaps an occasional game at drawing-room billiards."

The writer was imagining what would seem a highly improbable scenario in 1873, in which women went out to play sport and the men stayed at home – a complete role reversal of the two sexes. It was a response to the increasingly regular appearance of ladies' cricket teams on the village green and suggests an early anxiety felt by men that women were encroaching on their hallowed ground. Ladies' golf clubs had already begun to be formed, with one of the first in Scotland at St Andrews, in 1868. With hindsight, of course, the writer's prediction was closer to the truth than most people then could have imagined. Over the 140 years since the comment in *Punch*, women have steadily asserted their right to participate in a huge range of activities outside the home, which were previously the preserve of men.

Frances Teacher, Scottish Champion, 1907.

Westwood Ho! and North Devon, the second ladies' golf club in Britain, was formed in June 1868. At the opening event on 20th June, the sight of women on the links, caused nervousness and there was much male shoe-shuffling. The men responded either by passing remarks suggesting that women had neither the physique nor stamina to carry through a round of golf, or by displaying excessive gallantry in ensuring everything was done to assist the ladies' play. Sixty women had joined the club. The Honorary Secretary (a gentleman) and the Club professional (a gentleman) were on the course to help explain the game to 'beginners' (ladies)! In the event, the two rounds, each of nine holes, were completed by one of the 'debutantes' (ladies) in 61! *Trewman's Exeter Flying Post*, Wednesday 24 June 1868, commented on the day's play, with a wry sense of humour:

> **"The general play gave promise of such proficiency that the gentlemen may very possibly have to succumb to the superior prowess of the gentler sex in any contest over the short course. The fair sex may be congratulated on having added this outdoor amusement to the few hitherto allowed them."**

During the second half of the 19th century, the whole topic of social restrictions on women was beginning to be debated. Up until then, a married woman was entirely dependent on her husband: she couldn't properly own property in her own right until 1882; she couldn't divorce without an Act of Parliament: and if she left the marital home, she lost the right to have custody of her children. In Victorian Britain authority nearly always meant male authority. But change was in the air; the societal restrictions imposed on women in education, employment and family life, and the narrow-minded attitudes towards them, were gradually easing. The campaign for women's political rights was beginning in earnest through the suffrage movement, although it didn't meet with success until 1918, when women got the vote for the first time – well, as long as they were over thirty and householders or married to a householder. It was 1928 before women received the vote on equal terms with men. But that was another struggle!

In the early days of ladies' golf, there were alarming reports of women being 'warned off' courses in Scotland and made to feel unwelcome as spectators: "The golfer's hapless wife or daughter has been loath to accompany him to St Andrews or North Berwick and silently contemplates the pleasures she has not been permitted to share." (*The Queen* 18 November 1890).) Ladies were, in fact, always made welcome at the annual meeting of the old North Berwick Golf Club, a great social event in the East Lothian 'goff' calendar, but although they were included in the very fine luncheon served in the marquee, they were excluded from any match play!

"The second day's gathering of the members and friends of the old North Berwick Club was largely attended. Within the large marquee on the green a fashionable assemblage of ladies and gentlemen partook of the luncheon and afterwards engaged in foursomes. At first glance, one supposed the foursomes were mixed, but not so, the gents excused themselves from lunch and took to the links in groups of four, leaving their wives, daughters and maiden aunts to gather their skirts and follow on behind as spectators."

(*The County Gentleman: A Sporting Gazette & Agricultural Journal*, 8 Sept 1888)

A gathering of ladies and gentlemen at the Old Club Meeting, c.1923.

The gentlemen enjoying the Old Club Meeting at North Berwick, c.1923.

In spite of this perception of hostility to women golfers, it was generally accepted that Scotland was much more liberal in its attitudes to women enjoying a game of golf than England, but by the 1890s golf was gaining ground as an acceptable pastime for women there too – and the gentlemen were kind enough to point out that the standard of play at many ladies' golf clubs was 'rapidly improving'!

By 1890, women's publications were venturing to recommend golf to their readership. They were reflecting the changing attitudes towards female participation in sporting activities, rather than influencing the change. In February 1890, the *Girls Own Paper* ran a two page feature on the increasing popularity of golf, cautiously heralding its benefits for women:

> **"It is, however, only of late years that ladies have taken up a game which has nothing but favourable points to recommend it, embracing as it does all the advantages of open air, healthy exercise, education of the eye, and, like most games, developing control of temper and general judgement in deciding the best method of overcoming the various obstacles and 'hazards' of the links..."**
>
> (*Girls' Own Paper*, Saturday 1 February, 1890)

A comment in *Golf* in July 1891 about the NBLGC indicated the degree to which ladies' golf was taking off and also the extent to which the ladies were pushing out the boundaries, to make it acceptable for them to play on the main links, rather than always being confined to their nine-hole course: "The ladies' fine course was pretty busily occupied last week, the summer competitions of the North Berwick Ladies' Club being now in full swing, and over the long course, also, the fair votaries of the royal game were by no means conspicuous by their absence."

A step forward in the golfing world occurred when the magazine *Golf Illustrated*, encouraged by the development of the ladies' game, introduced a dedicated column on women's golf. The magazine was first published in 1890 under the title *Golf*. Its tone was light-hearted and its content covered most aspects of the game. It made passing and often patronising references to lady golfers, but in 1894 a regular feature, 'On the Ladies Links', appeared, which adopted a slightly more serious and informative approach to women's golf.

There were all sorts of complex notions put forward as to why golf was becoming so popular among women – they wanted to be in the fashion; they were idle; or they were 'pot-hunting', that is seeking to win the 'rather nice' prizes offered by most ladies' clubs. Another suggestion was that women played golf because it had become the correct thing to do. The obvious reason that women simply wanted to get out and about and enjoy a sporting activity was rather overlooked. By the 1890s golf was so popular, it was suggested it was affecting the dynamics of romance and marriage! Some suggested it was responsible for the decline in marriage, as young men and women concentrated to such an extent on the game, they were suppressing their 'natural inclination for romance'! Others claimed that men were taking up golf just to get a chance to get close to the 'objects of their adoration', who were generally to be found on the golf course! (*Golf Illustrated*, July 1894)

May Hezlet was quick to pick up that, by the turn of the century, golf was becoming socially acceptable in polite society. "Among the numerous games that are now being taken up by girls, Golf stands out as the most suitable." She was soon writing a regular advice column in a small ladies' magazine entitled *Madame*, emphasising that as well as being a particularly healthy sport, it could be played all year round – except when there was deep snow! A covering of snow on the North Berwick links on Saturday 17th January 1891, did not, however, deter the keener ladies from finding a way of enjoying a round of golf. While their husbands made heavy weather of playing on the 'snow-clad' links, a ladies' foursome comprising Lady Aymee Clerk, her sister-in-law Lady Napier, and Lady Louisa Hay and her sister-in law, Mrs Wolfe Murray, converted part of the beach into a golf course!

The feature in Golf Illustrated, 'On the Ladies' Links', which reported on women's golf.

ON THE LADIES LINKS

MRS. BOYS writes :—

" Many of the Scottish players remained on in Troon in order to be near Prestwick for the Scottish Championship this week. The Prestwick links adjoin the Troon links. The members of both play the 9 holes out at Troon or Prestwick, as the case may be, and crossing the boundary, play the 9 in holes on the other links, returning in the oon. The Prestwick links were reported to be—by the s who played there in the Scotch and Irish match—more lt than the Troon course. The first four holes on Troon few difficulties, but after those the holes are most sporting set with difficult hazards. The carries were not, however, too or even the medium players.

The short course

As ladies' golf increased in popularity, pressure mounted for separate courses. The setting up of short courses for the ladies could be regarded as a cynical move by the men to get the ladies off the long course; the men's argument was that they held up their play. A good number of the ladies wanted their own course, so that they would not always be subjected to the restrictions imposed on them by the men. The development could therefore be characterised as being 'for the convenience of both persuasions'.

Although ladies' clubs sprang up in quick succession in the 1880s and 90s, the courses laid out on which they could play were rarely up to scratch. St Andrew' Ladies Club, set up in 1867, had failed to move with the times. In 1890, the course was still no more than a glorified putting course. It covered about five acres and the length of holes varied between 40 and 90 yards. There were no long stretches where a lady could practise driving a ball. The rules stated that only a wooden putter could be used there and, given the severe limitation of women's dresses, it was unlikely that any ladies would attempt to use anything else!

Ladies on the long links

The subject of ladies continuing to play on the long links always aroused some comment or other. The North Berwick Green Committee had grown particularly agitated about ladies on the long links when they posted the following threatening notice, which would be regarded as blatant sex discrimination today.

> **"The links authorities here, recognising that the fair sex has a splendid green of their own and that the long course is otherwise sufficiently brisk in the height of the season, have issued the following notice to ladies: ladies are particularly requested to restrict their golf to the Ladies' Links from 10 a.m. till 5 p.m. during the months of July, August and September. If this request is not attended to, all permission to ladies to golf on the private links will be stopped."**
>
> (*Haddingtonshire Courier,* 1893)

The gents dominated play on the long links.

HOURS OF PLAY FOR LADIES, 1903

From 1st November to 31st May, excluding Easter week, ladies must not start between 10 & 11 a.m. and between 1.30 and 2.30 p.m. From 1st June to 31st October, during Easter week and on New Year's Day, the Edinburgh Spring Holiday, Victoria Day and Christmas Day, the ladies are obliged to start before 9 a.m. between 11 a.m. & 1 p.m. and between 3 & 5 p.m.

Anti-female comments laced with sarcasm, appeared all over the golfing press, such as those made by Henry Moncrieff, Lord Wellwood: "If women choose to play at times when male golfers are feeding or resting, no-one can object…at other times… they are in the way."

In April 1900, the North Berwick Green Committee decided that during July, August, September and October, the hours during which the ladies be allowed to start on the long course should be restricted to before 9 o'clock, between 11 & 1 and between 4 & 5. This was to ensure that the men would be able to tee off by 11 o'clock, for their morning round, and that they would be ahead of most of the ladies. The men reckoned this would be more convenient for everyone! Of course, few ladies would be out on the links before 9 o'clock and few, unless they were younger members, would want to start a game at 4, the time for afternoon tea! A short, late morning round would seem one of few workable options, if they wanted to test their skills on the long course and enjoy lunch. In January 1903, the rules, regarding the times ladies were permitted on the links, were amended. They were little better – the attitude seemed to persist that the ladies should be sticking to their own course and allowing them to play on the west links was most certainly under sufferance.

The men tended not to mince their words, as suggested in this comment in Golf Illustrated, 7 September 1900: "When men are everywhere beginning to allow play on their links under certain restrictions, these idiotic women by their bad golf, and worse manners, threaten the existence of a scratch player on long courses."

The next excuse men made against the idea of women golfing was to suggest that the female temperament was unsuited to golf: "She takes an unholy delight in chattering at all points in the game and worries the hardened golfer to distraction by being tremendously amused or delightfully flippant over all her unsuccessful attempts at play." (*Review of the Week, 1893*). Almost every aspect of ladies' golf was pulled apart by the ungracious male golfer. Even when the Ladies' Golf Union produced a handicapping policy, it was sneered at by some of the male golfers, who declared they were mystified by the system: "It is difficult for a mere man to understand how the par scores of ladies' links are arrived at!"

✦ ✦

Writing in the *Pall Mall Gazette* on the Ladies' Championship, Mr. J. L. Low says : " I cannot think there is anything pleasing in the idea of two ladies being pitted against each other in a struggle before three thousand people. Some ladies, but very few, play gracefully. I like to see them driving, when they do not overswing ; I like to see them putting ; and if they would play more with spoons instead of struggling with irons, their game would be happier to watch. I like to see two men well matched wrestling, or boxing, or coming to grips in any struggle of strength and nerve before a big, excited, critical crowd. But women are different, and their position is a false one when they enter the arena. If women wish to compete with each other they should do so in private, on a green where the common spectator is not present to unnerve and excite them."

This view on the Ladies' Championship expressed by one man was not uncommon in the early days of ladies' golf. This appeared in Golf Illustrated in May 1908.

The negativity to women enjoying golf on the same terms as men, didn't come entirely from men. Golfing champion, Amy Pascoe, blurted out in the column 'On the Ladies Links', in *Golf Illustrated*, September 1900:

> **"Someone must speak. Ladies on long links are blocking the course, and, ignorant and neglectful of golfing etiquette, are keeping men on the tee and off the green. Complaints from different clubs have been heard from time to time, but this season a flagrant trespass where the kindness of members allows women a free *entrée*, with the exception of one certain hour and day, obliges me to write against these negligent, stupid and selfish people."**

There were words of advice from the Daily Telegraph correspondent, reported in *Golf Illustrated* in August 1903, that ladies who were playing together without caddies, shouldn't wait until they were asked for permission to pass, but should "promptly accept of their own will what man may be loath to claim as a right"! The Telegraph correspondent appeared to be blinded by the general assumption that women were both slower and worse players than men – and particularly so when they were not accompanied by their (male) caddies. At almost every turn it seemed that women only played over the long course on sufferance of their 'superior' male counterparts.

The following piece which appeared in the *Haddingtonshire Courier* of September 1905, perfectly underlines not only the growing popularity of golf at North Berwick, but also the continuing male prejudice against women golfers, even though attitudes were beginning to soften by that time.

> ***"A Golfing Tale of Woe***
> ***Going over to North Berwick from Edinburgh last year, fairly late in the season, a lady golfer from the south, inexperienced in the crushes of the famous Scottish links, and believing that a full three and a half hours would give her sufficient time to play round the eighteen holes and get lunch, met with a rude awakening. In the first place the ladies were not allowed to start until 11 o'clock, so that she had to watch singles, foursomes and three-ball matches start before her, and, when fairly on the way, she and her partner, who were playing quickly and well, had to wait between every shot and for 5 or 10 minutes on every tee, so that by the time they had played twelve holes, she had to abandon her game and run for the train back to Edinburgh, which she just managed to catch by forfeiting her lunch. This was on a day when the rain was falling all the***

time, and occasionally rather heavily, so the condition of affairs on a fine day is better imagined than described."

Sexism

Sexist put-downs were commonplace and very often appeared in golfing magazines that were targeted at women as well as men. But it was also a habit that when a woman was referred to in the press, she was usually defined by her relationship to her closest male relative. This occurred time and time again. Annie Maxwell was generally introduced as the sister of the great amateur golfer Robert Maxwell and the Anderson girls as the daughters of the Rev. F. L. M. Anderson. When Molly Graham, who hailed from Nairn, but learnt much of her golf at North Berwick, began to emerge as a first class player at her Hoylake Club, the feeling was expressed that:

> **"Miss Graham, a sister of the Hoylake amateur, gives hope that she may some day in the world of ladies' golf, emulate the feat of her distinguished brother in the more serious work confined to the male sex."**

The gents didn't get it all their own way on the golf course. On Tuesday 13th July 1897, Theodora Orr and Annie Maxwell challenged two gentlemen, Captain Sadler and Mr John Menzies, the stationer, to a foursome at North Berwick and easily asserted their golfing superiority. A close match in the morning resulted in the ladies winning 3 up and 1 to play. In the return match in the afternoon, Miss Orr and Miss Maxwell, boosted by their earlier performance, exhibited superb form and soundly beat their opponents – 8 up and 6 to play!

By 1903, even Horace Hutchinson, a well-known English amateur golfer, responsible for the most cutting remarks about lady golfers – such as confining them to the short links, until they can drive beyond 75 yards - was coming round to an acceptance of 'new woman on the links'. In an article published in *Golf Illustrated* (24 July, 1903) he commented on the extent to which attitudes had changed towards women golfing over the previous 30 years: "Thirty years ago women did not play golf; they hardly played anything, except the piano, and that distressingly, and a little croquet with hoops about as narrow as a five barred gate." His acerbic style is still there, but at least he acknowledges the successful revolt of golfing womanhood and that women had proved themselves "worthy of the victory they had won".

Mixed Foursomes

There were relatively few occasions for young people to get together without the girl being carefully chaperoned. Mixed foursomes offered opportunities for discreet flirtations. There was much light-hearted banter about these potential 'sexual' encounters: "The fair one drives the mutual ball into the gorse bush. What an opportunity for her partner, by a brilliant stroke with his 'niblick', to extricate his dear one's, and land it comfortably on a piece of good turf. What girl could resist him after that?" (*Golf Illustrated* p208 vol. vi, 1899). The critics of female golfers also had their say about mixed foursomes – that it was 'peculiarly liable to the error of dawdling'. This was, of course, the fault of the ladies; they played slower than the men and didn't 'stride so rapidly through the greens'.

In spite of some rather negative attitudes, mixed foursomes became a popular fixture on the calendar of most golf clubs. A foursomes' competition for ladies and gentlemen, the Mixed Doubles Tournament, was first introduced as a feature of the North Berwick Ladies' Club at the September meeting in 1890. It was restricted to lady members and honorary gentlemen associates and generally brought out the very best golfers of both sexes. The play, two rounds of the ladies' course, was brisk and competitive. At the inauguration meeting, twenty couples participated and the competition was won by 16 year old Frank Dalziel (eldest son of committee member George Dalziel) and Ada Gillies Smith. The first prize of a gold crescent brooch set in pearls was given by George Dalziel and awarded to the lady of the winning partnership and presented by A.J. Balfour, then Chief Secretary for Ireland. Among the couples was Maud Anderson, one of the Rev F.L. M. Anderson's several daughters, and chartered accountant George Gordon Robertson – they finished well down the field. Perhaps there was more concentration on an attachment growing 'to passion in a very rapid fashion', than holing the ball, as they were joined in matrimony, at St Baldred's Church on 6th January 1891!

THE FREE AND FROLICKING FOURSOME

I know I am not steady
But everyone's the same
And in the club already
I've made myself a name.
I've played in ladies' foursomes
At the peril of my life: -
You know what I'm afraid of, is
That one of those said ladies
Designs to be my wife!

Playing mixed foursomes at North Berwick in the 1920s. The young woman 2nd left is demonstrating one of the new-found freedoms women could enjoy after the First World War – smoking in public!

Health benefits

A report of the annual meeting of the North Berwick Ladies in September 1890, referred to the 'brightness and healthiness' of the participants. There was a clear sense of approval of women engaging in physical activity, whereas not many years before it had been frowned upon and positively discouraged. The supporters of women's golf were strong advocates of its health benefits. It was seen as ideal for women as it gave them the opportunity to exercise a great number of muscles without any over-exertion or strain. Golf was often hailed as a panacea to mend all ills, male and female – it could stave off depression, protect regular players from gout and rheumatism and was a remedy against headaches, heartaches and 'mothers-in-law'. More extreme ideas were put forward that suggested that playing golf had a 'good moral effect', as it was impossible to win a match if one lost one's temper – a sort of notion of Victorian 'anger management'.

Elsie Grant-Suttie and Frances Teacher.

Golf's rising popularity brings more equality?

By 1900, there was a record number of women participating in competitions and tournaments. Yet, while pages of newspapers were devoted to minute details of men's golf, the ladies' game was often not reported. Even the greatest lady golfers of the day were not immune from the narrow mind-set of the press, which ignored the idea that women's golfing achievements might be newsworthy. In June 1911, the *Haddingtonshire Courier* reported Elsie Grant-Sutties's success in winning the Scottish Ladies' Championship at St Andrews in a couple of lines, even after a most exciting final round. It then went on to report, over several column inches, the all-male British Linen Bank's golf competition across the Old Course at St Andrews, which took place the following day, drilling down to details of the problems on the links caused by lack of rainfall.

Elsie Grant-Suttie's golfing talents were given more press recognition in May 1914, when she was battling for a place in the semi-final of the British Ladies' Open at Hunstanton: after being seven times in the bunker and three times in the long grass, she won her match. Sports journalist, Bernard Darwin, commented that Elsie Grant Suttie had the "most wonderful skill in recovery that I ever remember to have seen". He wrote of her:

Elsie Grant-Suttie's medals, presented to NBLGC.

> **"Put an ordinary lady in a bunker you may hope that she will stay there for a season – put Miss Grant-Suttie there and you may thank your stars if she does not lay her ball stone dead – Miss Grant-Suttie's putting was almost as good as her niblick play – an overwhelming combination."**
>
> (Bernard Darwin's report appeared in *Golf Illustrated*, May 1914)

Mary Bradshaw-Isherwood, writing in *Hearth and Home* in February 1894, made a daring suggestion that there was a possibility of a new employment for women – " the new employment that has presented itself to my mind as a suitable one for ladies who desire occupation, or to add to a slender allowance, is that of a Golf professional!" Twenty three year old Mary Isherwood, an enthusiastic golfer, was unlikely herself to be too concerned about a 'slender allowance'; she was brought up in Marple Hall, near Stockport, a member of a prosperous old English family. She belonged, however, to the generation of women who were pushing out the boundaries, to extend their limited role in society. Most respectable upper and middle-class women did not work, unless it was an absolute necessity. In identifying the reasons why women might like to work, she was probably thinking of her own position: possessing a good intellect made women restless, living at home was "deadly dull, unsocial, lonely, vacuous," and women wanted change and a bit of excitement!

Isherwood had raised a strong point - in the early days of golf there were no professional women golfers. Men could make a living from golfing, but not women. It is claimed that a North Berwick woman was among the first to break through this barrier. Helen Maud Anderson, one of the exceptional Anderson sisters, is reputed to have earned a living from teaching golf. In the mid-1890s, she and her husband George Gordon Robertson moved to Mitcham in Surrey, where Helen Maud became a member at the exclusive Princes Ladies' Club. Her sister Blanche moved from North Berwick to Streatham in 1898, to be near her and also joined Princes. Both Blanche and Helen Maud became well-known figures in ladies' golfing tournaments in the south. In 1906, Mrs Gordon Robertson (Helen Maud) is recorded as "The Instructor" attached to Princes Ladies Club. Had she been a spinster, like her sister Blanche, the appointment would not be so exceptional, but in 1906 she was a wife and mother of two children (then aged 11 and 14). It was highly unusual for a married middle-class woman to have any sort of job and the fact that she had children made it quite extraordinary. In Britain, the teaching profession was just opening up to single women and wasn't a possibility for married women until 1944!

Mary Isherwood inspired her generation writing and publishing short stories, which questioned long-held assumptions about women's submissive role. The stories were often centred round the themes of golf and women's lack of freedom to make choices:

"Gradually the young wife found she and her husband did not think alike on many subjects....the divergence between them came to a climax

on the subject of golf. Mrs Brookes adored the royal and ancient game, and was no novice at it.....[but] her husband forbade the subject being mooted or his wife to pursue a game that he declared was foolish folly."

(From *A Duffer of a Husband*, 1895)

Certainly many young married women, from among the prosperous middle classes, would find much that resonated with their experiences. Perhaps the Hon. Gwendolen Balfour, who golfed in North Berwick, was one. The following snippet appeared in the gossip columns of *Golf Illustrated*:

"The Rt. Hon. J. B. Balfour, the Lord Advocate....plays golf, but like his namesake [no relation] his ability is not equal to his enthusiasm. His son, however, is coming forward with a good game and will soon be heard of at North Berwick."

It is interesting and not surprising that the magazine focussed on one of the Lord Advocate's sons, in this case Patrick, rather than his talented daughter. Balfour, raised to the peerage in 1902 as Lord Kinross, had five sons and one daughter. Gwendolen was a sufficiently good golfer to compete on several occasions in the Scottish Ladies' Championships, both before and to a lesser extent after her marriage. As things turned out, Gwendolen was 'heard of' rather more than any of her brothers, because of the rather miserable circumstances surrounding the annulment of her marriage in 1917 (see chapter 5). One might speculate that her insistence on continuing to play competitive golf after marriage was frowned upon by her husband!

On 12 May 1893, *Golf Illustrated* enthusiastically congratulated the ladies on the formation of their Union (the LGU) and the speed with which they had made arrangements for the first Championship competition, which was to be held at St Anne's.

"Those who are fortunate to win the valuable trophy and the four medals will acquire as much fame as if they had graduated at Girton College, Cambridge."

This reference to the first ever ladies' college (founded in 1869) in connection with the first ever ladies' national golf championship reveals much of the attitude towards women making inroads into a male preserve. Although there was state provision for elementary education for girls and boys from 1870, it was the norm for upper and upper-middle-class girls to be educated at home by a governess and then go for a few terms to a finishing school. University education for girls was not considered necessary and just a little vulgar!

Far Left: The ancient kirk at Whitekirk, a few mile south of North Berwick.

Left: The smouldering ruins of Whitekirk, after the severe fire in 1914, which was blamed on the Suffragettes.

But by the early 1900s times were changing! There were many opportunities denied to women, but access to higher education was gradually being prised open. There was an increase in the number of careers on offer – to single women! However, women were still excluded from the political world. In 1897, the National Union of Women's Suffrage Societies (NUWSS), whose members were called Suffragists, campaigned peacefully for women to get the vote, but they were met with intransigent opposition from both sexes. In 1903, Emmeline Pankhurst formed the more dynamic Women's Social and Political Union. Her supporters, known as Suffragettes, were prepared to take violent action to draw attention to women's lack of political rights. They resorted to setting fire to post boxes, burning down churches and vandalising golf courses. They heckled and harried government ministers. Many young golfing women became caught up in this movement. The lettering 'Votes for Women' was cut into the turf of several golf courses. Asquith, who in 1908 was the new Liberal Prime Minister and a regular visitor to the North Berwick links, was a particular target. In August 1913, Asquith was attacked by two suffragettes while golfing at Moray, in north east Scotland. In February 1914, Whitekirk church, a few miles south of North Berwick, was destroyed by fire, in what appeared to be a suffragette outrage. A.J. Balfour's sister-in-law, Frances Balfour, President of the NUWSS, spoke of her horror and sorrow that women could do so much damage to a historic building and to the reputation of their sex. She had a valid point.

The outbreak of war in August 1914, gave women a chance to prove themselves. The suffragettes immediately ceased their militant campaign. Women across the country threw themselves wholeheartedly into the war effort. The members of the North Berwick Ladies' Club were no exception: Rita Gillies Smith, Elsie Grant-Suttie, her cousins Hilda and Ethel Grant-Suttie came forward as Red Cross volunteers and served in the Voluntary Aid

Detachments in northern France. Faith Laidlay channelled her energies into raising funds to provide fresh produce for the Fleet. Blanche Anderson became a driver for the army officers in the south of England. Madge Neill Fraser went out to Serbia with the Scottish Women's Hospitals and died there. Geraldine Blackwood Porter, whose family owned West Lodge in Hamilton Road, North Berwick, received the order of the Red Triangle in recognition of her work with the Y.M.C.A., teaching French to British troops. Her brother Aubrey was killed in October 1915 in France aged 24.

The efforts of these and countless other women challenged many previously-held attitudes. It was little surprise then, at the end of the war in 1918, women got the vote. The first woman to take a seat in parliament was American born Nancy, Lady Astor, elected for Plymouth in 1919. She became prominent as a politician and not just as a wife of a very wealthy man, Waldorf Astor. Nancy was also a keen golfer and did much of her golfing on North Berwick links.

The Great War (1914–18) had propelled women into a situation where they tasted greater freedom and independence, but for most women it was temporary and most appeared content that it was so. They gave up their war-time jobs and returned to domesticity. It is true they adopted new fashions, wore shorter skirts and tighter fitting clothes and had a political voice, but the men remained the main bread-winners and decision-makers. In North Berwick, as in other golfing communities, the gentlemen still sat on the management committee of the Ladies' Golf Club and, although attitudes towards women had softened, the culture of a male-dominated society remained.

Hilda Grant-Suttie (right) in nursing uniform, photographed after the 1914–18 war.

CHAPTER TEN

Notabilities at North Berwick (1920s & 30s)

"Probably no other corner of Scotland attracts so many distinguished visitors in the late summer than North Berwick. Already this attractive East Coast resort contains some interesting personalities – some of them 'regulars' – and it is expecting more as the season advances."

(*Glasgow Herald*, 8 August 1936)

In the first half of the 20th century, North Berwick continued to be a mecca for the rich, the famous, the influential, and the 'bracing centre' of the golfing world. Golfing in North Berwick was largely centred round the leisurely pursuits of the upper classes and the prosperous middle classes and this group maintained their dominance of golfing on the North Berwick links until the Second World War. Noble and well-connected families continued to arrive in town during the summer months and early autumn. They continued to take up residence in the large houses mainly to the west of the town, often having sent their staff ahead a few days earlier to make the necessary preparations. The families still generally travelled up by train. The London to Edinburgh train stopped at Drem, a few miles south of North Berwick, and their chauffeurs, who had driven up ahead, perhaps in the Daimler, would be at the station to greet them.

The Hon. Miriam Pease swinging her club with great verve on the links at North Berwick in 1927.

The Great War (1914-18) interrupted these patterns, but only temporarily. Although people still holidayed and golfed, most Clubs, 'naturally and properly,' decided to suspend competitions for the duration of the war. It hardly seemed right to indulge in such pleasant pastimes, when so many men were experiencing the horrors of trench warfare at the Western Front and in other theatres of action. By September 1914, *The Scotsman* and the *Haddingtonshire Courier* were reporting the deaths of young men who had spent almost every summer of their short lives golfing at North Berwick. Winifred Martin Smith's brother was an early casualty:

> **"Julian Martin Smith, a member of a well-known golfing family has succumbed to a wound received at the front. (Educated at Eton and Cambridge) he was an exceedingly able golfer and he was well-known at North Berwick where he often played."**
>
> (*The Scotsman*, 22 September 1914)

The same report mentioned the serious wounding in action of Lieutenant W.G. Houldsworth, the only son of the Rev & Mrs Houldsworth of Cranston, North Berwick, describing him as a well-known golfer and member of the North Berwick New Club. He died the following day on 23rd September.

The reluctance to be seen to enjoy oneself in the midst of the loss and sufferings of others lasted throughout most of the war. In April 1918, although the Edinburgh Spring Holiday brought over 400 holiday makers to North Berwick, yet *The Scotsman* reported that: "Owing to the war, the golf links had a less animated appearance than usual at holiday time."

The war finally ended in November 1918 and it wasn't long before the press was back at North Berwick, proclaiming the arrival of "Notabilities at North Berwick", who "are devoting much of their time to golf". In spite of the great levelling experiences of the First World War, society remained class-ridden and deferential and although the days of aristocratic ascendancy in the social, political and economic life of Britain were coming to an end, the concept of a high society of wealthy, privileged and influential people still flourished. Its character may have been changing with the influx of an expanding, prosperous middle class, many of whom had made large fortunes during the previous century of industrial development, expanding trade and a growing overseas Empire. North Berwick seemed to hold a unique attraction for this affluent society, with its wonderful golf links, which, in the early days of the game, had been willing and, perhaps in retrospect, far-sighted enough to accommodate ladies as well as men.

The links were popular all year round, but particularly in the late summer and autumn. At the close of the season in October 1927, the *Sunday Post* reported that "Several large villas in the favourite resort have just been let on a lease of from one to two years at rentals varying from £500 to £600 per annum."

PERSONALITIES AT NORTH BERWICK.

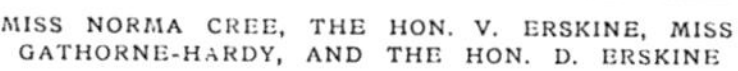

MISS NORMA CREE, THE HON. V. ERSKINE, MISS GATHORNE-HARDY, AND THE HON. D. ERSKINE

MISS PYM, MISS KATHERINE TENNANT, AND LADY HAMBRO

MISS JEAN BAIRD

MISS MABEL LIGHTON, MISS MONTEITH, AND MRS. PELHAM-BURN

MRS. DENNISTOUN

The Tatler and other society magazines delighted in publishing photos of the aristocracy and gentry who graced the links at North Berwick, during the season.

It would seem there was no abatement in the town's popularity. Late summer at North Berwick was largely about 'society' – the leisured classes moved from one venue to the next and North Berwick was just one of a number of fashionable venues to visit and golf was just one of a number of sporting activities to enjoy. Contemporary photographs, however, perfectly portray the reputation of the North Berwick links as one of the hot-spots. Hardly a week passed without snapshots appearing in the *Tatler* or the *Illustrated Sporting and Dramatic News* of society figures posing on the golf course, either as spectators or players, giving weight to the notion that the upper classes held sway on the town's west links. They were photographed lining up at the starter's box, waiting to be given the signal to begin play; they were snapped sitting on the bench at the Redan, waiting to go through; or standing chatting while partners and friends played on. Vivid captions such as *Personalities at North Berwick, Princess plays golf at North Berwick, Debutantes and Drivers*, added to the perception of the glamour of the place. Edinburgh photographer, James Balmain, opened a studio in North Berwick, opposite the station. He sold many of his photographs to society magazines like the *Tatler*.

Princess Helena Victoria regularly graced North Berwick links with her presence during the 1920s. She was a granddaughter of Queen Victoria and rather unkindly nicknamed 'Snipe', because of her rather long nose. She never married. During the golfing season, she chose to stay with her bachelor friend, Sir Courtauld Thomson, at Corner House, Gullane and travel the 4 miles to North Berwick in a chauffeur driven Rolls Royce. In the evenings, they hosted glittering parties for the golfing set. Princess Helena was a popular and active royal and a steady golfer. In 1929, she was appointed patroness of the Ladies' Golf Union.

Princess Helena Victoria and her friend, Edinburgh born Sir Courtauld Thomson golfing at North Berwick in 1927.

There were still references to North Berwick as the *Biarritz of the North*, the fashionable northern watering hole for the elite classes. The North Berwick Old Club still erected a marquee near the home green for its annual meeting, although members arrived in their motor cars rather than their carriages. The Old Club members remained the titled country gentry, but with the addition of a handful of bankers or merchants, who had fulfilled the stiff criteria for acceptance – taste and manners, as well as money. *The Scotsman* continued the habit of announcing the arrival of 'notable' or 'distinguished' visitors engaging in golf at North Berwick, into the 1930s. They might arrive in August and the gentlemen, at least, would leave for the grouse moors in time for the glorious twelfth and return in September. Sometimes they would reappear in October for a short golfing holiday.

LADY BAIRD AND HER DAUGHTER

The wife of Sir David Baird of Newbyth, the 4th baronet and an old "Forty Twa." She is the daughter of Major-General James Davidson, and is seen with her daughter, Jean

MISS SAUNDERSON AND MRS. WYLD

Two of the numerous enthusiasts who are congregated on the famous Scottish links, where the concentration of forces has been bigger than ever this year, and at present shows no sign of demobilisation

MRS. JAMIESON AND HER DAUGHTER, JULIET

Mrs. Jamieson is another familiar figure on the North Berwick links, and her little daughter, Juliet, shows every sign of having inherited the family talent for the great game

'More Snapshots from North Berwick' was the caption in the Tatler, 6th October 1920, to describe these 'distinguished' visitors on the golf links.

JAMES BALMAIN (1853-1937)

James Balmain came to Scotland from Philadelphia in 1873 and carved out a career as a photographer in Edinburgh. After he opened his North Berwick studio in 1914, he capitalised on the popularity of the town as a golfing resort among the rich and famous. He was tipped off as to who had made tee reservations and made sure he was at the Starter's Box to record the event. His son Kenneth later took over the business.

The Hon. Miriam Pease was back on the links in September 1919, after the disruption of war. She arrived, as usual, with her parents – her father was Lord Gainford, secretary to the Treasury in Asquith's government during the war and first Chairman of the BBC, when it was still a company and not a corporation. The upmarket Royal Hotel, situated in close proximity to the station, was the preferred location for Miriam and her parents during their September visits to North Berwick. War had not improved anyone's golf, but it was said that Miriam Pease, renowned for her 'pluck' and 'enthusiasm' kept her hand in by practicing in her garden at Edgebaston, 'with a garden seat for a hazard and a jam pot for a hole'. Unlike most women of her class and generation, she had a career as a Home Office Factory Inspector and after she retired, she took out a membership of the NBLGC and came to live in North Berwick. She had a flat in Tusculum, a large Victorian house in York Road, built and owned by the Cree family, and sub-divided in about 1950. Miriam was a colourful character and became a well-known figure around the town and a member of the town council. She was an ardent golfer, though never particularly successful. She didn't seem to mind – she played because she loved the game.

During August 1920, the Earl and Countess of Buckinghamshire were to be seen on the links enjoying golf with political celebrities such as Herbert and Margot Asquith. Georgiana Wilhelmina, Lady Buckinghamshire, had close ties with North Berwick and had property in the town. Her grandmother was the sister of Sir Hew Dalrymple Hamilton 4th Bart. of Leuchie and her aunt Lady Elizabeth Baillie Duncan owned St. Ann's, a mansion house with beautiful grounds set on edge of the links, and one of the earliest built to the west of the town. On Lady Duncan's death in 1886, her estate and house passed to Georgiana's father and then to Georgiana.

Among the society ladies identified by *The Scotsman* and *The Times*, as enjoying 'the goff' at North Berwick, in September 1920, were Lady Esmé Gordon Lennox, Lady Zia Wernher, Winifred Martin Smith (now Mrs Olaf Hambro) and her sister-in-law Mrs Evan Smith. They were rich and privileged and appeared to lead charmed lives: but it was not always the case. Hermione Frances Gordon-Lennox, daughter of Baron de Ramsey, was part of the London set who golfed regularly at North Berwick during the season. She had been married in 1909 to Lord Esmé Charles Gordon-Lennox and given a house in Eaton Square by her father. By 1920, her marriage was in difficulty; her husband, an officer in the Scots Guards, had been twice seriously wounded during the war and Hermione detected a change in his mood and attitude towards her. He hated London and society life and as a consequence, she

Margot Asquith and her half-sister Katherine Tennant enjoying golf on the links.

often travelled without him. In May 1923, she brought an action for divorce against him, on the grounds of his desertion. By the end of the year both had remarried. Lady Zia Wernher's family were frequent visitors and avid golfers, and indeed the war had not curtailed their golfing pursuits. Lady Zia's father, Grand Duke Michael, a cousin of the Russian Tsar, had been exiled for eloping with her mother, Sophie von Merenburg, (later styled Countess Torby), a minor Russian aristocrat, and marrying her without the Tsar's approval. The family would arrive in North Berwick with a huge retinue of servants and insist on lessons from no-one but Ben Sayers. The Grand Duke would play in shirt sleeves, with a specially made golf club with a shaft as thick a cricket bat handle! He always thought he was rather splendid at golf: Ben Sayers thought otherwise.

Winifred Martin Smith, or Mrs Hambro as she had become in 1917, had been the darling of both London society and the golfing world before the war, with her wealth, beauty, poise and marvellous talent on the golf course. Her father Martin Ridley Smith was a well-known and wealthy Lombard Street banker. The family home was the Warren in Hayes, Kent, which Martin Smith had taken on a long lease from another North Berwick golfing regular, financier Walter De Zoete. Martin Smith was a great philanthropist and was said to entertain over a thousand people every year at the Warren. Winifred, and one of her sisters, Sybil, married into the Hambro banking family, who also lived at Hayes. The Hambros owned Hayes Place, the mansion house with a great political rather than sporting provenance. It was built in the 1750s by

William Pitt the Elder (twice prime minister), and where his son, William Pitt the Younger (Britain's youngest ever PM at the age of 24, in 1783) was born. Pitt the Younger died overwhelmed by debt – not so the patriarch of the Hambro family, Sir Everard, who was one of the wealthiest and most successful international bankers of his generation. He and Lady Hambro (she was his second wife and years younger) joined the other society golfers in North Berwick in September during the 1920s and 30s.

Winifred Hambro had been a member of the NBLGC since she was a young girl (see chapter 6) and her talent had given her a place in the English International team and she reached the semi-final of the British Ladies' Open in 1914. She gave up serious competition after her marriage, but she continued to play for Sussex County and won the Sussex Women's Championship in 1929. In August 1932, during the weeks before the family made their annual visit to North Berwick, Winifred, her husband Olaf and their two young sons were staying at the Glendoe shooting lodge, near Fort Augustus, in the Scottish Highlands. On the afternoon of 28th August the family was enjoying a trip in a speed boat on Loch Ness, when the boat burst into flames. In the chaos that ensued, they jumped off the boat and attempted to swim ashore. Olaf and the boys made it, but Winifred, a strong swimmer, collapsed, disappeared under the water and was drowned. The boys' governess, who was with them, stayed aboard the boat and survived. The mood of gaiety on the North Berwick links was muted that September.

Redcroft Hotel.

Royal Hotel.

The Hambros tended to stay at the Marine, which was perceived as the grandest hotel in town. There were, however, plenty of other good hotels for 'visiting dignitaries' and they had a greater appeal for short stays than having to go through the cumbersome process of renting a house. Sir Victor and Lady Warrender and the Wernhers were ardent fans of the Redcroft Hotel, a stone's throw from the station, with its half a dozen excellent tennis courts for alternative recreation; the Speirs and their party preferred the more formal atmosphere of the Royal, while the Meysey Thomsons, Lady Wemyss and Lord and Lady Knaresborough were happier with the quiet seclusion offered by Bradburys.

The impact of so many high profile families visiting North Berwick provoked much discussion. There was a feeling, that those who rented or bought a house, for the purpose of holidaying in North Berwick, made a tangible contribution to the burgh's social and economic life, while the hotel visitors breezed in and out, and merely embraced the status that a visit to the famous resort afforded and bestowed little or nothing of value on the community. This idea is expressed in the following extract from *The Times*, 8th September, 1924:

"The hotel population forms hardly more than an accidental contribution to society. It is the semi-residents who are the backbone of the community: the people who own houses, or take them for the summer, or who return to the same lodgings in the little grey town year after year. In them, North Berwick has a closely-knit, and by no means unfashionable, society of its own, independent of the ebb and flow of hotel guests. It is an extremely pleasant society to be admitted to."

Mrs Isabelle Turnbull, Betty Lampson, Eileen Tweedie and Evelyn Baird waiting for their tee time, c.1930.

The view can be easily challenged; many 'semi-residents', such as Harry and Kate Armitage, stayed at the Marine on their initial visit to North Berwick, before taking the decision to buy a house. The Tennants, even with two 10-bedroomed houses in the town, had so many family members and friends who enjoyed golfing that it would have been impossible to have them all as house guests. The Hambros and Martin Smiths may have formed part of the hotel population, but they golfed on the links here 'year after year' and were members of one or other of the town's golf clubs, thus, it could be argued, forming part of that 'pleasant society'. The many socialites who came to golf who were not club members, nevertheless reinforced the notion that golf was the main business of the town.

In September 1928, the 'notables' at North Berwick included the Earl of Wemyss, Lord and Lady O'Brien, Sir John and Lady Lavery, Sir William and Lady Pulteney, Lady Angela Forbes, Sir George and Lady Clerk, Captain Fitzroy, Speaker of the House, Sir David and Lady Kinloch and Miss Joyce Wethered. The list is interesting. Sir John Lavery (1856-1941) was a well-known society painter and friend of the Asquiths and spent time with them at North Berwick, but more usually was guest of Patrick Ford, M.P. at Wester Dunes, the mansion house he built in 1908, overlooking the 7th green. Lavery's first wife had died in 1891 shortly after giving birth to their daughter Eileen. He later married a strikingly beautiful Irish-American, Hazel Martyn (1986-1935), whom he painted on innumerable occasions. He also painted a series of pictures of the links at North Berwick, the most famous of which was for many years said to feature Nancy Astor. In recent times, this has been disproved. When a layer of backing paper was removed from the painting, the caption with the true identity of the figures in the painting was revealed. The young woman golfing is Lavery's 15 year old step-daughter Alice Trudeau, (who became Mrs Alice Gwynn) and the man and woman seated watching are Herbert Asquith and Lavery's wife Hazel. Two other figures are identified in the painting – Patrick Ford and his wife Jessie.

Top: The Golf Links, North Berwick, 1921.

Bottom: The caption on the reverse of the Lavery painting, North Berwick Links, which confirms the identity of the golfing girl.

Extract from a letter written by Alice Gwynn, Lavery's step daughter:

"You ask about the golfing picture. It was done at North Berwick, Scotland, we went to stay there every autumn with Sir Patrick Ford who was MP for Edinburgh at that time. They had a lovely house Westerdunes... [My father] sent for his paints the week after we arrived and [asked] me to pose for a figure in the foreground..."

Patrick Ford was the son of an immensely successful Leith Wine and Spirit merchant, James Ford, who left a large fortune to be shared between his five surviving children, when he died in 1905. Patrick used part of his inheritance to build Wester Dunes with its magnificent 4 acres of grounds, for himself and his new wife Jessie Field, as a holiday home. Their main residence was a huge property at 8 Moray Place, Edinburgh. Patrick was called to the Bar in 1907, but after the war, swapped the legal profession for politics and was MP for Edinburgh North from 1920 until he retired in 1935. The Fords had a wide range of interests in art and drama, they were great entertainers and social golfers, but neither of them appears to have been a member at North Berwick for any length of time.

Whenever Nancy Astor did appear on the links at North Berwick the photographers were out in force. She always attracted a crowd of onlookers who followed her play across the course. On one occasion, at least, at the end of her game, she dropped to the ground, and retaining her poise, delighted the gathering by signing her autograph for anyone who managed to get close enough. She was observed playing a single, over the 'Old Course' one Saturday afternoon in February 1924, with Ben Sayers' son George, who was by then the pro at the Merion Club in Philadelphia. George was on a visit to North Berwick to see his father who was terminally ill with stomach cancer and who died three weeks later on 9th March.

BEN SAYERS (1857-1924)

Ben Sayers' golfing achievements are legendary. Sayers, from his humble background, could play golf – he was brilliant at it. He never won the Open but tied for 2nd place in 1888 and took 3rd in 1889. He was regarded as one of the best professional golfers of his day. He set up a business making golf balls and then clubs, and he established his credentials as a great teacher of golf. He had a lucky break when

Edward VII, on his historic visit to North Berwick in October 1903, requested a meeting with Sayers to pick his brains about the subtleties of the game and commissioned a set of Sayers' golf clubs. After this, Sayers was able to charge out for lessons to the most elevated members of society. He realised the potential for teaching the wives, daughters, nieces etc. of the aristocratic and well-to-do gentlemen who were already confident in their game. They didn't mind a bit of extra coaching from Sayers, and it perhaps satisfied their vanity that they were employing one of the best professional golfers, who had received the seal of approval from no less a person than the King.

Nancy Tennant leaving Ben Sayers' shop, 1926. During his lifetime, Ben Sayers prided himself on teaching some who became golfers of note, e.g. Elsie Grant-Suttie. He had patrons among members of the Royal family and aristocracy – several women among them.

Sir William and Lady Pulteney started golfing at North Berwick after the end of the war and remained members of the New Club and the Ladies' Club, respectively, for many years. Sir William had married Jessie Arnott, the daughter of an Irish industrialist, in 1917, when he was 56 and she 40. They had no children. Sir William had had a long and successful military career, serving in various posts in the British Empire. During the 1914-18 war he was promoted to Lieutenant-General. Unfortunately, he was said to have distinguished himself by his incompetence in the field. Criticisms of First World War generals are often harsh, but many of them, fine soldiers like Sir William, lacked modern military training and became involved in decisions which had disastrous consequences for the fighting men on the Western Front. He was saved from disgrace by influential friends and in 1920 he was appointed Black Rod to the House of Lords, a position he retained until his death at the age of 80 in 1941.

Left: The Hon. Lady Clerk (front row rt.) with other members of the Ladies' Club after the Spring Meeting, April 9, 1930.

Far left: The Speaker, Captain Edward Fitzroy and Mrs Fitzroy walking along the coast at North Berwick, 1930s.

Sir George and Lady Clerk were following family tradition golfing at North Berwick. The Clerks of Penicuik, male and female, had been club members for decades. In September 1928, Sir George's 80 year old mother Aymée, the Dowager Lady Clerk, was already installed at Lyndhurst, in Melbourne Road, for the golfing season, 'with maid'! Sir George's wife, the Hon. Lady Clerk, (formerly Honor Dutton) often took part in the Club tournaments in the 1920s and 30s. The day she was photographed at the Spring Meeting (above), she must have had a disastrous round, for even with a handicap of 36, she made no return.

Edward Algernon Fitzroy (1869–1943), second son of Baron Southampton and directly descended from an illegitimate son of Charles II, was a Conservative member of parliament for over forty years and was elected Speaker of the House of Commons in 1928. He and his wife Muriel Douglas Pennant were regular visitors to North Berwick after the war, and were great friends of Sir Hew and Lady Hamilton-Dalrymple.

Miss Joyce Wethered's appearance at North Berwick always grabbed the interest of the press as she had already won the British Ladies' Open Championship on three occasions, in 1922, 1924 and 1925 and the English Ladies' for five consecutive years between 1920 and 1924. Indeed, she won the British title for the fourth time in 1929 at St Andrews. Her record was unsurpassed. She enjoyed playing at North Berwick and particularly so in the late 1920s and early thirties during her romance and short engagement to Major Cecil Hutchison, a Scottish International golfer and a member of the New Club since 1904. They were long-standing friends, though there was a considerable age gap; Joyce was 31 and Cecil 54. They became engaged in November 1931, to the delight of the golfing world, but broke it off suddenly the following March. Joyce continued to visit Scotland after she had given up championship golf and was snapped in June 1935 as a spectator at the Open at Muirfield. The following year, she married Sir John Heathcoat Amory, chairman of the famous Victorian Devon lace-making business, J. Heathcoat & Co., and a great amateur sportsman.

Joyce Wethered enjoying the Open at Muirfield in 1935.

The Earl of Wemyss, mentioned in the press report as a North Berwick visitor in September 1928, was the 11th Earl, Francis the 10th Earl having died in 1914 at the fine age of 96. The 11th Earl was not accompanied by his wife, Lady Wemyss, but unofficially in the company of Lady Angela Forbes, whose name appeared in the newspaper article further down the list. There is no hint of public scandal in the report, but in fact the Earl and Angela Forbes had conducted an intimate relationship for many years, which was well-known within the family circle. Hugo Charteris, the fourth, but eldest surviving son of the 10th Earl had married the languorously beautiful but reluctant Mary Wyndham in 1883, when he was styled Lord Elcho. Mary had pleaded with

Mrs Lubbock (seated centre) Margot Asquith (2nd right) and ladies gathering by the starter's box .

her father for the marriage not to go ahead and it was never happy from the start. By 1928, while Lady Angela was installed with Hugo at the Wemyss family seat, Gosford, Mary Wemyss was content to stay at Harestanes, a small house on the edge of the Kilspindie golf course. Over the years in the private correspondence she shared with A. J. Balfour, she wrote fondly of golfing at North Berwick and as the years went on, she commented ruefully on the dwindling opportunities for golfing:

> **"I suppose the number of Septembers in which I shall be able to play golf at N. Berwick is now getting pretty small and one week out of four seems a formidable fraction."**

Mary Wemyss had been a part of the golfing expeditions to North Berwick since the early days of her marriage to Hugo in 1883. She was very often in the company of her great friends and contemporaries the five older Tennant sisters, the daughters of Sir Charles Tennant's first marriage. Those days had passed; war had intervened and had robbed Mary of two of her sons and the Tennant family of several of their young men. By 1920s only two of the older Tennant

6

7

8

9

10

sisters were alive: Lucy, then in her 60s and the widow of a Wiltshire landowner, Thomas Graham Smith, and Margot Asquith, who was in her late 50s. Lucy was crippled with arthritis and it was Margot, slim, reasonably fit and full of energy, who was still golfing. Margot was often photographed in the company of her much younger half-sisters Peggy, Katherine and Nancy, who were still in their twenties and their mother Marguerite Lubbock. Widowed in 1906, Marguerite, Lady Tennant, had married Major Geoffrey Lubbock and had two sons by him, Peter and David. Marguerite Lubbock remained one of the central figures of the NBLGC in the 1920s and 30s, until her death in 1943.

In September 1926 and 1927, the 'semi-resident' Tennant/Lubbock ladies were out in force on the links with visiting friends. Among the group were: Lady Barbara and Lady Mary Bingham, daughters of the 5th Earl of Lucan; their cousin Phyllis Spender-Clay, whose mother was Pauline Astor, sister-in-law of Nancy Astor; and Lady Mary Thynne, daughter of the 5th Marquess of Bath.

The weather in the east of Scotland is variable at the best of times, but September is usually a good month. September 1926 was apparently the warmest since 1821, with temperatures reaching into the 70s (degrees fahrenheit) on some days. Photographs taken of the ladies show most of them wearing close-fitting cloche hats, tweed skirts and knitted cardigans - but of course, the North Berwick links are notorious for sharp, cold winds whipping off the sea, at any time of year. Although fashions had become much more relaxed in the 1920s, conventions were still observed and ladies would not go out in public unless they were appropriately dressed and well-covered up. Skirts were much shorter, but still well below the knee, and full, or fitted over the hips with inverted pleats for ease of movement. Even golfing, however, allowed for a string a pearls to be worn around the neck.

There were a number of contemporaries of Katherine Tennant, who had been swinging their clubs on the links from childhood. In the early 1920s, they were to be found battling against each other in competitions like the Cree Medal, held annually on the ladies' links for children aged between 7 and 14. In August 1920, it was won by Olive Teacher, the younger half-sister of Frances Teacher. The first handicap prize of £1 was won by twelve year old Eileen Tweedie. (The boys, it has to be said, didn't seem to shine in this event!) The following August, Eileen won the Cree Medal and in 1922, aged 14, was playing in the Ladies' Gold Medal competition where she picked up the third handicap prize. Eileen's father owned Edradour, a villa overlooking the links and the family were regular visitors to North Berwick during the 1920s and 30s. They golfed, they sailed, they played tennis and they socialised. Eileen was an excellent golfer, with a swing as graceful as it was powerful. She played

Golfing ladies at North Berwick in the 1920s and 30s from the previous pages:

1. Phyllis Spender-Clay, Sept 1926.

2. Eileen Tweedie & Evelyn Coats stride out on the links.

3. Players and spectators from l. to r. Joan Peck, Evelyne Grahame, Patrick Adam and Mrs Lampson

4. Barbara Bingham, Mary Thynne, Mary Bingham, Sept 1926.

5. Nancy Tennant driving off from the 14th tee, on North Berwick West Links, 1927.

6. At North Berwick, 1930. From left, Winifred Clark, Mr Illingworth, Edith Laurie and Sir Algernon Rumbold.

7. Barbara Wyld in full swing.

8. Mary Thynne taking a putt, 1926.

9. Gathering at the 1st tee, Eileen Tweedie centre and James Waterlow (rt).

10. Golfing at Archerfield, 1926 l. to r. Peggy Loder, Nancy Tennant, Margot Asquith and Katherine Tennant.

in almost every Club Medal and tournament until her marriage in 1940 to Gervase Riddell-Carre and was a great asset to the Ladies' Club, becoming Lady Captain in about 1937.

Right: Eileen Tweedie golfing with friends at North Berwick c.1930.

Far right: Betty Rumbold and Evelyn Baird.

Eileen was often photographed golfing in those years with friends and contemporaries - Violet and Sheila Grahame, Betty Rumbold, Mary Berry, Rosemary Hope Vere, Betty Lampson, Dione Jamieson, Evelyn Baird, Mary Martin Smith, Peggy Hambro, Joan, Diana and Barbara Wyld, Barbara Steele, Pam and Lara Deuchar, Evelyn Coats, Angela and Priscilla Couper, Edith and Sheila Lawrie. They were all much of an age and all shared a love of golf. With their air of confidence, privileged lifestyle and talent, they defined the membership of the North Berwick Ladies' Club during that era.

Diana, Sybil and Lulu Esmond joined the other youngsters in competitions on the ladies' course. Their father Edward Esmond (1874–1945), a wealthy Parisian race horse owner and sportsman, purchased the stylish Lorimer house, Marly Knowe, set on the rise to the south of the town, in about 1920. The family would arrive in North Berwick every summer, with many servants and a great deal of luggage. Edward Esmond was keen for his daughters to golf as well as anyone else, and he employed pro golfer Henry Cotton to come to North Berwick to give them lessons. They also received lessons from another pro, George Duncan. It paid off; all three girls became exceptional golfers, but particularly Diana and Lulu. In 1926 Diana, aged 17, won the Girls' British Open Championship at Stoke Poges. In 1928, she was runner-up in the French Ladies' Amateur Championship. In August 1936, Lulu Esmond, brought her fiancée, Baron Geoffroy de Waldner de Freundstein to North Berwick. They were spotted striding across the course: "he in a wind-resisting beret and warm pullover and she in a heavy-weight checked skirt fashioned on the cross." Perhaps it was a cool summer. They were married in Paris in October. Lulu Esmond gave up golf after the war to take up gardening for which she then became famous. She entertained everyone with her great sense of humour. Her caddy Lawrie Lumsden used to say he was paid with a chocolate bar!

Edmond Esmond (seated 4th left) with his daughters on the links.

Edward Esmond became a popular figure in North Berwick. He was renowned for his generosity. He inaugurated a tennis event at the Redcroft Hotel and presented a handsome silver trophy for the competition. He gifted an elaborate silver trophy to the artisan Bass Rock Club. It is still played for every year in July. His granddaughter, Isabelle de Waldner, continued the family connection with golf and North Berwick, by returning to North Berwick whenever possible each July, to present the trophy to the winner. Ella Vlandy, who joined the Ladies' Club in the 1930s recalls Diana and Lulu playing golf: "They were both exceptional golfers, she recalls, and graceful with it." Ella's parents owned the Redcroft Hotel and Ella was invited by the Esmonds to take part in a putting match on the lawn at Marly Knowe, after which there was a splendid tea. Sir John Simon and Lady Simon were guests of the Esmonds. John Simon, an eminent Liberal politician was Foreign Secretary at the time. Ella was a shy teenager, but recalled with great clarity at the age of 102, in 2016, how incredulous she thought it was that the Esmonds were so inclusive of her. She never forgot their kindness.

By the starters box from l. to r. Mary Hill-Walker, Mrs Martin-Smith, Barbara Gordon-Lennox, Betty Lampson and Eileen Tweedie.

Betty Lampson was one of Eileen Tweedie's regular golfing partners and a friend. Betty's great-grandfather, Sir Curtis Lampson, an American fur merchant who was involved in early attempts to establish the first transatlantic telegraph cable, had been Depute Governor of the Hudson Bay Company in the 1860s and had created much of the family's wealth. Although Betty was brought up in Chelsea, her grandmother, Helen Blackburn was a Scot and her father and his siblings were born at Killearn House in Stirlingshire. It was probably the Scottish connection which led to the golfing holidays in North Berwick. As a young woman Betty travelled to more exotic locations. In 1933 she visited her much-loved uncle Sir Miles Lampson in China, where he was British Minister and in 1934 went to Egypt when he took up the post of High Commissioner and then Ambassador. She later married a diplomat John Rayner and spent time overseas.

During the late 1920s and 1930s, many of these 'bright young things' married. In April 1934, Marguerite Lubbock's daughter, Katherine Tennant, married Cabinet Minister, Walter Elliot, at St Baldred's Church in North Berwick. It was reported that a large crowd gathered to watch the arrival of the bride. Katherine was a popular figure in the town and that was reflected in the guest list that included many members of the local community with whom she had regular dealings. She had recently been elected the first female Vice President of the North Berwick Burns' Society and her proposer Willy Struth, the butcher, received an invitation. Many of her guests were members of the NBLGC, including Elsie Grant-Suttie and the rather elderly Misses Gillies Smith, the acclaimed golfing sisters of the early days of the Ladies' Club.

Kathleen Tennant's wedding.

For many of the regular young golfing ladies, marriage meant ties with North Berwick were broken, but a remarkable number retained their connections with the town and their membership of the Club. The descendants of the Tweedies, the Tennants, the de Zoetes, the Wylds, the Steeles, the Lawries and the Coupers still return to North Berwick to golf. It is of course a very different place, but the enjoyment of a round of golf on the links today doubtless holds good.

Barbara Wyld, daughter of Marion Wyld and granddaughter of Eulalie Houldsworth, one of the first lady golfers at North Berwick, married David Hely-Hutchinson son of 6th Earl of Donoughmore in June 1934, and continued the family tradition of supporting the NBLGC with the birth of five daughters. The youngest, Deborah, remembers the annual summer excursion to Scotland in the 1950s. They would arrive at Whitsun and stay at Cranston, their holiday house on West Bay Road. In mid-August their father would disappear up north to the grouse moors and return for golf in September. Mrs Hely-Hutchinson was left in charge of the household, setting up accounts in the grocers, the butchers etc. and organising regular deliveries to the house. When their father was there, or their parents were entertaining, the five sisters had meals with their Nanny in a separate room and according to Deborah almost always ate lobster!

The Hely-Hutchinson girls. Rose, Jean, Kate, Deborah and Poll c.1953.

Sybil Steele and her daughter Barbara with a friend on the links in the 1930s.

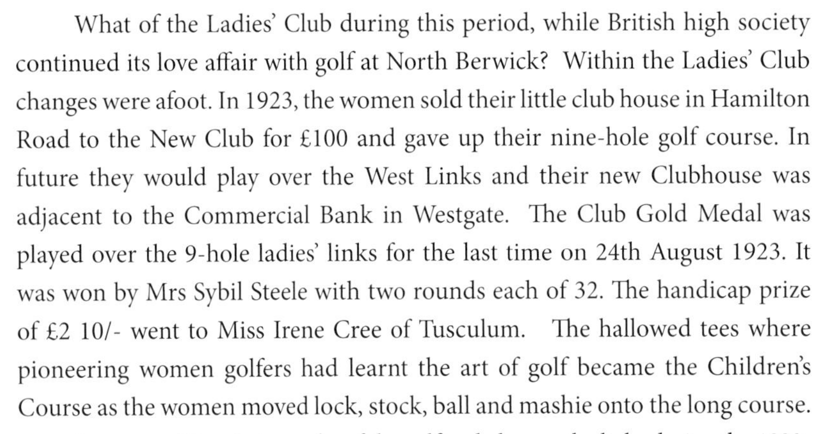

What of the Ladies' Club during this period, while British high society continued its love affair with golf at North Berwick? Within the Ladies' Club changes were afoot. In 1923, the women sold their little club house in Hamilton Road to the New Club for £100 and gave up their nine-hole golf course. In future they would play over the West Links and their new Clubhouse was adjacent to the Commercial Bank in Westgate. The Club Gold Medal was played over the 9-hole ladies' links for the last time on 24th August 1923. It was won by Mrs Sybil Steele with two rounds each of 32. The handicap prize of £2 10/- went to Miss Irene Cree of Tusculum. The hallowed tees where pioneering women golfers had learnt the art of golf became the Children's Course as the women moved lock, stock, ball and mashie onto the long course.

In many of the photographs of the golfing ladies on the links during the 1920s and 30s, the young caddies can be seen hovering in the background. After the Second World War, all that changed; caddies were few on the ground and ladies had to get used to carrying their clubs. When it was pouring with rain, they had to cope with water-proofs and dripping umbrellas, as well as slippery grips on their clubs. It was hard-going for keen players; the caddies had been a feature of the ladies' game since the early days of the club and every self-respecting lady golfer employed a caddy.

Two young caddies hover in the background of this photo of Nancy Tennant and Mrs Geoffrey Lubbock c.1929.

Lady golfers waiting at the Redan. From left: Katherine Tennant; Lady Oxford (Margot Tennant); Lady Dorothy MacMillan; Mrs Sylvester Gates (neé Tennant); Lady Constance Hatch; Mrs Geoffrey Lubbock. This photograph by Balmain appeared in the Tatler 16 Oct 1929.

Relinquishing the Ladies' Course marked the end of an era for North Berwick's golfing ladies. For over thirty years it had symbolised the presence of women's golf in the town, during which time, the women had established themselves as a driving force in the development of the ladies' game. The nine-hole course had been comfortable and convenient, but by the 1920s, most women were choosing to play over the West Links. They had outgrown their short course. The Ladies' Club, of course, continued and membership was prized in the world of women's golf. The running of the Club became more democratic, as the men stepped back and the women took up positions on the Committee.

It was not just a question of the gentlemen giving way to the ladies, the exclusivity of this golfing paradise was slowly breaking down. In September 1939, war intervened once again and gaiety and golf were suspended at North Berwick and across the entire country. Britain was consumed by the Second World War for six long years. When it was over and normal daily life resumed, there were strong indications that society was changing. There was a fundamental shift in public attitudes and a desire for greater equality in society and a denting of class divisions. The post war years brought a visible affluence to the majority of the population in the 1950s. People had spare cash to enjoy leisure pursuits. Activities such as golfing and being a member of a golf club were, for the first time, within the reach of most working men – and women!

CHAPTER ELEVEN

Striking Change

"I would only like to add that I trust the proposed amalgamation with the New Club may prove a success and eventually put both Clubs in a more favourable position than they are at present. I'm afraid I have doubts."

(Extract of letter from John Cook, Trustee, NBLGC to Miss Millicent Couper, Hon. Sec. NBLGC, 29 October, 1934)

In the dining room of the North Berwick Clubhouse, gilded wooden boards with the names of past Lady Captains and Club Champions, hang above the old lockers, which line two sides of the room. The roll call of Lady Captains is strangely incomplete; a list of a dozen names in alphabetical order come under the collective dates 1919 to 1950, before the list takes on a conventional appearance, starting in 1950-51 with... *Miss M J Couper*.... and continuing to the present day. The problem for the NBLGC is that there are few records before 1950. There is no definitive evidence to say who was appointed the first Lady Captain of the Club, or when that event occurred. It is certain that the club was run by a committee of gentlemen until after the First World War, but it would appear that no Minute Book from the Ladies' Club survives from the early period. Even after the ladies took over the running of the club, there is a frustrating lack of documentation until 1969.

By chance, one small, but important, relic of the NBLGC's past history has been preserved. In 1967, a Mr Campbell Davidson got in touch with the Club in order to present it with a first edition of *History of the Scottish Ladies Golfing Association*, 1903-1928, published in 1928, to celebrate the Association's first 25 years. He explained that his gesture was in memory of his great aunt, who was the golfing champion Dorothy Campbell. The book was received with

Catriona Matthew, one of Scotland's great women golfers, encouraging a rising North Berwick golf star, Clara Young.

thanks. But there was something more, for clipped inside the front cover was a small strip cut from a postcard: on one side most of a halfpenny stamp bearing Edward VII's head and on the reverse, Dorothy Campbell's signature.

Presented to North Berwick Golf Club (Ladies Section) in memory of my grand aunt Mrs Dorothy Campbell Hurd by G. Campbell Davidson. 15th August 1967.

Other more substantial relics of the Ladies' Club's history survive in the form of trophies and medals, presented over the years by individuals who wished to support the Club; commemorate an important event; or preserve the memory of one of the Club's great golfers. The Scratch Medal, played for in the opening season of the North Berwick Ladies' Golf Club in summer 1888 and won by Margaret Gillies Smith, was commissioned by Sir Walter Hamilton Dalrymple, who had done so much to encourage the founding of the club. The medal was made by the renowned Edinburgh jeweller, Mr Inches, in his premises on Princes Street. It was the size and twice the thickness of a crown piece and of solid silver, gilted. On the reverse side was a copy of an old print of the Bass Rock and the front bore a copy of the ancient arms of the Douglas family, copied from a seal which had been discovered on the sea shore at North Berwick in 1737, with the legend 'Sigilum Wilhelmi dei de Douglas' – the seal of William Lord of Douglas. Local legend supports the origin of the seal; in 1735, three coffins were apparently washed away from the old kirk burial ground on the promontory by the harbour and one of these was said to have contained the remains of Earl Douglas. Such symbolism firmly roots the Ladies' Club as an established feature of the Burgh's heritage.

Dorothy Campbell's signature cut off a postcard, probably sent to one of her siblings between 1902 and 1910.

In the early days of the club, apart from the prestigious scratch medal, an assortment of desirable prizes were donated for each competition. At the Ladies' Club autumn gathering on 24 August 1889, Benjamin Hall Blyth presented a gold brooch as 1st handicap prize. There was a gold bangle as 2nd prize, a silver pin tray as a 3rd, a set of gold sleeve-links as a 4th and for the 5th successful contestant, William Bloxsom, the Club Secretary, gifted half a dozen pairs of gloves – girls wore a different pair of gloves for every occasion in those days! It made it worthwhile for any golfing girl, anxious about competing against the formidable North Berwick 'cracks', to enter the competition on the off-chance she might play a decent round and take home a nice piece of jewellery to wear for the next county ball. It is said that these high value prizes attracted 'trophy hunters', but there is not a great deal of evidence of this at North Berwick. However, the Campbell sisters, the Anderson sisters and the Gillies Smith sisters must have pocketed a cache of pretty pieces of gold and silver collectibles in their day.

The North Berwick Lady Captains' board in the present clubhouse.

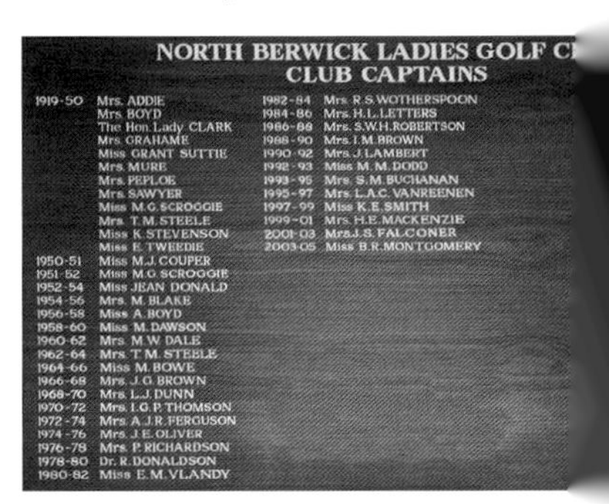

NORTH BERWICK LADIES GOLF C

CLUB CAPTAINS

1919-50	Mrs. ADDIE	1982-84	Mrs. R.S.WOTHERSPOON
	Mrs. BOYD	1984-86	Mrs. H.L.LETTERS
	The Hon. Lady CLARK	1986-88	Mrs. S.W.H.ROBERTSON
	Mrs. GRAHAME	1988-90	Mrs. I.M.BROWN
	Miss GRANT SUTTIE	1990-92	Mrs. J.LAMBERT
	Mrs. MURE	1992-93	Miss M.M.DODD
	Mrs. PEPLOE	1993-95	Mrs. S.M.BUCHANAN
	Mrs. SAWYER	1995-97	Mrs. L.A.C. VANREENEN
	Miss M.G.SCROGGIE	1997-99	Miss K.E.SMITH
	Mrs. T.M.STEELE	1999-01	Mrs. H.E.MACKENZIE
	Miss K.STEVENSON	2001-03	Mrs.J.S.FALCONER
	Miss E.TWEEDIE	2003-05	Miss B.R.MONTGOMERY
1950-51	Miss M.J.COUPER		
1951-52	Miss M.G.SCROGGIE		
1952-54	Miss JEAN DONALD		
1954-56	Mrs. M. BLAKE		
1956-58	Miss A.BOYD		
1958-60	Miss M.DAWSON		
1960-62	Mrs. M.W.DALE		
1962-64	Mrs. T.M.STEELE		
1964-66	Miss M.BOWE		
1966-68	Mrs. J.G.BROWN		
1968-70	Mrs. L.J.DUNN		
1970-72	Mrs. I.G.P.THOMSON		
1972-74	Mrs. A.J.R.FERGUSON		
1974-76	Mrs. J.E.OLIVER		
1976-78	Mrs. P.RICHARDSON		
1978-80	Dr. R.DONALDSON		
1980-82	Miss E.M.VLANDY		

In June 1902, North Berwick Ladies' Club held a tournament under the special title of a 'Coronation meeting', to celebrate Edward VII's accession to the throne. For the first time, a silver cup – the Coronation Cup – was offered as the scratch prize. Several 'front-rank' players, including the three redoubtable Gillies Smith sisters, took part. The competition was keen, but Rita Gillies Smith out-played her 29 rivals to lift the trophy with a score of 62 for two rounds of the Ladies' Course.

The presentation of silver cups, or Quaichs, became increasingly common and gradually replaced the tradition of valuable prizes being offered by generous donors for each match. In 1914 a silver Quaich was presented to Frances Teacher, as runner-up in the Scottish Ladies' Golf Championships held that year at Muirfield. The Quaich was for keeps and so didn't have to be handed back in time for the competition the following year and today is a Teacher family heirloom.

Left: The silver Quaich awarded to North Berwick golfer Frances Teacher in 1914, is still held by her descendants.

Right: The Dalziel Rose Bowl presented to the Ladies' Club by George Dalziel one of the original committee members of the NBLGC.

The Dalziel Rose Bowl was presented in 1913, by George Dalziel, one of the original committee members of the Ladies' Club. It was to be played for at the Gold Medal Autumn Meeting of the North Berwick Ladies' Club over the West Links and was awarded as the first handicap prize. The first recipient was Mrs James Craig of Carlekemp, who with a handicap of 16 produced a winning score of 84. In September 1914, the Autumn Meeting was one of the last of the club events played before war intervened and the Rose Bowl was won by Miss J K Sherriff. The meeting was not held again until 1919, after the war had ended, when Catherine Macfie produced one of the highest scoring winning rounds of 106, although it should be borne in mind that her handicap was 4. The Rose Bowl was won on three consecutive occasions from 1920 to 1922, by a young Millicent Couper, who carried forward the tradition of great women golfers at North Berwick into the 1930s. The indefatigable Elsie Grant-Suttie saw off the younger competitors when she won it in 1938 – with a handicap of 9 – her winning score was 72. In a century of competition for the Dalziel Rose Bowl, the lowest handicap score to date is 64, achieved by Katherine Smith in 1999.

Elsie Grant-Suttie (far right) with a group of lady members attending the first Scottish Boys' Championship tournament, in April 1935, which was held on the links at North Berwick. Lady Hamilton-Dalrymple is pictured 2nd right.

The Hunnewell Quaich was presented to the Club by American golfer Maude Hunnewell, who lived for some years in England as a child and learned her golf at North Berwick, during regular family holidays. She was a powerful golfer and potential champion, but never got further than the final eight in the Ladies' British Open. In September 1921, she took part in an exhibition game at North Berwick with Joyce Wethered, who was runner-up in the Open at Turnberry, earlier that year. Playing to the home green, Hunnewell took the hole in 2, to the delight of the following crowd. It was not often that Joyce Wethered was defeated. In 1928, Maude married Ray Atherton, American Chargé d'Affaires in London. The Hunnewell Quaich was first played for at the Spring Meeting on the West Links, in July 1923, as the first handicap prize and was won by Miss Dagmar Sawyer, daughter of Florence Sawyer (née Anderson), with a score of 83.

Special conditions were attached to both the Dalziel Rose Bowl and the Hunnewell Quaich: "No player with a handicap of more than 18 strokes can win, [except that] a player with a handicap of more than 18 may win if her handicap is reduced to 18 and her score is then the best" and that "the club in each case to present the winner with a replica." Both trophies are still played for today.

In 1927, Lt. Col. & Mrs George Campbell Grahame presented the Grahame Cup to the Ladies' Club. It was competed for in an annual hole-for hole (knock-out) competition. The Grahames had three daughters Evelyn, and twins Violet and Sheila, all of whom were good golfers and lived for part of

Maude Hunnewell and Joyce Wethered draw a crowd during their exhibition game on the West Links in September 1921. Miss Hunnewell's score for the round was 78, while Miss Wethered's was 86.

the year at Ingleholm, in Clifford Road, North Berwick. The winner of the inaugural competition for the Grahame Cup was Millicent Couper, while Eileen Tweedie was runner-up.

The names of the early Lady Captains are to be found inscribed as winners of the various trophies and medals many times over, between 1919 and 1950, but offer faint clues as to the dates of their respective captaincies. The Captain was elected annually at the AGM held in August, but was eligible for re-election for a second year. Florence Sawyer's granddaughter, the late Ann Dymond, was sure that Florence was either the first or one of the first Lady Captains. The photograph of her in the ladies' changing room today records

Right: Violet Grahame watches her opponent Eileen Tweedie driving off at Perfection, 1927.

Far right: Millicent Couper with Eileen Tweedie, winner and runner-up of the Grahame Cup, played for the first time in 1927.

her as Captain in 1921. The Ladies' Golf Union official yearbooks fill in some important gaps: Mrs Sawyer is recorded as Lady Captain in 1925 and again in 1926, though this is not to say she was not also captain in 1921.

Florence Sawyer, one of the daughters of the 'golfing cleric', the Rev. FLM Anderson, had gone out to India in the 1890s, with her new husband, Charles, an army officer, but had returned to Britain after the birth of her daughter and persuaded her husband to settle in her beloved North Berwick. She was an indomitable character and had golfed on the long links before the formation of the Ladies' Club in 1888. In the competition in September 1923, the first over the west links after the ladies had officially given up their links, Florence won the Scratch Prize in 86. A pencilled note on the official results record reads: "Mrs Sawyer's handicap will be reduced at next competition." At 8 it was almost the lowest among the competitors that day!

Florence Sawyer (née Anderson) one of the first Lady Captains of the Club.

We do know from other sources that Mrs Eleanor Addie was Lady Captain in 1933 and there is a reference to Elsie Grant-Suttie being elected to take over for the 1935 season. The Ladies Golf Union yearbooks provide further information, but their records do not tie in entirely with the names on the board in the Clubhouse. For example, Lady Hamilton-Dalrymple, Mrs Marion Wyld and the Hon. Mrs J. M. Balfour are missing from the board, yet according to the LGU yearbook, all were Lady Captains during the 1920s and 30s. It would be a clear acknowledgement of the contribution made by the ladies to the history of the golf in the town, to update the board and put the record straight.

Lady Hamilton-Dalrymple and Lady Helen O'Brien on North Berwick links c.1930. Lady Dalrymple is one of the past Lady Captains whose name is not recorded on the board.

Looking forward – young men and women awaiting the start of the Inchdura Mixed Foursomes over the West Links, North Berwick, c.1935.

LADY CAPTAINS OF NBLGC 1921-1948

1921 Mrs Florence Sawyer (née Anderson)

1925 Mrs Florence Sawyer

1926 Mrs Florence Sawyer

1927 Hon. Mrs J.M. Balfour

1928 Lady Hamilton-Dalrymple

1929 Lady Hamilton-Dalrymple

1930 Miss Elsie Grant-Suttie

1931 Miss Elsie Grant-Suttie

1932 Mrs Eleanor Addie (née Turnbull)

1933 Mrs Eleanor Addie

1934 Miss Elsie Grant-Suttie

1938 Mrs Marion Wyld (née Houldsworth)

1939 Mrs Marion Wyld

1948 Mrs Catherine Peploe (née Macfie)

The Amalgamation

All through the summer of 1934, the only subject of conversation on the lips of golfers was 'to amalgamate or not to amalgamate'. The issue was officially aired at the Annual General Meeting of the New Club, North Berwick, on 21st September 1934, when its Committee took an historic decision to open negotiations both with the Ladies' Golf Club and the Tantallon Golf Club to discuss the possibility of all three Clubs coming under one 'umbrella' and sharing a club house. Both the Ladies' Club and Tantallon were in favour of an amalgamation and talks started. All seemed well.

A year later, however, the scheme had fallen through; negotiations with Tantallon had not proceeded as smoothly as anticipated and after protracted and sometimes uncomfortable discussions between the parties, the New Club Captain, Robert Addie, regretted that the Committee could "no longer see its way to recommend the inclusion of Tantallon in the scheme". The resolution was quickly amended to the effect that "the Ladies' Club only be invited to join up with the New Club". It was carried almost unanimously.

In the months that followed there was copious correspondence between the Ladies' Committee, their Trustees, legal agents and the New Club Committee, to sort out the details. Funds were needed by the New Club to carry out an extensive upgrade to the existing Clubhouse. The five Trustees of the Ladies' Club, Sir John Couper, Robert Maxwell, T.L. Grahame Reid, John Cook and John Dunlop handled the negotiations, including financial matters, on behalf of the Ladies' Club. As Secretary, Millicent Couper, daughter of Sir John, communicated the views, wishes and concerns of the Ladies' Committee and lady members in writing, often asking for, and always following, advice from the Trustees.

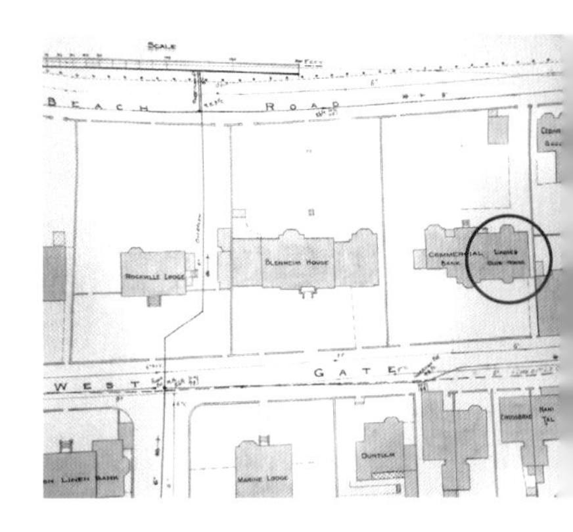
Extract of 1934 plan of North Berwick, showing the position of the Ladies' Club premises.

On 30th January 1935, Millicent wrote to Boothby, the New Club Secretary: "Dear Sir, I am instructed by my committee to write to ask you when is the earliest date on which you can let me know whether the scheme for the Amalgamation of the New Club and the Ladies' Club has been passed, as it is very awkward not to be able to inform our members of anything definite….and we are anxious to know how long we will have to have temporary premises."

The ladies' anxiety was to continue for some time. In December 1935, no agreement had been reached and indeed the Trustees were advising caution over any financial arrangement into which the ladies might enter with the New Club, which might disadvantage them in the longer term. Sir John wrote to the ladies' agent, Gifford, suggesting that the New Club was being less than transparent in its dealings:

> **"I feel the Committee of the New Club is not treating the Ladies in a generous manner as regards prizes and petty disbursements. At the joint meeting of the Sub-Committees, Mr Deuchar represented the New Club and Mrs Deuchar was acting Captain of the Ladies' Club, which I consider not quite playing the game. The New Club wants to take every penny it can from the Ladies."**

Eventually the financial negotiations were concluded and at the general meeting of the NBLGC in August 1936, the members approved handing over £800 as a condition-free loan to the New Club to provide accommodation for the ladies and an additional sum of £100 to be spent on furnishings for the ladies' common room. This was set against a capital sum required by the New Club of £2300 for the overall upgrade of the clubhouse. There was further wrangling over possible changes to the rules in favour of the ladies, but this was firmly over-ruled by the men. By December 1936, the Minute of Agreement had been signed by the Trustees of both Clubs and the amalgamation was sealed.

How much of a difference it made to the women golfers is difficult to assess now. Alterations were made to the New Club clubhouse, situated on the edge of the West Links, with separate entrances for men and for women and separate sitting rooms and facilities for tea, simple lunches and other meals.

The women were able to give up their less than satisfactory accommodation in the premises of the Commercial Bank in Westgate and enjoy the convenience of custom-built facilities close to the starter's box and the 18th green. For most of the time since its inception in 1888, the Ladies' Club had been run by the men. In a way, it was little different, except they were all under one roof and the bulk of the healthy bank balance of the Ladies' Club was tipped into the coffers of the North Berwick New Club.

The New Club's annual Rule Book of 1937 reflected the amalgamation. Rule 1 read as follows:

> **"The Club shall consist of not more than 290 Ordinary and 10 Extraordinary Members, exclusive of those on the Supernumerary List, and of Service Members admitted under Rule XIV, and of Honorary Members, and of not more than 150 Playing Lady Members, 10 Non-Playing Lady Members and 10 Extraordinary Members of the NBLGC admitted as Associate Members."**

To the modern eye, that looks like one set of rules for the men and another for the women. From the start, the women were not full members of the Club – they were Associate Members. Only Members of the NBLGC were eligible for election as Associates and then they had to go through an election process. The throng of 300 members of the Ladies' Club, noted in their 1933 Rules and Regulations, had somehow been cut to half that number – and against a background of the continuing popularity of the game of golf. The Committee, which of course, was all male, made the bye-laws and managed clubhouse and links.

Semi-finalists in the Scottish Women's Foursomes at North Berwick, in June 1934. From l. to r. Eileen Tweedie, Issa Anderson, Margaret Stewart and Jessie Anderson (Scottish Girl Champion).

'The very best lady golfers!'

In the twentieth century, North Berwick continued to attract and produce some of the very best lady golfers. The names of several have found a place in golfing history. Whether they were native to the town, like Jean Donald and Marjory Fowler; or settled there because of strong family connections, through years of summer golfing on the links, like Millicent Couper; or took up membership of the NBLGC, because of its fine reputation, like Charlotte Beddows; whatever the reason, the result is a panoply of extraordinary women playing some extraordinary golf across the links at North Berwick, over more than a century.

Charlotte Beddows played golf into her eighties.

Charlotte Beddows (née Stevenson) was born in October 1887, almost a year before NBLGC held its first meeting in July 1888. She was seventeen when she won her first medal in the Scottish Ladies' Championship at North Berwick, in 1905, as a semi-finalist. It was the year Dorothy Campbell lifted the championship on home ground. At that time Charlotte was not a member of the NBLGC. She was born into a middle-class Edinburgh family on October 22nd 1887. Her father James St Clair Stevenson had a drapery business, in a prime position at the west end of Princes Street, which he ran with his brother-in-law, Robert Maule. The business developed into the popular Edinburgh department store of R P Maule, which was bought by Binns in 1934 and much later by House of Fraser. Charlotte, her younger brother and sister, and their Maule cousins were all encouraged from an early age to play golf. Charlotte attended George Watson's Ladies' College in Edinburgh and as a schoolgirl distinguished herself as a hockey international and outstanding golfer. Both her brother Tom and cousin Robert Maule, like so many of their generation, were killed in the First World War. In 1917, she married an Edinburgh optician John Watson. Charlotte was widowed in 1941 and in 1947 she married Brigadier Edward Beddows R.A.M.C., who had been her childhood sweetheart!

Charlotte was indefatigable on the golf course. It was said of her that she never walked around a course, but always played a round in double quick time, sometimes leaving her opponents exhausted and exasperated. She was happiest when she was setting the pace on the course – and winning. She played for Scotland in 1913 and went on to represent her country on 21 occasions. She had an extraordinarily long golfing career – she represented East Lothian first in 1909 and on the last occasion in 1966 when she was 78 years old. As Mrs Watson, she won the Scottish Women's title in 1920, 1921, 1922 and 1929. She played in the Curtis Cup in 1932. She appeared regularly on the North Berwick links in the early 1950s, joined the Ladies' Club and competed fiercely in almost every competition for the next twenty years, winning the Club Gold

Medal in 1959 at the age of 72, after completing the course in 79.

In 1964, she was awarded the Frank Moran Trophy in recognition of her fine golfing achievements. On a cold day in May 1968, when the course was heavy-going after rain, Charlotte Beddows and her partner Mrs Buchanan won the winter foursome's competition at the Club Spring Meeting. She had just celebrated her 80th birthday. Her reputation for storming around the course at a great rate and her impatience with slow players remained intact until the end of her life. Ella Vlandy, Lady Captain 1980-82, recalls her as a terrifying opponent and particularly when Ella defeated her in round 2 of the Grahame Cup in1962! Charlotte Beddows died at North Berwick in August 1976 at the age of 88, and is regarded by some as one of the finest golfers of her age.

Ella Vlandy practising her stroke c.1938.

As Charlotte Beddows was achieving her run of successes in the Scottish Ladies' Championships, in the early 1920s, a new champion was taking her first steps across the West Links. Jean Donald, one of three daughters of North Berwick GP, Dr Douglas Donald, was born in 1921. The Donald's house, St Helen's, in the Westgate was yards away from the 18th green and playing golf was a normal part of growing up for Jean. She shone in competitions on the children's course and in 1935, at the age of 14, she entered the Ladies' Spring Competition and won the school girls' prize. The outbreak of war in September 1939 caused a break in golfing tournaments, in much the same way as it had done in 1914, and Jean's golfing progress was delayed as she was deployed to work in the Foreign Office. In 1947, she won the Club Gold Medal and a few months later, the Couper Cup. By this time she was competing at national level and, in 1948, was runner-up in the Ladies' Amateur Open at Royal Lytham, where she was defeated by one hole. The same year, she helped the British team in its first victory over the United States in the Curtis Cup. The previous year she had won the Scottish Ladies' Championship and distinguished herself by setting a record margin for the event of 13 up and 11 to play.

Below left: Jean Donald (2nd from right kneeling) among a group of young prizewinners after a competition on the children's course c.1932.

Below right: Jean Donald matured into one of North Berwick's great golfing ladies.

She married late in life (in 1958 to John Anderson) and had no children. She died very suddenly as she was walking down between the car park and the club house at Gullane with her great friend Monica Dunnett to have a game of golf! It seemed a fitting point of departure. Jean was remembered by many of the North Berwick members as kind and encouraging to young golfers. She was a great supporter of Leuchie House, when it was a respite home for MS sufferers and was Chairman of Friends of Leuchie for many years, raising money and working hard to support the Servite Nuns who ran it.

Jean Donald was still a school girl, when Millicent Couper was catching the attention of the golfing world with her excellent play. The 16th June 1933 was a great day for NBLGC, as Millicent won the Scottish Ladies' Golf Championship at Turnberry, by beating Helen Holm (Elie & Earlsferry), the holder, in a very exciting final which stretched to the 22nd hole. The NBLGC acknowledged their pride and satisfaction in her achievement and at a special gathering, Mrs Cook, the Lady Captain, presented Miss Couper with a diamond brooch to mark her success.

Millicent Couper, Scottish Ladies' Champion, 1933.

"Much satisfaction was expressed in North Berwick last evening when the news of Miss Millicent Couper's victory in the Scottish Ladies' Golf championship reached the town. Miss Couper plays most of her golf there and is the Hon. Sec. of the NBLGC. In winning the title she has accomplished a great deal towards placing North Berwick in its rightful position as one of the foremost of Scottish golfing centres."

(*Haddingtonshire Courier*, 23 June 1933)

Millicent was at the top of her game. At the Ladies' Club Autumn Meeting the previous year, she had won the Gold Medal and 1st scratch prize, defeating veteran Elsie Grant-Suttie by one stroke. She went on to win the medal every year until 1938, notching up seven consecutive wins and surpassing Margaret Gillies Smith's record of five consecutive wins, fifty years earlier. In October 1970, it was proposed that Millicent Couper receive Honorary Membership for her "unfailing interest and previous duties undertaken in the club." The proposal was carried at the following AGM, in May 1971, after "permission had been granted by the Men's Committee"! Millicent did not have long to enjoy the honour, as she died a few weeks later. Not only was Millicent Couper a great golfer, she was a town councillor and became North Berwick's first female Provost. Couper Avenue in North Berwick is named after her.

Millicent's record still holds, although two North Berwick ladies have come close and have raised the bar in a different way. Moira Thomson (1950–2011)

Marjory Fowler, (1937–2003).

won the Club Gold Medal twelve times between 1982 and 2007, and on the last occasion achieved a record score of 70. Even more astonishing was the performance of Marjory Ferguson, who lifted the Gold Medal twenty one times. Marjorys run of consecutive wins between 1963 and 1971 was interrupted only by Barbara Hely-Hutchinson (née Wyld), who won the competition in 1965.

Marjory Ferguson (née Fowler) was born and brought up in North Berwick. Her father John Fowler, a local businessman took her out on the children's course as a youngster and taught her how to play. She quickly developed an extraordinary talent for the game and built up an impressive record of golfing achievements. She was a semi-finalist in 1957 and 1964 in the Scottish Championships and runner-up in 1966 and 1971; she represented Scotland in Home Internationals on many occasions; she played for Great Britain in the Vagliano Trophy Match and she won the East of Scotland Championship several times. She monopolised the East Lothian Ladies' Championships with her successive wins in the 1960s. In 1966, she was selected for the British Curtis Cup team: it was a great personal triumph. Marjory was fiercely competitive and her determined attitude to the game brought her high praise and great victories, but she was not a good loser. She should, however, be remembered for the contribution she made to furthering girls' golf, by setting up the East of Scotland Girls' Golfing Association in 1977, organising competitions and matches – and always expecting the girls to adopt her own high standards of play!

Moira Thomson, (née Dewar), (1950–2011).

In 1970, the Ladies' Committee introduced an annual competition, to determine the club's champion golfer. To enter, members had to take part in the Spring Meeting and the sixteen lowest scratch scores from that event would qualify to compete for the championship. A silver salver was donated by Lady Betty Weston, an active member since the 1950s. Most fittingly, Lady Betty was among the qualifiers in the first contest. It was won by Marjory.

Moira holding the Scottish Girls' Championship Cup in 1968.

Moira Thompson's connection with the Ladies' Club started after her marriage in 1972, to Alistair Thomson, whose family had lived in North Berwick since the 1920s. Moira (née Dewar) came from an Edinburgh professional family and attended George Watson's Ladies' College. The ethos was to develop good all-rounders. Moira was a high-achiever in class and a good sportswoman and equestrian. But it was golf at which she excelled. In 1968, she won the Scottish Girls' Championship. Her contemporary and school friend, Gillian Kirkwood (née Macdonald) was runner-up. Moira went on to be a stalwart of the East Lothian County team, but really came into her own as a member of the Scottish Seniors' International team for the last ten years of her life. She died after a short illness at the age of 61, in 2011.

Moira's mother-in-law, Catherine (Babs) Thomson was Lady Captain 1970-72. She was the only child of Dr Alexander McEwan and Christian Haldane Roger. The McEwans had interests in a whisky distillery, Abbots Choice, and Christian's father had founded the successful Leith timber merchants Garland & Roger in 1878. In 1924, Dr McEwan bought Greenhythe, previously the home of Mary Orphoot, one of the original members of the NBLGC. It was a beautifully appointed house, but before the family moved in, a garage was built to accommodate Dr McEwan's 1907 brown and black Daimler, registration number S 809. Babs enjoyed a privileged upbringing, at Greenhythe, with doting parents and as she recalled in later life: 'There seemed to be servants around to do everything – even to drive the car.' The McEwan's comfortable lifestyle was very typical of the North Berwick golfing families in the 1920s and 30s. From a very early age, Babs was out on the children's course learning how to swing a club and aged five was captured in action by photographer, Balmain, always on the lookout for a good golf story.

Babs, aged four, giving a promising swing, at North Berwick in 1927.

It has long been a tradition in the NBLC that the lady members help with the children's' competitions. The Hon. Mrs Edith O'Brien organised the events for the youngsters, during the 1970s and Lady (Hermione) Malcolm took over in the mid-1980s. Both kept meticulous records of the matches played and the results. Members were detailed to mark the young competitors' cards as they went round the course. Joan Oliver, a past Lady Captain recalls:

> **"On one particular occasion, it must have been in about 1975, I was teamed up with one of the younger competitors, a six-year old girl. All went well 'till the fourth hole when she had an 'air shot'. She looked across at me furiously when she saw me marking it as a shot. However, she quickly recovered her composure, buckled down and fired off an amazing shot right onto the green. I was struck by her sportsmanship, her determination and her skill!"**

The little girl was Catriona Lambert. Her burgeoning talent was recorded in the minutes of the meeting of the Ladies' Club about ten years later, on 6th August 1986, when the Lady Captain, Mrs Letters, noted the success of a junior member, 16 year old Catriona Lambert, in winning both the Scottish Schoolgirls' Championship and the S.T.V. Scottish Girls' Match Play. The early promise did not fade and Catriona Matthew (neé Lambert) went on to win the British Women's Amateur title in 1993, before turning professional a year later.

Over twenty years she established herself one of Britain's best and most

The Children's Course:

1. Elsie and Jean Hamilton-Dalrymple facing a 'stymie'!

2. Cheerful young golfers in Summer 1934.

3. Checking the clubs before play commences.

4. Keen competitors!

5. Virginia De Zoete lines up the ball, 1963.

6. A good strike!

7. Henrietta Loder aged 5, 1927. Head up and ready to play!

1

2

3

4

6

7

consistent women golfers and maintained a strong presence in both the LPGA Tour and the Ladies European Tour. She has played several times in the prestigious Solheim Cup match, where the top 12 European women play against their US counterparts. She has successfully juggled the demands of home and family with her career, most notably in August 2009, when she won the Ricoh British Women's Open at Royal Lytham & St Annes. It was a great personal victory as it was her first win in a major tournament; but more remarkable, she achieved it only eleven weeks after the birth of her second daughter, Sophie. In March 2016, Catriona, ranked among the world's best women golfers, received Scottish golf's lifetime achievement award and became the first woman to enter the Scottish Golf Hall of Fame. She is a firm believer in encouraging girls to play golf. That is evident in the attention and advice she has given to an up-and-coming young North Berwick golfer Clara Young.

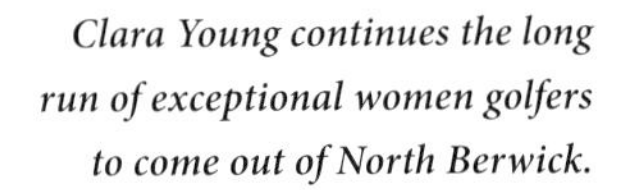

Clara Young continues the long run of exceptional women golfers to come out of North Berwick.

In 2015, at the age of 18, Clara became the youngest Scottish Ladies' Amateur Champion in over 30 years. She started golfing on the children's course while she was at primary school, when it was soon clear she had a prodigious talent. In 2010, barely 14 years old, Clara won the coveted Ladies' Club Gold

Medal – she is possibly the youngest winner. She has already represented Scotland in the under 16s and under 18s and played for Great Britain and Ireland. In 2015, she was awarded a full scholarship at the University of Missouri to study golf – and marketing. It presented a golden opportunity for Clara and will prepare her to take on the world's best women golfers, if that is her ambition. She has a host of extraordinary role models, from her own home town. The opportunities afforded Clara were not there for Rita Gillies Smith, Elsie Blyth, Annie Maxwell and Blanche Anderson and the other pioneering members of the NBLGC. For Dorothy Campbell, women's golf was opening up just as her game was developing. But it was a brave step for a single young woman, brought up in a safe, cosseted environment, to sail across to the other side of the world and carve a career in golfing and win international renown.

In 2005, the Ladies' Club was fully integrated into the North Berwick Golf Club, giving the ladies full voting rights and fair representation on the Committee. One hundred and seventeen years after the gentlemen had graciously provided separate facilities for ladies to enjoy a game of golf without the stress and strain of the long course, which was considered too much for the ladies to tackle, the lady members had finally achieved parity with the men.

North Berwick has witnessed some exceptional talent among the women who have golfed on its beautiful links, but every single woman, whose golfing endeavours are recorded in these pages, has brought something of her own experience and her own character into play and has contributed to the creation of this unique story.

Here's wishing Clara a par, or under, at every hole she plays, as she takes forward the legend of the golfing women at North Berwick.

APPENDIX

The LGU and the SLGA and their links with the NBLGC

By Gillian Kirkwood,

Chairman LGU (2010–2013) and Chairman SLGA (1999–2000)

When North Berwick Ladies' Golf Club was founded in 1888, there were only 16 older ladies' clubs in Great Britain and Ireland and only 7 in Scotland. Golf was a new phenomenon, and there were not many lady golfers around. The growing middle class meant that there were more people with the leisure time to follow healthy pursuits and Victorian gentlemen came to accept golf as an acceptable pastime for their female relatives, as it did not compromise their modesty.

The early women golfers were likened to ships in full sail; they rustled as they moved, and any kind of wind would cause their skirts to lift and their bonnets to take off. If it rained then the long skirt would soak up mud and water and it made progress uncomfortable, if not impossible. The fitted blouse and jacket impeded the swing, and the high collar chaffed the neck. The skirt would get tangled up with the putter. As for teeing the ball and getting it out of the hole, these feminine galleons had to rely on a caddy, as they could not bend far enough to reach the ground themselves. It was considered unladylike to swing higher than your shoulder, or to show a glimpse of ankle at any time. These ladies played on shorter courses, as extensions of the Men's course, either as putting courses or what we would consider a six or nine-hole pitch and putt course.

But the ladies persevered, and by 1893 there were over 50 ladies' golf clubs in the British Isles – and these ladies were raising the club above the shoulder – and some could hit the ball as far as the men.

Women are always good organisers. In 1893, a call came out from the Wimbledon Ladies' Golf Club to form a Ladies' Golf Union. It took men several more years to form any kind of Golf Union for themselves. North Berwick Ladies was one of clubs which gave early approval for the formation of the Union and announced their intention to send delegates to the inaugural meeting. The meeting was held in London on Wednesday 19 April, 1893. Perhaps they sent apologies, but in the event, no-one from the North Berwick Ladies' Club attended. Nor did they affiliate until 1913!

The main aims of the 1893 Rules of the LGU were as follows:

1. **To promote the interests of the game of golf.**
2. **To obtain a uniformity of the rules of the game by establishing a representative legislative authority.**
3. **To establish a uniform system of handicapping.**

A governing body was needed to provide the infrastructure for communication between clubs, and comparison of players which would allow them to compete in Inter-club and Open meetings on an equal footing. Up until the 1890's handicaps were in a chaotic state, because each club calculated its own par of the green and players' handicaps, by its own method. The most popular was that the best player in the club was considered scratch, and everyone got shots from them. But what if the best player was not very good? Another club could have a true scratch player, and their club handicaps would be much higher. When it came to having a handicap match between the two clubs, the latter club would be at a distinct advantage.

Handicapping was something that Issette Pearson, the founding secretary of the LGU, and Mr Laidlaw Purves, one of its first Vice-Presidents, felt passionately about. Initially, Laidlaw Purves had worked hard to rally the men to form a governing body but without success. When he encountered a willing and like-minded ally in Issette Pearson, he put all his energies into devising a system for the ladies and it was enthusiastically adopted by the LGU members. Mabel Stringer in her book *Golfing Reminiscences*, said: "In my opinion the greatest achievement of the LGU is undoubtedly its handicapping system....a life-sized statue of the present Mrs Miller (Issette Pearson) ought to be erected in every golfing country in the world - not so much as founder of the LGU, but as the successful solver of the riddle of women's handicaps."

A method of comparing the 'par' for the course was fundamental in providing the standard needed for handicapping. In those early days, some courses had extremely low pars, such as Freshwater (60), whilst Southport (104) was at the upper end of the spectrum. With such a variation, what hope had ladies playing at these low-par clubs from competing against their high-par sisters in an Open Meeting? Issette and her colleagues instituted a system of calculating a scratch or bogey score for each hole of the course based on the score taken by a 'champion scratch player'. There were only a few of these 'champion scratch players', and although busy with their own golf, they saw it as their duty to go round the country taking 'pars' whenever requested. If no "champion scratch player" could be found, then the best golfer in the neighbourhood was prevailed upon to estimate the score such a champion would take, based on information that a hole under 140 yards was designated as a 3, under 260 yards as a 4 and under 360 yards as a 5.

When the 'par' of the green had been settled, the handicap was then calculated with the following formula: (Best score x 2 + next best score) divided by 3 – Par of green = Players handicap, e.g.

(75+75+81) divided by 3 –72 = 5.

In 1907 the LGU claimed: "the handicap shall be some clue to a player's form; there shall be no 'plus'; no one should be 'scratch' unless she has proved her right to the title; a player receives the same handicap in every club to which she may belong and as every player handicaps herself by the scores she returns, there can be no complaints to the handicap committee not recognising her merits". The country was divided into groups, each with a handicap manager. Once a handicap was obtained, it was the duty of the handicap manager, to revise all medal scores returned by each member.

Mr Laidlaw Purves did not like the idea of doubling the best score. He considered that a handicap based on a suppositional score was fundamentally flawed. He advocated basing the handicap on the average of the three best scores, and in 1913 the ladies eventually agreed with him.

There were lively discussions as to the limit of the handicap which should be allowed in a club. In most, 24 or 25 ranked as the highest, but in several places they rose to 40 or 50. May Hezlet, a British Ladies' and Irish Champion, felt that when it rose so high, handicapping became a farce:

Issette Pearson created the LGU's first handicapping system.

"A player who needs 40 or 50 strokes to help her around an 18 hole course is either so hopelessly bad that she ought not to enter competitions at all, or returns scores which with the handicap subtracted bring her down to the 60s or low 70s and so are manifestly absurd. 18 or 20 is quite enough for the ordinary beginner who has played about a year and is not a hopeless duffer."

In order to obtain LGU Handicaps for its members, the club had to be affiliated to the LGU. It is not known why the North Berwick Ladies did not affiliate until 1913. Perhaps it was the nature of the membership, for many of the good players were members elsewhere, and possibly obtained their handicap from their home club. The entry for North Berwick, in the 1914 LGU Handbook, lists all the members with club handicaps and 19 with LGU Handicaps. There were 23 members who had a club handicap of scratch, but only 3 had an LGU scratch handicap. They were Madge Neill Fraser, Elsie Grant-Suttie and Frances Teacher.

Although the LGU no longer runs a handicapping system, nor provides the LGU scratch scores, it still runs all the Ladies' Amateur Championships at

GB & I level. The Ladies' British Open Amateur Championship was held over the West Links, North Berwick in 2008, when the final was contested, not by any home-grown golfers, but by two Swedes! The LGU organises the British Girls, British Seniors and British Stroke Play, as well as Home Internationals between Scotland, England, Ireland and Wales. At least one major match occurs every year, either Curtis Cup (v USA) or Vagliano Trophy (v Continent of Europe). The LGU organises the teams and, when it is a home fixture, the event. As well as all these amateur matches and championships, the LGU runs the Women's British Open, currently sponsored by Ricoh. North Berwick member, Catriona Matthew won the Ricoh at Royal Lytham and St Anne's in 2009. The management and running of these events is the LGU's major responsibility, but it also recognises that ladies' golf needs an advocate to make its voice heard in a sport still dominated by men.

Enough of the LGU.... What about the Scottish Ladies' Golfing Association (SLGA)? It was founded in 1904, originally to run the Scottish Ladies' Amateur Championship which had started the previous year. Dorothy Campbell of North Berwick was on the first committee. As its name suggests it now runs all the Scottish Championships, national events, Scottish international teams and act as the advocates for ladies' golf in Scotland. Course rating, using the USGA system, is administered through the SLGA, and handicapping queries go to them. If there are any contentious issues the clubs are the voting members. North Berwick, as a large club, gets two votes at the SLGA AGM. North Berwick has held the Scottish Ladies' Amateur Championship on six occasions, with such illustrious winners as Dorothy Campbell (1905), Jessie Valentine (1951), Joan Hastings (1967), Gillian Stewart (1983) and Elaine Moffat (1998).

North Berwick members have had their fair share of success, both at National and International level, and some of their exploits are documented elsewhere in this book. Without the LGU and the SLGA running things, they would have nothing to play in, and no infrastructure with which to run the club. Hooray for the LGU and SLGA!

In October 2015, the SLGA amalgamated with the men's Scottish Golf Union to form Scottish Golf. It was inevitable – not just for financial reasons; funding and sponsorship are found more easily if the is a single organisation, but also because the two separate organisations had become an anachronism in this day and age. Many of the old guard will regret the passing of the SLGA, but the future of golf starts with development from grass roots level and that has to come from the clubs – the clubs need to be all en-compassing, so no gender issues should be present!

INDEX

The index lists the characters and places which feature in the book but is not fully comprehensive.